Also by Lee Gale Gruen

Memoir: Adventures with Dad: A Father and Daughter's
Journey Through a Senior Acting Class

Books/Speaker Website: LeeGaleGruen.com

Blog: "Reinventing Yourself in Your Retirement Years"
(link: LeeGaleGruen.wordpress.com)

REINVENTING YOURSELF IN YOUR RETIREMENT YEARS

Find Joy, Excitement, and Purpose after You Retire

Lee Gale Gruen

Reinventing Yourself in Your Retirement Years

ISBN: 978-1-7358481-0-5

Published by

Big Hat Press
   Lafayette, California
   www.bighatpress.com

Cover Design by Milos Rocenovic

For All Retirees Who Have Struggled

Table of Contents

Foreword

"Retire from work, but not from life." – M.K. Soni

For 37 years I always looked forward to teaching my developmental psychology course until, that is, the last three weeks of each semester. The class began with the miracle of birth and advanced through the stages of infancy, childhood, adolescence and adulthood, an accelerating curve revealing new human skills and capabilities at every turn. Then came trouble, the gerontology segment.

The scholarly literature about the last phase of life was mostly dispiriting, detailing multiple, often forced transitions into decline and loss of status. Opportunities for productivity and personal fulfillment narrowed, only to be replaced by physical complications and cultural obstacles. To end the course on such a downer note was difficult for my young students and for me as well, especially as I approached that milestone called "retirement."

Once retired, of course, one realizes that along with the pitfalls associated with getting older are choices to be made. Today, the choices are more varied and interesting, partially fueled by technological advances and the recognition that today's older population is a formidable consumer base worthy of being catered to.

In *Reinventing Yourself in Your Retirement Years*, Lee Gale Gruen offers two distinct tools to assist in making those critical life choices. The first eight chapters set the stage for post-retirement and offer a myriad of activities that are wide open for seniors, most of which offer new ways to discover fulfillment, pleasure, and purpose. The last chapter is a long one, consisting of a collection of remarkable short essays from her online blog, *Reinventing Yourself in Your Retirement Years*.

Often presenting an experience plucked from Gruen's own life, it turns to also be about you. These stories are best described as an interplay between you and the author and should be contemplated and savored before moving on to the next entry. You will have much to learn about yourself, and you will be the better for it.

Patricia Keith-Spiegel, Ph.D. Recipient of the California State University Trustees Award for Outstanding Professor and The Distinguished Professor Award by the American Psychological Foundation.

Preface and Acknowledgments

After completing my first book, a memoir, *Adventures with Dad: A Father and Daughter's Journey Through a Senior Acting Class*, I found a small, boutique publishing company, Author Mike Ink Publishing (now AM Ink Publishing), interested in publishing it. Working with the publisher, his editor, and his book cover designer was another new learning experience. That day in 2013 that I received a copy of my memoir made me feel like I had birthed a child—so precious, so amazing, so unbelievable.

I thought my book writing job was finished and that my publisher would handle marketing it. Not true! I quickly learned authors are expected to promote their own books. Suddenly, I was a salesperson hawking a product. I developed a website to promote the book: LeeGaleGruen.com. I had killed off my stage fright by becoming a professional actress in my senior years, so I found that I loved speaking to groups. My natural aversion to self-promotion was disappearing, too. The more I did it, the easier it became. I contacted various clubs, organizations, libraries, and senior programs, and soon I had bookings for author talk/book signing events. I appeared on writing panels and was interviewed by radio and podcast hosts.

So many retirees, baby boomers and seniors I encountered during my talks told me that they were lost and depressed. I understood those feelings because I once had them, too. I came through it and lived to tell my story, and so can you. The takeaway is that we can stand up to the forces that beat us down: society, peers, media, significant individuals, and on and on. We can triumph and reinvent ourselves at any time in our lives, even in our later years.

I received many inquiries about how I had gotten to where I was in my life, and I realized that I had a message that was inspiring to others. So, in 2013, soon after the book was published, I started writing a free, online blog, "Reinventing Yourself in Your Retirement Years," as a way of passing along what I have learned—a giving back. It is composed of my thoughts, observations, and experiences which I think are universal to my own age demographic—that of retiree and senior. My blog postings from over six years are printed in Chapter 10. My blog can be accessed online at: LeeGaleGruen.wordpress.com.

I, then, began to receive invitations to speak on the subject of retirement and healthy/successful aging. I developed a lecture titled the same as my blog, "Reinventing Yourself in Your Retirement Years." I have been a guest speaker at clubs, organizations, health agencies, senior communities, wellness fairs, colleges, and other places where retirees, baby boomers, and seniors congregate. The link to my guest speaker webpage is: LeeGaleGruen.com/guest-speaker.html.

Audience members asked if I had a book based on my speech that they could purchase. That was my motivation for writing this book. I have tried to present a down-to-earth discussion of what it means to retire: the fears, the pitfalls, the closing of a door on your life up to that time. This is an honest view of what most people facing retirement worry about and how to address those worries. I examine what life is like after retirement and how to find your own niche in this puzzling, new world. Then, I offer an in-depth look at what is available for retirees including activities, pursuits, and even employment. However, it doesn't just stop there with a final message of "get a life" as so many similar books do. I gently take the reader by the hand in a step-by-step journey on how to identify what might even be of interest to them and how to go about finding activities to tap into those interests—how to reinvent themselves. The latter part of the book is composed of the blog posts I have written for more than six years on my free, online blog, "Reinventing Yourself in Your Retirement Years."

My goal with this book, my public talks, and my blog is to help and inspire baby boomers, seniors, retirees, and those about to retire to find joy, excitement, and purpose in their lives during retirement. I believe that starts with finding a passion which will motivate you to want to get up in the morning, get dressed, get out of the house, and embrace life. I'm going to show you how you can reinvent yourself after retiring just like I did.

Many have helped or supported me in my quest to publish this book. I want to thank Patricia Spiegel for lighting a fire under me and for her help in editing this book and writing the Foreword; the members of my Published Writers Club for sharing their valuable information; my lecture audience members for their appreciation and encouragement; those of my blog followers who have responded to my various postings with comments and validation that I have touched their lives in some way; and my son for always supporting me in all my endeavors.

* * * * *

Some names, locations, and other minor details have been changed to protect the privacy of the individuals involved.

CHAPTER 1

My Story

———

Since retiring at the age of sixty, I have become a professional actress, author, public speaker, and blogger. I have discovered that sought after "second act" of my life. Even ten years ago, I never would have believed I could do that.

I grew up shy and worried about what others thought of me. My long-term, crippling stage fright stayed with me until I retired from my thirty-seven-year career as a probation officer. I didn't have any idea what I was going to do with the rest of my life. One day I had the identity of probation officer, and the next day I didn't. It was devastating. I was divorced and a mother and grandmother. My children lived hundreds of miles away, my career was gone, my parents were gone, and I was estranged from my only sibling.

I still remember that first day with no job. I woke up in the morning and had no office to go to, no people to interview, no reports to write, and nothing to do. Everything seemed surreal. I got out of bed and moved very slowly through the house in an almost frozen state. I can recall feeling hungry and wanting to go to the kitchen to get some breakfast. I kept saying to myself, *Okay, now you put one foot in front of the other.* It felt like walking through molasses.

Over the next few weeks, I had some lunch dates with friends, went shopping a lot, and read the newspaper from the front to the back for the first time in my life. However, a few months into that existence, it was clear that just wasn't enough. I'd been active, driven, and on deadlines most of my college, working, and child-rearing years. Now, I was lost, bored, and didn't know what to do with myself. My new lifestyle was getting old very fast, and I questioned whether I was wasting away.

Eventually, my disoriented state passed and restlessness set in. I contributed my efforts to an unsatisfying, volunteer job for a while. I was unstimulated and fretting that would be the description of the rest of my life. One day, I was bellyaching to my friend, Maya, on the phone.

"Why don't you check out Emeritus College," she said.

"What's that?"

"Oh, it's a school for seniors in Santa Monica."

"Is that what I am now, a senior?"

"Get used to it, honey" was her snappy retort before signing off.

A few days later, the lack of stimulation in my life motivated me to drive to the school Maya had recommended and check out the classes. I sat at a table in the clerk's office rifling through the pages in the Schedule of Classes. I came to the Theater Arts section and almost passed it by. I had never had any interest in acting—my lifelong stage fright saw to that. Although I had worked with robbers, drug addicts, murderers and the like during my career, I had never conquered my fear of speaking in front of groups.

Before moving on to the next page, I noticed a class called "Scene Study." I had no idea what that meant. Briefly perusing the class description, I imagined that the students just sat in their seats and went around the room with each reading a line or two from a play before the class discussed and analyzed it. I'd always liked plays and figured I could handle that, so I signed up since nothing else in the schedule grabbed me.

I walked into the classroom on the first day. Everyone else there seemed to know each other; they had obviously been taking the class for a while. I was the new kid on the block. Nobody talked to me, and I felt intimidated, but I took a seat.

Before the class started, a man walked up to me and handed me some papers.

"Do you want to read this with me?" he said.

I didn't understand what he meant, but I answered, "Okay."

He walked to the front to the room. I, on the other hand, continued sitting where I was. He turned around.

"Well, come on," he said with a spark of irritation in his voice.

"Where?"

I was getting nervous. He couldn't possibly mean up to the front of the room to join him, could he?

"Up to the front of the room."

Oh my God, yes, he did mean that.

My stage fright kicked in big time, and I could barely move let alone talk. I looked at the door, seriously considering leaving. However, I was too embarrassed to walk out. After all, I was a mature senior; how could I just slink away?

During my career, I usually interacted with my probation clients on a one-to-one basis and had no problem with that. I managed to avoid situations where I had to speak to groups of people, knowing that my stage fright would keep me up the night before, wreck emotional havoc on me, and choke the words in my throat as I tried to talk. I'm sure it started as a child in grammar school when I had to give a book report in front of the class. The other kids always snickered and teased the poor sucker trying to read his darned essay. That fear of being judged mercilessly and potentially failing in a public arena stuck with me.

Slowly, I made my way up to the head of the class, dragging it out as long as possible. I was shaking; I felt flushed and weak. I looked at the papers I was holding, barely able to read as my hands were trembling. For the first time, I saw that it was the opening scene from *Death of a Salesman*. I didn't think I could feel any worse about my situation, but the title of a famous and complex play made me freeze up even more.

Help! How do I get out of this?

My first line was one word: "Willy."

I wasn't sure I could say it. A croak came out. I could hear my heartbeat banging against my eardrums.

My partner said his line. I read the next, still very nervous, but just a bit more relaxed by the end of the sentence; the heartbeat ratcheted slightly lower. We went on for another few lines, and suddenly the strangest thing happened to me. I became so immersed in my role that I forgot that a roomful of strangers was watching me and judging me and maybe snickering.

After ten minutes, our scene ended, and the class members dutifully clapped as they do for everyone I learned later. It snapped me out of my trance.

Oh, I'm not Linda Loman in my bedroom wearing a robe and talking to my husband, Willy. Oh, I'm standing in front a roomful of people and I JUST SPOKE FOR TEN MINUTES!

I couldn't believe it. I'd never had an experience like that before. What a high! From that moment on, I was hooked on acting. I had found my passion.

A few weeks later, my mother died, and my father was depressed and withdrawn. Typically the life of the party, it was so uncharacteristic of him that it scared me.

"Come with me to my acting class, Daddy," I blurted out while visiting him one day.

I have no idea where that came from. Maybe I thought it would help shake him out of his funk. He had been so down since Mother passed. Maybe it was because it seemed a natural fit for his usually outgoing, charismatic personality. He had always craved attention and loved to be the main attraction. I would have done anything to bring him back to his old self. I figured he would come with me to the class once, maybe twice at the most, and just be an observer. It would take his mind off his despair, and then he'd segue back into his usual activities like playing bridge at the senior citizens center, shopping at his favorite discount stores, or having lunch with my sister or me.

"No, I don't want to go."

"Come on, Dad. You'll love it"

It took some convincing, but I finally wore him down. He didn't have the energy to resist.

I picked him up a few days later. We rode in almost complete silence.

"We'll just sit in the back of the class. You don't have to do anything," I assured him.

We walked into the packed room and took seats in the last row. About half-way through the class, the teacher called on my father to come up to the front and participate in an improvisational exercise with another student.

Oh, he's not going to like this, I thought.

Before I could protest, Dad was on his feet walking jauntily toward where his scene partner had positioned herself. He quickly got into the spirit of the improv theme and really seemed to be enjoying himself. While driving home, Dad wanted to know, "So, what time are you picking me up next week for our class?"

That began our magical journey attending the class every week. We bonded more during those three years than we had in the previous sixty.

I soon discovered we were expected to appear with our acting partner in a class showcase onstage before a live audience with costumes, props, blocking, and memorizing. My stage fright was working overtime juxtaposed against my new passion for acting. Slowly, the passion was winning.

I had another problem. Class members were supposed to find appropriate scenes from professional plays to perform. Well, there just wasn't anything available for an eighty-five-year-old man except *The Sunshine Boys* by Neil Simon, and that had already been done the previous semester.

I wasn't sure what to do. A few class members had written their own material. I didn't think I could do that. As a probation officer, I had written reports for judges to assist them in sentencing criminal defendants. That was technical and investigative in nature. I'd never done any creative writing in my life. However, it was clear that I didn't have a choice. I had to try to write something for us.

I came up with a humorous dad and daughter scene. The theme was that the dad character was an irascible old man, and his daughter was tearing her hair out with his antics—not too far from the truth.

The class and the teacher loved our scene. Dad was thrilled. He was just where he belonged. So was I as I grew more and more confident in myself.

We eventually performed our scene in the class showcase. The audience went wild. They and the class members thought we were very special; the first father/daughter team ever in that senior acting class. Audience members surrounded us at the end, wanting to talk to us. They were not just the friends we had invited, but strangers invited by other class members or folks from the community who were enjoying a free show they'd read about in the local newspaper. Dad couldn't get over it. A thespian was born!

We performed in the showcases twice a year for the three years we attended the class together. I was becoming confident in my writing ability as I penned scene after scene. They were all based on my father himself—things he had done or might have done in certain situations, but exaggerated to find the comedy. All had the same framework: crotchety dad and over-whelmed daughter, but each had a different storyline.

There was:

Going to the Movies with Dad
Going Camping with Dad
Going to the Airport with Dad
Dad Goes Mod
Dad Goes Digital
Going to the Market with Dad

Dad and I had our artistic differences. His old, controlling nature returned as his grief declined. Nevertheless, he respected my achievements, and most of the time we were very compatible as acting partners. Acting was the platform for our ever increasing closeness.

As I became comfortable in the class and got to know the other students, I began networking with those who were going on real auditions and booking real acting jobs. It sounded intriguing, and I decided to try it.

I went to my first audition, gripped by stage fright all over again. I walked into the waiting room dressed like my character, an English spinster, as my acting books had advised. All the other actors were dressed in jeans and tee shirts, even the ones my age obviously there to audition for the same part as I was. Just like the first day of the acting class, I considered bolting, but my new, stronger self forced me to stay. I bumbled though and hurried out, just a bit stronger and more confident. I went on more auditions still nervous and unsure. However, each one helped build my confidence and catapulted me onto the next.

I soon booked my first paid, acting job. It was a commercial. I had professional headshots taken. I got an agent, went on more auditions, and booked more acting jobs. However, even if I didn't book the job, I grew to love the whole process whether it was just an audition or actually performing in a production.

My original resume consisted only of the few scenes I had done in acting class; there was a lot of white space on the paper. After a while, as I completed more and more acting jobs, it started to fill up, and I started to feel like a real actress.

Of course, I shared it all with Dad who was living in a nursing home by then. He was experiencing it vicariously through me. We loved talking acting whenever we could.

It's been several years now, and I have appeared in commercials, television, theater, music videos, print jobs, voice-over jobs, short films and live-interactive roles. In 2011, I was one of six backup exercise/dancers in the "Jane Fonda Prime Time Firm & Burn" workout DVD which was made to appeal to the baby boomer/senior market. I played the mother of show host, Patton Oswald, on the 2014 Film Independent Spirits Awards Show. In 2016, I was in a pre-Super Bowl commercial for Toyota Prius. For many years, I have portrayed various patients at university medical schools as part of student training. I have played such diverse roles as a granny rapper; a sexy senior; a trash-talking, gangster granny with a machine gun; and a regal queen. I have been dressed in a space suit, ridden a mechanical horse, fallen on an air mattress, had my lips sewn shut (by makeup), been hoisted up by college students for a beer binge, and on and on. Once, I taught an Acting-for-Fun class on a large cruise ship.

The story of my transition from retired probation officer to professional senior actress has been written about in *Time Magazine*, the *Los Angeles Times* newspaper, *AARP Life Reimagined* (American Association of Retired Persons), and in Marlo Thomas' 2014 book: *It Ain't Over...Till It's Over* which profiles different women who have reinvented themselves.

About two years into the acting class, Dad and I were sitting in the classroom, and the notion popped into my head of what a poignant memoir our experience would make. I first thought I would write something for my children, but then I wondered if the public might be interested. I dropped the whole notion with the thought, *That's ridiculous, I'm not a writer.*

However, the idea wouldn't leave me alone. For years, I followed a pattern of discarding and revisiting the book idea. Finally, after not having consciously thought of it for a few years, I woke up about three o'clock in the morning with half the book written in my head. I had chapter headings, full paragraphs, and dialogue. I kept trying to go back to sleep, but new thoughts were coming rapid-fire. I bargained with myself that I'd get some sleep and then write it down in the morning. Well, that didn't work, and after a few restless hours, I got out of bed and searched for some paper in my room as I wasn't about to walk down the hall to my office to find proper paper. So, my memoir started on a pack of Post-its, the only thing I could find. This is the metamorphosis of my writing:

Forced to create scenes to perform with my father in the acting class showcases, I discovered my talent for writing. Thoughts began to spill out of nowhere and culminated in my composing an account of that magical time we shared. The process has been grueling, consuming, fun, demanding, frustrating, exhilarating, and an incredible growth experience. The very act of writing the book became a catharsis, allowing me to deal first with the death of my mother and, several years later, my father. It has enabled me to look at my own fears, inadequacies, and the forces that have controlled me all my life. Now, I can understand why therapists encourage their patients to journal. Things are so much clearer when you write them down. Feelings and memories flowed from my brain to my fingers that I never even realized I had. I have often been stunned by what I've just written. It's as though it has a life of its own with me trailing helplessly behind.

From the day I first thought about writing the book to the day I held a published copy in my hands was a span of nine years. My memoir, *Adventures with Dad: A Father and Daughter's Journey Through a Senior Acting Class*, is available on Amazon.com and contains all the scenes I wrote and performed with my father. My books/speaker website is: LeeGaleGruen.com.

Creative writing came to me late in life, and it has been a gift. Writing the scenes my father and I performed was my first stab at it. I delved in much deeper by writing my memoir. I now write regularly and have had several short stories and articles published in online newsletters, e-zines (online magazines), and in a book: *Chicken Soup for the Soul—Think Possible*. I've also completed a stage play and a screenplay based on my memoir. And, of course, I've written this book.

I found a second life after I retired. Just as Michelangelo viewed himself chipping away the chaff of the marble to free the wheat of the statue hidden inside, I studied the raw materials and carved out the new life waiting for me. I couldn't find anything available to help me and had to stumble around finding my way, so I decided to pass along what I'd learned to simplify the process for others.

CHAPTER 2

Fear of Retiring

———

Contemplating retirement can be frightening. It has so many negative assumptions associated with it. It is a major life passage and is identified with being old. In our youth oriented culture, people try hard to avoid the label of retiree or senior.

Here are some common reasons people fear retiring, and that means from any activity you have done most of your adult life which defines you: a job, profession, stay-at-home parent, homemaker, etc.

LOSS OF IDENTITY

My professional identity for thirty-seven years was that of probation officer. Yes, I also had the identity of mother, wife, daughter, sister, friend, and more. Most of those would remain. My career and working identity for the bulk of my adult life, however, disappeared forever once I retired, and that was the activity that filled much of my waking hours for decades.

BECOME IRRELEVANT

Our youth oriented society seems to categorize retirees as being irrelevant—no longer useful—don't contribute anything to society. The majority of advertising and the like is aimed at younger people. That type of pigeonholing works on our self-esteem, and we come to believe it, too. We view our aging with fatalism, we despise it, and we rail against it.

BECOME INVISIBLE

Many seniors talk about how they feel invisible. Others seem to talk past them. Younger people don't include them in conversations. They have nothing in common with what seems like the rest of the world.

BECOME UNIMPORTANT

Your job identity gives you a sense of importance. Whatever your daily pursuit was, others in that field appreciated your importance or expertise. Without that position, are you even important anymore?

COMFORTABLE IN YOUR OLD ROUTINE

You may have been burned out at your job, but at least it was a known. There's a certain comfort level in routine.

FEARFUL OF TRYING SOMETHING NEW

You don't know what you're going to face once you retire. You're entering the unknown, and it can be very unnerving.

ALL YOUR FRIENDS STILL WORK

Many of us form strong friendships with co-workers while on the job. You might worry about who you'll hang out with once you retire. Perhaps, everyone you know is still working, maybe even your spouse. You'll be all alone.

BE BORED

What will you do with yourself? How will you fill all those waking hours that your job used to take up?

BE A BURDEN

No one wants to become dependent, needy, pathetic, and a burden on others. Will they roll their eyes when you call or appear? Will they be with you just out of duty, or even worse, pity?

LACK VALIDITY

A job gives us validity. It makes us feel we fit in—we are one of the group. When we retire, will we become the proverbial "square peg in a round hole"?

NO LONGER USEFUL

You might feel like you have nothing more to contribute that anyone wants. What good are you? What is your purpose in life?

LACK STRUCTURE

A job provides structure in our life. We know what our duties are and how and when to do them. To retire means that structure will be gone. You're afraid that you'll be floundering—at loose ends.

LOSE STATUS

Jobs confer status. Within our group, we get respect and admiration commensurate with the level of experience and expertise we have on our jobs. We pass along that knowledge to the newbies. We'll lose that when we retire.

NOT HAVE VALUE

Will you still be valuable when you're not contributing to society through your work? What good are you?

DON'T KNOW WHAT YOU'LL DO WITH YOUR LIFE

You have years to live, and you have no idea what you're going to do with all those days, months, years, and decades ahead of you. How will you fill all that time?

NOTHING MEANINGFUL, WORTHWHILE OR STIMULATING IN YOUR LIFE

Jobs provide stimulation and meaning. Without your job, you might have nothing to live for.

FEEL OLD

Only old people retire. Thoughts such as: *I don't want to be part of that group. I feel fine. I'm not old,* creep into our minds as we contemplate retirement. People fight getting old with actions such as dying their hair, wearing more and more makeup, undergoing plastic surgery and other procedures, taking supplements, lying about their age—doing anything to fool themselves and others into believing they're not aging.

FEEL WORTHLESS

You might have thoughts like: *Who wants me? Does society just want to throw me on the trash heap? Maybe that's all I'm good for; I deserve it.*

FEEL LONELY

Will you feel all alone—have only yourself to be with? Does anyone want to be with you anymore?

LACK MOTIVATION

Many sink into feelings of: *If I can't contribute anymore, why even try?*

LACK CHALLENGES

You might worry that life will be dull and no longer challenging.

DISAPPOINTMENT

Will you feel that nothing is any good or meaningful anymore?

DEPRESSION

Depression is the scourge of retirement. It's a hiding place driven by concerns about: *What will happen to me?* Many seniors start making statements like, "I don't know why I'm still here." Others insert into conversations references about waiting to die. Suicide begins to seem attractive to some.

SUBSTANCE ABUSE

A plague on retirees and seniors is substance abuse. So many in their later years began to withdraw into addictive behaviors such as drinking, drug abuse, over-eating, marathon television watching, and hours spent in front of the computer. They might even abuse their own prescription medication. It goes hand in hand with feelings like: *I'm worthless. Why bother anymore?*

ILLNESS

Aging does bring decline which can result in illness, physical and/or mental. Concern about that is valid and frightening. Your conversations may begin to center around illness-related topics. You may find yourself with such thoughts as, *Will I have a heart attack, get cancer, or get dementia or Alzheimer's Disease like (fill in the blank) did?*

DISABILITY

It's bad enough when you become ill, but maybe it can be treated, controlled, or cured. However, what about when you become temporarily or permanently disabled? What if you can't walk, can eat properly, shake, or any other number of conditions? That is certainly a part of aging for many. It's easy to obsess about such concerns to the neglect of everything else.

ANXIETY

Many retirees become anxious and worried. They only focus on negatives. This is driven by fear of the unknown and feelings of helplessness.

NOTHING TO LOOK FORWARD TO

So many worry that life will just go on and on in a depressing, boring manner.

NOT ENOUGH MONEY

A huge concern when contemplating retirement is: *What if my money runs out? Will I be out on the street?* One financially comfortable friend confessed to me her greatest fear was that she might become a bag lady someday. Retirees must educate themselves on how much money they really need and perhaps consider living a less expensive lifestyle than they had been used to when they were younger. Do you really need such a large home? Must you really drive such an expensive car? There are a lot of free or low cost activities available to seniors; you have to be proactive and seek them out.

CHAPTER 3

Why People Retire

———

As I stressed earlier, retirement can be from a job, career, profession, parenting, or whatever your main activity was for the bulk of your mature life. It's a shock when suddenly the job is gone and the kids are launched. It's scary not to have that routine of doing what you've done most of your waking hours throughout most of your adulthood. Have you ever wondered, *Is this how it's going to be for the rest of my life?*

The people who retire usually fall into the baby boomer and senior categories. Let's define those terms.

BABY BOOMER: Those born between 1946 and 1964. They are now between the ages of fifty-six and seventy-four.

SENIOR: Replaced the term "Old Age Pensioner." It refers to those in their sixties and older. The youngest segment of baby boomers is now close to the beginning of the senior classification, and the oldest are well into it.

Here are just a few statistics to get a broad picture of the age-fifty-and-over demographic in the United States. Although some are a bit dated, the numbers are increasing, and you can extrapolate.

According to the 2010 United States Census, people age fifty and over made up approximately one third of the total population—about 100,000,000 people. The entire population in 2015 in the United States was estimated to be 320,000,000. Those age fifty-plus were thought to make up about forty-five percent of that population—144,000,000 people. The U.S. Census Bureau estimated the 2019 United States population at around 328,000,000 people, an increase of well over 1.5 million per year. According to the Social Security Administration, 10,000 baby boomers a day are reaching the age of 65. The U.S. Census now predicts that by 2035 there will be more seniors than children.

Here are some common reasons people retire:

TIRED OF WORKING
Most people work the majority of their adult lives. After years and decades, jobs become repetitive. Many just burn out. The thought of not having to do the "same old thing" becomes very appealing.

ILLNESS
Some people become ill from the natural progression of aging or a fast onset of a debilitating condition. Others have accidents that disable them. Whatever the cause of the illness or deterioration, they are forced to retire as they can no longer do the work they've been doing.

NOT MENTALLY SHARP ANYMORE
Aging brings to some a decline of their cognitive abilities.

They might find that their diminishing mental acuity impacts their ability to do their job.

PENSION MAXED OUT

For those who have worked for decades at the same job with a pension plan, they find that their pension equals or almost equals their salary. Continuing to work and not collecting their pension means that they are almost working for free.

LAID OFF

The job may disappear for whatever reason. Some jobs may no longer be needed. Perhaps the business is sold and other workers in the acquiring company take those jobs. Maybe the business is outsourced. In recent times, new technology is taking over the work of human beings at many businesses.

DON'T CONNECT WITH YOUNGER CO-WORKERS

Some people find themselves feeling isolated and not fitting in with their co-workers. As older people retire, younger ones take their place. When you are in the top age category, there are fewer people with whom you might have something in common. You might begin to feel uncomfortable in that type of a setting and want to get out.

MANDATORY RETIREMENT AGE

Although a mandatory retirement age for most jobs in the United States is now illegal, some remain that do have such a requirement. Once a worker reaches that age, they are forced to retire whether they want to or not.

AGEISM

Although technically illegal, it still exists. Management might be easing you out in ways so subtle that you can't confront them on it. You might be given the worst assignments or transferred to work very far from your home.

WANT TO TRY SOMETHING ELSE

Perhaps you've always had a desire to do something specific, your job interferes with it, and you've finally positioned yourself to be able to pursue your dream. It could be anything from starting your own business to sailing around the world.

MOVE AWAY AND CAN'T FIND A NEW JOB

People are forced to change their residence for many reasons. If your new home is too far from your old job, you might have to quit. In the over-fifty age category, it is hard to find new employment.

SPOUSE WANTS YOU AT HOME

Sometimes, one spouse may retire before the other and wants the still-working spouse to be home with them. Perhaps, a non-working spouse requires caretaking.

CHILDREN NEED YOUR HELP

Your children might need your assistance for things like babysitting for their children (your adorable grandchildren) while they work. Or, you may be needed to drive the grandchildren to and from school or to extracurricular activities, doctor/dentist appointments, and the like.

YOUR PARENTING SKILLS ARE NO LONGER NEEDED
If your career has been as a full-time parent, once the kids move out and are on their own, your job is gone or significantly diminished.

CHAPTER 4

Finding Joy, Excitement, and Purpose in Your Retirement

As you reach your retirement years, you enter a new chapter of your life. You have no choice in the matter. You are probably a baby boomer or senior and have retired or are about to. Within that inevitable progression, we all make choices about our lifestyle as we press on. You may not even realize you are making a choice before each step you take.

Some choices are done with great deliberation, forethought, planning, research and discussion. Many are done unconsciously and instantaneously just before acting. Then, there are many styles in between. However you live your life, don't think you aren't making a choice. Life happens; unplanned things occur. However, as they present themselves, if we are thinking, breathing and have some level of intelligence, we make decisions as to how we react to them.

There is no turning back; we are propelled forward. We are forced to make decisions as we progress just by virtue of being alive. Nevertheless, they can be wise; we can have informed input.

Rather than just letting life happen and then making your choices as to how to react, you can plan and craft a new life that suits your unique personality. The rest of this book will deal with how to do just that. It will enlighten you as to what activities and opportunities are available for you in this new stage of your life—your retirement, how to identify what you might want to pursue, how to seek out and find it, and how to put your efforts into action.

It is vital to realize that you are still important, still worthwhile, and still relevant. Retirees and seniors are not just elderly people to be put out to pasture; they contribute much to society. They pass down the family and societal history. They are caretakers. They are role models. They are the guardians of wisdom and experience—society's stewards. Just take a look at the President, most members of the Senate and House of Representatives, and most state governors—overwhelmingly seniors.

Social: Many retirees and seniors are at a point in their lives where they are able and willing to give back to the community. They constitute the bulk of volunteers at places like hospitals, parks, museums, schools, police departments, and so on. Many of our institutions cannot afford to hire enough staff. They couldn't function without volunteers. Seniors have the time, interest and enthusiasm.

Economic: Retirees and seniors form a huge demographic. They control vast amounts of wealth which translates into purchasing power of significant amounts of goods and services.

Political: Retirees and seniors constitute a massive voting block. For example, in the 2016 election, 30 percent of voters were age 50 to 64, and 15 percent were age 65 and older. Seniors sway elections.

Retirees and Seniors are a demographic which should be pursued and courted by businesses and politicians, not ignored. Just as we spend time, energy, and resources on our children for the sake of our future, so must we spend the same on our seniors for the sake of our present.

WHAT MAKES PEOPLE HAPPY?

The World Health Organization advances the view that health is not just being free of illness but should include physical, mental, and social fitness as well.

Too many people have the wrong idea of what will make them happy. According to the 2011 documentary movie "Happy," you should do things that excite and gratify you; it's the doing, not the end result. Once you meet your basic needs such as food and shelter, money alone doesn't make you happier.

The difference between someone who earns $5,000 and $50,000 per year is significant in their amount of happiness. When you're struggling for basic necessities, it's very hard to be happy. However, there is not much difference in happiness between someone who earns $50,000 and $50,000,000 per year.

It has to do with something called the Hedonic Treadmill. More and more material possessions don't make you happier, they only make you crave more and more material possessions. Put another way, the more money you have, the more your expectations and desires rise. The things that make you happier include:

- personal growth
- relationships
- community feelings
- recreation
- new experiences
- friends and family
- meaningful activities
- appreciating what you have

So, to achieve true happiness, focus on: *What do I have?* rather than *What don't I have?* Do things like committing unplanned kind acts. That concept is very trendy these days. We hear it in commercials and read about it in magazines and newspapers. Don't dismiss it just because the idea is overused. Let's break it down and see what it really means and how it might be valuable to you.

It's not really complicated to commit an unplanned kind act. It simply means doing something nice for someone else. It doesn't have to be a major undertaking, cost money, or take much of your time. It can be as simple as smiling at a stranger when you pass them on the street or in a hallway. You might give a hug or a pat on the arm to someone who seems to need it. When your server in a restaurant pours you another cup of coffee or glass of water, look directly into their eyes and say, "thank you." That could be very significant to a person who is probably used to just being part of the background and rarely acknowledged.

It might be contrary to your nature to do as I suggest, but force yourself. Try it for one day—just do one kind act. See if it makes you feel good being kind to another human being. Stress behaviors such as:

- Gratitude
- Compassion
- Caring
- Love
- Altruism

I know that a lot of people will think it's hokey, silly, not worth their while. My response to that thinking: you need an "outlook makeover." It's such a win-win situation because that type of behavior not only beings joy to the recipient, but also to the giver. It simply feels good to be nice to others. So, do it for yourself as much as for the other person. Again, I simply encourage you to try it just for one day. If you don't like it, it's just not your thing, or it doesn't work, you have my permission to resume being depressed, pissy and miserable.

There is a country whose citizens are rated to be among the happiest people in the world. It bases its goals on the people-centered measurement of Gross National Happiness. That country is Bhutan, located in the eastern Himalayas near Tibet and India. It is ruled by a constitutional monarchy and has a population of three-quarters of a million people. That's about as much as a medium-sized city in the United States.

What an amazing concept: Gross National Happiness. We could use a dose of that philosophy in those oh-so-superior, first world countries whose main success indicator is the economically based Gross Domestic Product (GDP). GDP is strictly financial—a philosophy predicated on making money. Citizens in those countries are amassers—just keep grabbing more and more, whether or not they are happy, content, or satisfied as they do it.

So many retirees, baby boomers and seniors are depressed, isolated and lost. With their jobs over and their children grown, they don't know what to do with themselves. Studies have found that those who keep active physically and mentally live longer.

I don't have a magic bullet. All I have are ideas and suggestions you might not have thought of or been too intimidated to try. I can share them with you, encourage you, and tell you how to start, but you have to do the heavy lifting. You have to be proactive, seek them out, and then execute them. Even if you feel scared, awkward, intimidated, or uncomfortable, DO IT ANYWAY! All those happy people you see out there living the good life had those same feelings once. Everyone has to start at the beginning.

You have choices. You can sit home and be depressed, or you can get out and grab life in the time you have left. We always have to be doing something, all the time. There's no such thing as doing nothing. At the least, you're breathing, thinking, seeing, hearing, and you must move your body around to enable the basic requirements of life. So, if you have to be doing something all your waking hours, it might as well be something that brings you joy, excitement, and purpose. It's just a matter of what you choose.

CHAPTER 5

The Secret

———

The "secret" has an oxymoronic nature—so simple, yet so complex. It's probably something you've heard sometime in your life, but maybe the timing was never right. Maybe it wasn't for you back then. Maybe hearing it this time will click. Are you ready? Here it is:

Find something to be passionate about. Dig deep and search for an internal flint to start the kindling. We all have it somewhere. It's just a matter of uncovering it.

Yes, passion is something that makes you excited—makes you want to get up in the morning, get dressed, get out of the house, and embrace life! You'll have thoughts like: "Oh, boy! Today I get to (fill in the blank.)" I want to state again, if it's hard, scary or intimidating, *do it anyway!* Everyone else felt that way once. I sure did!

I found my passion by accident. It is acting. I love it and find it so exciting.

Okay, I know it's easy to say, "find your passion." A lot of people, especially if they are depressed or don't have anyone to encourage them, have no idea how to go about finding a passion. Here are some ways to identify your passion:

1. **What have you always wanted to do but never had the time, never got around to it, or were too scared to try?**

   You might have to think about this for a while. Make some notes. Ask your friends, relatives, or children for input. They might have ideas that you haven't even thought about. They've observed you over the years and have seen what you gravitate toward—what you appear to enjoy.

2. **What always seems to interest you?**

   What types of books, movies, or television programs do you pick? For example, one thing that I gravitate toward is science and natural history. I always read the scientific articles in newspapers and magazines, and I always enjoy scientific discussions. I realized that I'd love to do something connected to science. I also love animals. I found an activity that really grabbed me which combines the two: I became a volunteer tour guide at the world famous La Brea Tar Pits in Los Angeles, California, when I used to live nearby.

3. **What matches your talents, abilities or prior experience?**

   For example: what type of job did you do before you retired? If you were a teacher, you might like to tutor students. If you were a musician, you might like to mentor another budding musician.

4. **Try something different—something you've never tried before.**

   There's a comfort level in doing the same old thing, but it gets old and boring, and you don't get the opportunity to grow. Try lots of different things, even things that at first you don't find interesting or appealing. One might stick (ex: my acting).

When I was the coordinator of a study-discussion group at a senior, learning-in-retirement program, I compiled a list of topics under the umbrella theme for the participants to research and report on. Each class member picked a number from a hat, and in order of their ranking, they each chose a topic from the list. The lowest ranked member complained that someone else had chosen the topic he wanted which he knew a lot about as it tied into his former occupation. He didn't like the one remaining topic he got by default. When, several weeks later, he began his oral report, he started by saying that he loved learning about the subject and never would have studied it if he hadn't been forced to.

So, when you're presented with something, think of it as an opportunity rather than a curse. Better yet, don't just wait until you happen upon something. Seek out things that are different from your normal interests.

There are pursuits available for all types of personalities— if you're a people-person, if you're reclusive, and all degrees in between. This is not a contest. You don't have to do what I did and you don't have to perform to the level of some of the examples I will cite.

Make it work for you. Take it as far as it satisfies you, as far as it makes you excited that, "Oh good, tomorrow is Thursday, and that's the day I (again, fill in the blank.)"

You have a window of opportunity. Your working years are over and your kids are on their own. So, assuming that you're financially stable and in decent health, now is the time to do the things you've always wondered about or seek out others you never knew existed.

I have a cousin who was a successful, self-employed businessman. Far into his senior years, he refused to retire because he couldn't imagine what else he might want to do.

Years ago, I worked with a man who also lived in my neighborhood. He retired, and I ran into him walking his dog about a month later. He told me how lost he was; he didn't know what to do with himself. He died the following month.

Make sure you survive and thrive. It's doable and not that hard. Here are a few additional statistics I've run across since you liked the first ones so much. Then, I promise, we're done with statistics.

1. January 1, 2011 was the start of the 77,000,000 baby boomer generation turning 65. From that time, a baby boomer will turn sixty-five every eight seconds for the next eighteen years.

2. In 2015, the group of those age fifty and over living in the United States was thought to be a higher ratio to the total population than in 2010, and it is believed that they will soon control over seventy percent of disposable income.

3. Those age 50-and-older are believed to buy two thirds of all new cars, one half of all computers, and one third of all movie tickets. They spend seven billion dollars

per year shopping online and more than eighty percent of all credit card purchases of premium travel.

4. Adults over age 50 in the United States are the third largest economy in the world, just behind the gross national product of the United States and China.

5. The age 50+ demographic of consumers is projected to grow by thirty-four percent by 2030.

6. Loneliness and lack of socialization have the same impact on your health as smoking one pack of cigarettes per day.

7. People who retire to nothing have a life expectancy of five years.

8. Workers ages 55 and older are predicted to make up a quarter of the work force in 2022 which will be four percent higher than in 2012.

CHAPTER 6

Activities and Pursuits

———

I know it's easy for other retirees to give advice such as, "There are plenty of things to do," or "Get a life." They might complain, "I'm so busy I need to go back to work to rest." It may seem that the Holy Grail is forever out of your reach. You don't have any idea what you can do to jump on that elusive bandwagon and join the complainers who are so busy in their retirement they need to take a vacation from it.

It's difficult to even know what's available "out there." To make it easier and stimulate your thoughts, I've compiled a list of activities and pursuits you can explore. You may think of things not on my list, or you might expand on an idea I've included. There is something for all personality types on the scale from introverted to extroverted. And, the bonus is that once you find an activity you like, it's a natural place to meet like-minded people and make friends.

ATHLETIC ACTIVITIES
Hiking
Most locations throughout the United States and in other countries have hiking groups. For example, the Sierra Club in

California is an environmental organization founded in 1892 by John Muir, a naturalist and early advocate for wilderness preservation in America. They sponsor many outdoor recreational activities including free, day hikes several times a week in the local mountains. I was a member for many years and often hiked in my local mountains. Just show up at the designated meeting place listed in their online Day Hiking Section, join the others who have congregated, and start your hike. I've also skied with Sierra Club group members on organized club outings. I made many good friends there. I'm sure similar groups exist wherever you live.

Walking

There are organized group walks at malls, beaches, parks, and the like. Check local senior centers for their group walks. Or, just take solo walks in your neighborhood, and you'll meet lots of other walkers. Walk around the track at the local high school when classes are not in session.

Court and Field Games

This category would include games such as: tennis, badminton, handball, lawn bowling, bocce ball, baseball, and soccer.

Most parks or schools have public courts. There are also private clubs with these amenities. Many offer lessons. I have some friends in their eighties who play tennis a few times a week at a local, public court. Court and field games offer good exercise, fun, and provide opportunities for socializing.

Golf

There are public golf courses in parks and private courses at country clubs or some retirement communities. Instructors are available to teach you to play. You can just show up and be matched with other players.

Boating

If you live near the ocean, river or a lake, there are public docks. There are also boating clubs you can join to learn about it and have access to a boat.

Bicycling

Bicycle in your neighborhood alone or with a friend. Bicycle to the market instead of taking the car. It's cheaper, easier on the environment, and good exercise. Bicycle on public bike paths alone, with a group, or with a bicycle club. Club members meet at a specified location and pedal together, often to a destination to share a meal.

Swimming

There are public and private pools in most areas. They have instructors to teach you how to swim or help you improve. They have classes where you can meet like-minded folks.

Skiing

I became a skier in my late thirties. The senior ski club I eventually joined, Over the Hill Gang, even has members in their eighties. People of like ability meet up to ski together.

Exercise facilities

Check out local gyms. I belong to one that has exercise machines and background music. I go at my own convenience and have developed the level of intensity that works for me. I encounter the same fellow exercisers and have become friendly with some. You can also find groups organized around exercise at senior centers and parks.

CLASSES AND LECTURES

Do you enjoy studying or learning about new subjects? There are many non-credit programs in most areas that offer classes or lectures for seniors. Check them out at senior centers, high schools, colleges and universities.

For six years, I attended a learning-in-retirement program now called The Plato Society of Los Angeles. There were others in my area such as Sage, Omnilore, and Osher Life Long Learning Institute (OLLI) which is a national program.

You can explore auditing a class at your local college or university which means that you attend and just listen but don't participate, don't take tests, and don't get a grade. Or, you might consider attending classes for credit and getting that college degree you never quite attained, or a higher degree, or a different degree. You can also attend virtually online. Check to see what's available in your area.

CLUBS AND ORGANIZATIONS

A club is simply a group of people who come together to pursue a common interest or activity. You can find a club for just about anything that interests you. Some are strictly social; some have a specific purpose; some raise money for a cause. All have a social component to them. It's a great way to meet people.

If you hear about a club or organization that sounds intriguing, call the group coordinator and inquire about it. Attend a meeting to check it out.

Advisory boards for clubs and organizations need board members. This is a great fit for the take-charge personality. If you're more of a worker bee type, sign up for a committee that fits your personality.

There are many types of clubs. They can revolve around any organizing theme: charity, cars, knitting, quilting, cooking, trains, clocks, and on and on. I know folks in clubs for each of the examples cited. Another cousin started a club based around her speech impediment.

If you have an idea for a club but can't find an existing one, consider starting your own. Just invite a few friends and acquaintances and suggest they invite others. In a short time, you should have a well-attended gathering.

Here are some examples of clubs you can join:

Athletic Activity Clubs

As I made reference to earlier, I belonged to a group called "Over the Hill Gang" which is a national organization for the fifty plus crowd that has group athletic activities like skiing, hiking, canoeing, bicycle riding, and more. I've mentioned the Sierra Club on the West Coast which promotes activities in the mountains. Country Clubs usually are built around a golf course for club members' use, and they have clubhouses to hold events. Check your area for similar organizations.

Book Clubs

Book reading clubs are very popular. They are formed at community centers, groups, organizations, the library, or just by some friends who decide to start one. The modus operandi is usually that club members put forth book titles, and the group decides on which book to read next.

The way the club is structured can vary. Often, all the members read the same book, and they meet once a month to discuss it. They may rotate the meeting location among the homes of the different members. Many times, it's in conjunction with dinner, maybe a potluck, at the meeting location.

The ground rules can vary. Sometimes, the meeting is always at the same location. Sometimes the types of books follow a theme or pursuit. Sometimes, each member reads a different book of their own choosing and then gives a book report on it at the club meeting. I know a few people who belong to multiple book clubs.

Movie Clubs

Here, members may all go to the same movie together, or they may go to the chosen film separately. In both scenarios, members then meet together to discuss the movie. Again, it can be done in conjunction with food: in a restaurant, at a home dinner, dessert only, or alternating those possibilities.

Service Clubs

There are many service clubs where members support a charity or cause. The idea is to raise money to contribute to their chosen venture. They hold money-raising events, and the members put their combined efforts into planning and executing the affair. It's a worthy pursuit, an opportunity to give back to the community, and a way of socializing and making friends.

Some examples of service clubs are: Lions Club, Kiwanis Club, Rotary Club, American Association of University Women, and political clubs to name a few.

COOKING

Are you drawn to cooking or have always loved to cook? Creating a dish from a recipe or from scratch can be very gratifying and therapeutic. Your mind is fully engaged in the process, like a scientist in his/her laboratory.

You can shop for ingredients at local and distant markets and farms. You can have parties where you make all the dishes. You'll love the accolades from your invited guests.

Buy recipe books or borrow them for free from the library. You can find just about any recipe you want on the Internet. Watch cooking shows on television to learn about new dishes and methods. Practice them in your own kitchen.

Attend a cooking class. Many are offered locally. It's a fun experience shared with the other class members. Take a cooking vacation. Many tour companies offer cooking opportunities on their trips, often featuring dishes of the countries you visit.

DANCING

Dancing may be a multi-level pill. It is purported to be good exercise, reduce stress, and increase cognitive acuity (because it integrates several brain functions).

My Aunt Helen and Uncle Abe studied ballroom dancing as seniors. Then, they taught dancing at the active, retirement community where they lived. Another senior couple I know took lessons and became very accomplished at ballroom dancing. Now, they periodically teach it on luxury cruise ships in exchange for free cruises. Two other friends, a married couple, discovered dancing lessons at their local Arthur Murray Studio. They love it, and it's an activity they can share.

Senior centers have dances with live bands or recorded music. I've been to many of these. At one, I saw a woman with dementia dancing with her caretaker. Her steps were limited, mostly just a swaying motion to the music, but she was on the dance floor the whole time. Many there did not dance but just went to listen to the music and be among people.

I recommend seeing the inspirational 1975 movie: *Queen of the Stardust Ballroom*. Lonely and lost after becoming a widow, the main character starts attending a dance club which changes her life.

FOREIGN LANGUAGE

Have you ever wanted to learn a foreign language? Now is your chance. There are beginner's classes available as well as more advanced classes if you already know another language and just want to brush up.

I attended a community Spanish class for years sponsored by the local high school but held at the library. I also attended a total immersion program in Mexico three different times where I lived with a Mexican family and went to classes daily at a local school specializing in teaching Spanish to foreigners. It was a combination vacation and study program. It was low-cost and a lot of fun. These types of programs are offered all over the world.

GAMES

There are numerous types of games, both of a solitary and group nature. The latter offer a wonderful opportunity to socialize and meet new people. They're also fun to do with children and grandchildren.

Active: See Athletic Activities above

Sedentary:

Solitary Games: sudoku, crossword puzzles, video games, and cell phone and computer games

Group Games: mah-jongg; charades, board games such as chess, checkers, and Monopoly; card games such as bridge, poker, and gin rummy; and lots more.

GARDENING

Have you always been attracted to working in the soil with your hands? Find a plot of land in your backyard; front yard; public gardens; or just pots around your residence, inside or outside. Get some seeds or cuttings, and go at it. Buy books on gardening or borrow them from the library for free. Grow your own vegetables, fruit trees, flowers, or anything else in the flora category that interests you.

Community gardens are available in many vicinities. You are assigned a plot in a large area and can work your land next to your neighbors who are working theirs. Grow your own lunch or dinner, and socialize with others doing the same. Give your excess produce to friends or for charitable causes.

I used to snip cuttings from interesting plants I found when I was out and about to plant in pots at my house. Most folks are happy to give you cuttings from their yard if you ask for them.

One friend got heavily involved in two different rose societies. Not only did she have a lovely, self-tended garden at her own home, but she also helped tend the rose garden at the headquarters of the Pasadena Rose Parade. Whenever I talked to her, she was usually busy gathering cuttings from friends' gardens (mine included) and driving them to another location to be sold at money raising events sponsored by her gardening clubs. Another friend has a large plot of land abutting her home, and she planted her own orchard with many different fruit trees.

GENEALOGY

Websites such as ancestry.com or 23andme.com help you research distant relatives using your DNA.

My late friend, George, investigated not only his own family genealogy but that of his deceased wife. He went as far back to their roots as he could on his own. Then, he hired a professional genealogist to trace the family history even further back. Because of the wonder of the Internet, George was able to make contact with many unknown relatives. He took trips to faraway lands meeting some of those family members and visiting graveyards where ancestors were buried.

The Mormon Church honors genealogy of all people as part of their religious beliefs. To that end, they maintain a genealogical library. There are volunteers to help you search their records. Their genealogy website is free to the public.

I have visited the Mormon Genealogical Library in both Los Angeles, California and Salt Lake City, Utah. With the help of docents, I was able to access centuries old maps and decades old census records and ship manifests. It was exciting to see my mother listed on the 1920 census at age five as being a member of my maternal grandparents' household in Chicago, Illinois.

HOBBIES

You can continue with a hobby you've had for many years. Conversely, you can pursue a hobby that's new to you, maybe one that's always intrigued you or one you just heard about. Here are some examples:

Collecting

People enjoy collecting things from stamps to cars. It's fun to scour the Internet, newspapers, flea markets and the like searching for another item to add to your collection. There are even clubs devoted to specific collectables. Check the Internet to find them. You'll meet like-minded folks in your endeavors.

Crafts

My cousin, Gail, makes usable items such as Kleenex boxes, photo album covers, glass cases and more from a stitchery kit called "plastic needlepoint." She gives them as gifts to family members and friends or donates them to organizations to sell and raise money.

Another cousin (I have a lot of cousins), Ellen, taught herself to make beaded jewelry. Then, she started her own jewelry business. She now has a website and sells at craft shows, home parties that friends arrange, or at online crafter's websites such as etsy.com. She'll custom-make earrings or a necklace to match a buyer's clothing.

Flower Arranging

You can buy flowers and arrange them artistically. Or, you can start a step earlier and grow your own flowers to arrange. You can also take classes in flower arranging. You can use your flower arrangements to decorate your own home, to give as gifts, and to donate to hospitals and charity events. Flower arranging can be an art form. The Japanese culture has perfected it in Ikebana.

Photography

Many people find photography fascinating. My friend, Jim, has been taking photography classes for years at a local community center. He's always shooting photos and emailing them to the event participants.

A couple I met on a trip to New Guinea took hundreds of photos. They plan to cull them into a slideshow and show them at local clubs and community centers where they live. If your photographs are good enough, you can print them in books to sell or enter them into contests. Some even pay money to the winners.

Scrapbooking

This takes making a scrapbook to another level. Although a few hundred years old, making scrapbooks has had a recent rebirth and is now a verb: to scrapbook. There are both online websites and brick and mortar stores that sell scrapbooking supplies and offer classes in how to do it.

Scrapbooking consists of arranging and preserving such things as art, photographs, souvenirs, printed material, and anything else you can think of to compile in an album/book form or in boxes. Each item can have text to describe it, and their containers can be decorated.

Scrapbooks can be created for a variety of objectives from gifts to legacy items to pass down family mementos to the next generation. A family scrapbook will help your grandchildren remember you and enable your future generations to know about you and their family history before they were born. A scrapbook project could be done with your children or grandchildren.

MUSIC
Study a Musical Instrument

My Uncle Barney had a career as a postman, back when those sturdy souls hauled that heavy bag of mail on their shoulder—no wheels for Uncle Barney. When he retired, he took up the piano. He had never studied a musical instrument in his life, but the idea intrigued him. Uncle Barney plunked away, just loving it. It wasn't great music, but it was his music.

I attended a free piano concert at a senior center a few years ago. The 75-year-old pianist had a PhD in Physics. He had taught himself classical piano at the age of 60 and started giving free concerts at the age of 71. He performed many of his pieces without sheet music. He was wonderful and so excited about playing the piano.

I know someone who plays piano in a small band. All the performers are seniors. I know another man who teamed up with a friend to form an act. One plays the songs of a well-known composer on the piano while the other tells stories about that composer. They perform at senior centers and community venues, sometimes for pay.

There is a ukelele club for beginners and advanced members at the retirement community where I live.

Learn about Opera

There are opera clubs where you can hear talks about the current opera being performed in your location. You can connect with others to attend together.

One of my friends is an opera buff. He gives talks at grammar schools about the upcoming opera through a program sponsored by the Los Angeles Opera.

NEEDLEWORK

Do you like to work with textiles? Learn to sew, knit, crochet or embroider, or expand on your current ability? Try other forms of needlecraft such as: lace-making, quilting, applique, tatting, macramé, braiding, tapestry, or needlepoint. Look into the art of weaving textiles and fabrics. Seek out classes, clubs, or mentors to help you.

Make clothes for yourself, your grandchildren, the kids down the block, pets, or children in placements. Use your skills for costume making or altering for the local community theater. Make items to be sold by a club or charity as a fund raiser. A friend used to make baby quilts and donate them to a local children's hospital.

These activities aren't only for women. I read about a man who crocheted sweaters for oil soaked penguins so they couldn't groom themselves and ingest the oil. Rosey Grier, a big, burly NFL football player for the New York Giants and then the Los Angeles Rams in the 1950s and 1960s, was famous for his fondness of needlepointing, crocheting, and knitting. He even wrote a book for men about needlepointing.

PAINTING

Remember my Uncle Barney, the retired mailman? He also took classes in painting after he retired, another pursuit he had never done in his life. He would usually paint simple scenes in oil on small, twelve inch canvases. They were far from museum quality, but he was passionate about it. He would give his paintings to family members and friends. Everyone in the family had one of Uncle Barney's paintings hanging on their wall.

A former co-worker had always loved painting. When she retired, she continued to paint and took many painting classes. She became very accomplished in her seventies.

Have you heard of a painter called Grandma Moses? Her real name was Anna Mary Robertson Moses. She started painting at the age of 78 and lived to the age of 101. She took up this pastime because she developed arthritis in her hands and could no longer do the embroidery work she loved. She painted over 1500 canvasses. Unlike my Uncle Barney, her paintings do hang in museums. In 2006, one of her paintings sold for $1.2 million

PERFORMING
Acting

Have you always had a bit of the thespian in you? Enroll in an acting class. They are offered at senior centers, private studios, and schools. You might check out the acting classes at a senior program like I did. It changed my life! I became a professional actress after the age of sixty.

The local community theater offers an opportunity to get involved in the acting life. If you don't want to act but love the milieu, you can direct, build sets, sew costumes, sell tickets, and lots more.

I met my late friend, Angela, at an acting job. She had studied acting in college. However, she quit that passion after she married and had a family. As a senior, she rediscovered acting and was cast in many good roles including a juicy role in an academy award nominated movie. She was still pursuing acting in her seventies despite the cancer that racked her body. She told me that even if she was tired or didn't feel well, if she was called for an audition or booked an acting job, "It energizes me." I love that phrase. If you find a passion, it will energize you.

Stand-up comedy

Have you ever thought about being a comedian? Have you done it informally at work or at parties? Think about taking it to the next level. There are classes in standup comedy or sketch comedy.

I know four different women who as seniors started performing stand-up comedy at local comedy clubs. I'll periodically receive an email invitation to one of their comedy gigs.

SINGING

Do you like to sing? Here are some thoughts: sing in church choirs; sing at senior center musical programs; sing in barbershop quartet groups. If you don't know how to sing or can't carry a tune, there are classes to teach you.

TRAVEL

There are many ways to travel. You can find groups of seniors to travel with. Road Scholar (formerly: Elder Hostel) has trips throughout the world mainly geared to seniors. A similar company is ElderTreks.

Senior centers, schools, churches and the like offer low cost day trips, often with the bus, lunch, and a guide included.

Sign up to work at a National Park. They'll usually give you a free space to park your RV if you have one as well as pay you minimum wage. Some also offer dormitory style housing for their staff.

Do you like cruises? See if you have a desired skill you can teach or a lecture you can give on a ship in exchange for a free cruise. They will allow you to bring one other person as part of the deal. You'll each have to pay for your own transportation to and from the point of embarkation and debarkation. However, most everything onboard is free for both of you: the cost of the cruise, food, and entertainment. You will have to pay for any off-board excursions offered by the cruise as well as items purchased in the gift shop. You'll have to go through a booking agency which will also charge you an agent's fee. These agencies have Internet websites and are always looking for new recruits. One such agency is Posh Talks.

If you're a man, can dance, and have a pleasant personality, you can get a free cruise in exchange for being a dance host to dance with the many, single women who frequently take cruises. I once taught a class, "Acting for Fun," on a cruise ship. Another acquaintance gave bridge lessons. As mentioned earlier, a couple I know gives dancing lessons on cruise ships.

WRITING

Write on a computer. If you can't do that, write by hand. If your hands don't function so well anymore, dictate into a dictating machine and have someone else transcribe it. You can also dictate into your computer and the words will be typed automatically using certain computer programs such as Dragon. If you don't have a computer, ask someone to interview you and write it up. If you don't have anyone you know, you can hire a ghost writer. Ask members of local writers' groups for referrals, or google "ghost writers in (your location)."

Write your memoir or autobiography

You don't have to do it for publication as I did. You can write it for your children and grandchildren. They will value it as they grow older. If you can no longer write or type, you might try dictating it to a friend or relative—maybe your child, grandchild, or a niece, nephew, or other significant person. If you don't think you're articulate enough to tackle writing, a hired ghost writer will interview you to tease out the material you want to convey and then write it in a style that suits you. Many local or online publication houses can make your final manuscript into a book form. You can add photos and be as creative as you like.

My mother took a class called, "How to Write Your Autobiography." She solicited input from her older siblings about their family when she was too young to remember. She gave a copy to my father, sister, and me. I cherish it, especially now that she's gone! I've shared it with my cousins, too.

Another way to record memoir or autobiographical material is to be videotaped telling your story. My cousin made a video of my great uncle recounting his life story. She and his wife prompted his memory by asking relevant questions. Video and audio recordings can either remain in that format, or they can be transcribed into written form.

Write articles
Write for your local newspaper.
Write for your retirement newsletter.
Write for online newsletters. (I've sold two.)

Write short stories or a book
Have you ever gotten an idea for a story or even a book? Write it! Take a writing class if you need help in how to go about it. Join a writers' group to network with other writers. These can be published or you can distribute them to friends and relatives or email them to whomever you like. I read about a man who loved to write poetry. He set up a box on a post in his neighborhood and filled it with free copies of his most recent poem to the delight of his neighbors.

Write blurbs or longer accounts to go with family photos
Put the photos and stories in an album (see Scrapbooking above). This is another project that might be fun to do with grandchildren.

Write your own obituary

I've included this here because an audience member at one of my lectures told me she took a class in writing your own obituary. I'd never heard of that, but I think it's fascinating.

Write a blog

A blog is like a newspaper column, but it's published on the Internet. You can write things of interest to your readers. As an example, check out my blog, "Reinventing Yourself in Your Retirement Years," at: LeeGaleGruen.wordpress.com. I'll discuss blogs in greater detail in Chapter 10.

CHAPTER 7

How and Where to Find Activities and Pursuits

———

I'm sure many people reading the suggestions in Chapter 6 are feeling that they have no idea where to even find the activities and pursuits I have discussed or that they've heard about elsewhere. Yes, it can be difficult at times, and you have to put some effort and energy into seeking them out. Here are some methods to help you:

INTERNET

The Internet lets you access websites. These are simply computer screen pages of information posted by any person, agency, company, or organization regarding what they do and offer. Type into Google, Yahoo, Bing, or any other search engine an activity that interests you. Navigate the websites you encounter. Navigating a website is much like doing so with books, magazines, and newspapers. If an Internet article refers you to another one, find it on the Internet and read it, too. Do your research on where to find what you're looking for. It exists and is there for you.

If you don't know how to use a computer or the Internet, take classes offered at senior centers and local schools. As my son said to me many years ago when I resisted learning to use a computer and the Internet, "Come into the modern world, Mom."

If learning it is just too hard, ask for help from your children, your grandchildren, the kid next door, or anyone else. If you never learned to type or you can't type anymore do to finger coordination problems, there are voice activated programs for the computer such as Dragon. Again, if that is too overwhelming, ask for help from your friendly librarian. They'll check the Internet for you or help you do it.

Caveat: Always be cautious about anything you discover on the Internet. Try to check out the legitimacy of a website through other sources such as the librarian, friends, or newspaper and magazine articles. Try calling the contact telephone number on the website and talking to a live person.

LIBRARIES

Ask your librarian to help you find information about activities that are available in your area or help you get information about one that interests you. There are books and computers at the library. He/she will help you use them to find what you're seeking.

NEWSPAPERS AND MAGAZINES

Read newspapers, magazines, newsletters, and study online sources and the like looking for opportunities. I read in my retiree's newsletter about a volunteer opportunity at my local natural history museum. I eventually called, talked to the person in charge of the volunteers, made an appointment, and was taken on a tour. The volunteer coordinator mentioned that she also handled volunteers at the La Brea Tar Pits. I hadn't thought of that but was very excited because it was so much closer to my house. That began my volunteer work there for four years, and I loved it.

NETWORKING

Ask family members, friends, acquaintances, and even strangers you encounter in your daily activities what they do, what clubs they belong to, how they first heard about it, how they found information about it, and anything else you can think of. Or, if you have an idea of something you'd like to try but don't know where to start, ask them about that, too. If they don't know about it personally, they may know of someone who does and can refer you.

I started attending an acting class only because a woman I sat next to at an organization dinner started chatting with me. I told her I was about to retire and didn't have plans. She was acting in plays at a children's charity program and invited me to attend. I did, and it looked like the actors were having so much fun. That was the moment that put the idea of acting into my mind. Although I wasn't aware of it consciously, it might be one of the reasons I stayed in that senior acting class after discovering I had to perform instead of running out as I had wanted to do.

SENIOR CENTERS

Most areas have a local senior center. It is your friend. Stop by and pick up their schedule of activities. They have so much to offer baby boomers and seniors such as classes, movies, lectures, dancing, entertainment events, day trips, games, etc. My father played bridge at his local senior center for years.

SOCIAL MEDIA AND SOCIAL NETWORKING

Social media websites are more for broadcasting information, whereas social networking websites are more for communication between parties. Now, however, the lines are often blurred. Social media and social networking are ways to interact with people through the Internet. There are many social media and social networking websites where you can post things you want to say, photos, videos, etc. Conversely, you can see what others post. These "others" can be family members, friends, acquaintances, celebrities, or strangers. These platforms enable you to connect virtually to anyone in the world who also uses that same social media or social networking website. They are good vehicles for locating and eventually engaging with others. An old friend from decades ago found me on Facebook. com, a social media website, and she contacted me.

People post information about events, get-togethers, parties, classes, lectures, and all manner of gatherings. If they are of interest, you could attend, also. Between 2012 and 2015, there was an 80% increase in Facebook users age 55+.

Here are some of the most popular and free social media and social networking websites:

Facebook: facebook.com
This is a website where you can search for friends, colleagues, relatives or strangers. It is mainly for sharing information of

all types including personal thoughts, photos, videos, links, and other matters of interest.

Twitter: twitter.com
Twitter's platform allows users to communicate using 280 characters or less called "tweets." This has become very popular with celebrities including upper echelon politicians

YouTube: youtube.com
This is a video sharing service. You can upload your own videos and view those of others. You can often find professional videos, too.

Pinterest: pinterest.com
This is mainly a photo sharing service. You can "pin" photos on your page and view photos on the pages of other members.

Tumblr: tumblr.com
This is a cross between websites like Twitter or Facebook and a blog where the writer shares his thoughts on an ongoing basis, often with an overall theme; it's like a newspaper column.

Instagram: instagram.com
This is another photo sharing website that makes it easy to shoot photographs on your smartphone and upload them to Instagram or other social media sites

LinkedIn: linkedin.com
This is geared toward networking for business purposes. It lets

you connect with people seeking your skills or whose skills you are seeking.

Meetup: meetup.com

This site is for enabling members to find each other and form real time groups over shared interests. A friend who wanted to practice and improve her Spanish found a group through Meetup.com that got together once a week at a local coffee shop.

WordPress: wordpress.com

This is a blogsite that lets you create a free blog. You can share your thoughts with others or read their blogs. If folks like it, they will start "following" your blog and receive a notification each time you post a new blog. There are also other blogsites such as blogger.com. Chapter 10 consists of my blog posts for over six years on my blog, "Reinventing Yourself in Your Retirement Years." Follow my blog at: LeeGaleGruen.wordpress.com.

CHAPTER 8

Volunteering

———

This is a huge category with so many volunteer opportunities available. It's a way of contributing your time and effort to something worthwhile by helping others. A large percentage of volunteers are seniors, so it's also a great chance to interact with people your own age and make new friends with common interests.

The secret to turning a volunteer job into a passion is to volunteer for something that you find exciting. That becomes a win-win situation: you are giving back to the community while doing an activity that you enjoy or find meaningful.

To identify my perfect volunteer position, I used the method of thinking what types of articles I always read in newspapers and magazines. I realized that I always read the science and natural history articles. I had only taken a few science classes in school, and I hadn't worked in a scientific field as a career. Nevertheless, I was always drawn to science.

I scouted around for opportunities near where I lived. As mentioned earlier, I soon learned that the world famous La Brea Tar Pits was looking for volunteers. The thought was enticing, and it was only a few miles from my home. I checked it out and liked what I found.

I started slowly, reading the literature provided for potential volunteers. I liked it even more, so I attended a few of their docent training sessions. I went from like to love.

After completing my instruction, I toured groups around the grounds of the park, lecturing about the geology, animal life, and how the tar pits were formed. I also led groups inside of their attendant building, the Page Museum, discussing the skeletons on display of the extinct animals who were trapped in the tar as long ago as 60,000 years. The experience also tapped into my newfound passion to act and perform in front of people; being a tour guide is a type of performance. I loved it when participants thanked me at the end and told me how interesting and clear I had made it for them.

There are volunteer positions for all personality types on the continuum from introverted to extroverted.

Are you an in-charge type? Volunteer programs are always looking for people to take leadership roles: head committees, plan functions, decide on procedures, and other decision making or administrative matters.

Are you the reclusive type? There are lots of volunteer jobs to suit your personality. My friend, Jim, volunteered in what he called the "bone room" at the National History Museum of Los Angeles County. He would help catalogue ancient animal bones. That is a by-yourself type of job but fascinating to the right person.

Are you a caretaker type? Hospitals, crisis clinics, and other such locales need people with caring personalities to interact with their patients and victims.

Do you like kids? My girlfriend, Maya, used to volunteer as a grammar school classroom aid. She was supervised by the teacher and had direct interaction with the children in the class.

AARP has partnered with the Peace Corps to place seniors in volunteer jobs worldwide.

Here are some examples of volunteer opportunities:

ANIMALS

Do you love animals? The local rescue agencies and animal shelters are always looking for people to walk dogs, clean animal enclosures, and other duties. Also, they need people to staff their occasional animal adoption clinics.

Be a pet therapy team with your dog (or bird or other animals) at hospitals, retirement homes, and the like. My dog and I were a pet therapy team for a few years at a local hospital. We visited patients who had requested a dog visit. They were so grateful and often talked about their pet waiting for them at home. For the short time of our visit, it took their minds off of why they were in the hospital. I got as much satisfaction from the encounter as they did.

AQUARIUMS

Do you like what lives in the oceans, seas, rivers, and lakes? If you have a local aquarium, check out what they have to offer. My friend, Caroline, used to volunteer leading school groups at a small aquarium in Santa Monica, California.

CHILDREN

There are lots of opportunities to work with kids. Check local schools, child day care centers, and google key words to find them in your area. Big Brothers/Big Sisters is a national organization helping to match an adult with a needy child. The adult serves as a mentor—a type of parental figure. I know of many of these relationships which have formed into lasting bonds between the mentor and mentee.

COACHING

Are you good at athletics? Little Leagues and other youth athletic groups are always looking for volunteers to coach their budding athletes. Special Olympics is an athletic event for handicapped youth. If this appeals to you, contact them and offer your services.

COMPUTER

A former high school classmate volunteered to be the webmaster for our high school reunion website. He updates it when new information comes to him. People who hadn't seen each other in years can now connect—and do. Old friendships have been renewed and new ones formed. We are only able to do that because he contributes his time and effort. If you are a computer techie type, offer your services to places in the community needing such services.

CRISIS CENTERS

There are crisis centers of various kinds in most cities. There is usually a training program to help you work with those coming for assistance. A friend volunteered at a rape crisis clinic. The protocol is that the volunteer sits with rape victims in the waiting room until they are seen by the social worker. Just the volunteer's presence and willingness to chat about normal, matter-of-fact things gives the victims some comfort at a traumatic and frightening time in their lives.

DOCENT (VOLUNTEER TOUR GUIDE)

I mentioned that I was a tour guide for four years at the La Brea Tar Pits. I was also a tour guide at the Virginia Robinson Gardens in Beverly Hills, California. It is a century-old, historic estate with gardens covering six acres. I got to hang out in that beautiful atmosphere and perform in front of people by leading them on tours of the house and garden. What could be better! Museums, art galleries, and historic sites open to the public are always looking for docents.

GOVERNMENT AGENCIES

Google "Public Service and Volunteer Opportunities" to begin navigating the Internet to find out what's available in your area. One idea is being a juror on the Grand Jury for the court system. The State of California has the "Health Insurance Counseling and Advocacy Program (HICAP)" where volunteers help Medicare beneficiaries make informed choices as well as acting as advocates when health care benefits and rights are threatened or denied. Other states may have similar programs.

HOSPITALS

There are many volunteer jobs available at hospitals. A former neighbor volunteered for years at the information desk at a local hospital. I've mentioned earlier how I volunteered with my dog as a pet therapy team visiting patients at a nearby hospital. It was exceptionally gratifying to me to bring a bit of joy into the life of someone hurting. Another friend does the same with her dog. Hospital gift shops usually use volunteers to work there as salesclerks and stock the shelves.

The "No One Dies Alone" Program was started in 2001 and exists at many hospitals. It provides a volunteer companion to dying patients who would otherwise be alone. The patient must be assessed by the doctor as being seventy-two hours away from death. For the right personality, this can be very satisfying.

LIBRARIES

Ask at your local library if they need volunteers. A former classmate who is adept with computers helps with the library website in his neighborhood.

Many libraries have an affiliated group called "Friends of the Library" or some similar title. They help sell the library's castoff books, they find guest speakers, and so forth. I have a friend who volunteers at her library, and she booked me to speak there about my memoir, *Adventures with Dad: A Father and Daughter's Journey Through a Senior Acting Class*.

MARRIAGE CEREMONY OFFICIANT

Perform civil wedding ceremonies. Search the Internet for this unusual opportunity in the city or county where you live. There will probably be a training program you'll have to complete.

MEALS ON WHEELS

This is a national program aimed at senior hunger and isolation. Volunteers deliver free or low cost meals to the homes of low income, vulnerable, or isolated seniors who are unable to prepare or purchase their own. There are similar programs operated by private charitable agencies or faith-based organizations.

MEDIATOR

Mediate disputes between people or groups for government and private agencies. Google "Volunteer Mediator" to find opportunities where you live. This will probably require you to complete a training course.

MUSEUMS

I've mentioned that I led tour groups at the Page Museum which houses the fossils dug up from the La Brea Tar Pits. Of course, there are many other types of museums. I know several people who are volunteers at their local art museum. Pick a nearby museum that intrigues you and call to see if they have a volunteer program.

POLICE AND SHERIFF DEPARTMENTS

Yes, local law enforcement departments use volunteers to staff phones and desks for public contacts as well as other volunteer duties.

POLITICAL PARTIES

Here's a category that's always looking for volunteers. If you have an affinity for a political party, volunteer at their neighborhood office to do such things as secretarial work, phone calling, distributing literature, letter writing, door-to-door canvassing, or other duties. Some of that work can often be done from your own home.

RELIGIOUS INSTITUTIONS

Faith-based groups such as churches, temples, and mosques depend on volunteers to help operate their establishments. If you belong to one, inquire if they need help. They have office duties, repair work, religious study instruction, and a myriad of other tasks that need to be done.

TAX AID

AARP has a program to assist needy seniors in preparing their income tax returns. They are seeking volunteer client facilitators, technical and management assistance aids, interpreters, and finally volunteer tax preparers who will receive tax preparation training and certification by the IRS.

TEACHING

Were you a teacher in your earlier years, or have you ever wanted to teach? Schools, clubs, religious organizations and more all utilize volunteers to help pass along their knowledge and expertise to the next generation.

TOUR GUIDE

See "Docent"

TUTORING

Tutor a child or even an adult. Many students are lagging behind in their studies or find difficulty with some school class. If you're adept at a particular subject, help them catch up.

USHER

Many performance venues use ushers. Check out your local theaters, outdoor amphitheaters, sports stadiums, and other similar spaces. In exchange for ushering, you get to see the performance for free.

I had a friend who used to usher at the Hollywood Bowl in Los Angeles, California. Another friend ushers at Dodger Stadium in Los Angeles. An avid baseball fan, he gets to see the baseball games for free, and he is also paid.

VOLUNTEER VACATIONS

There are tour companies that plan vacations all over the world where you can do volunteer work for the local people. It's a fascinating experience interacting with inhabitants of faraway lands by helping them improve their lives.

VOTING POLL WORKER

Help staff the voting polls in your area when elections are held. It's a wonderful public service, and you can meet your neighbors. For years, my father worked at the voting precinct in his area. Although you are paid a stipend, it is more a volunteer activity.

ZOOS

Are you drawn to animals that live in wilderness areas or exotic locations? Your local zoo has many of them. Docents lead tour groups and staff gift shops and other spots there. Jim, the same friend who volunteered in the museum "boneroom," was also a tour guide at his local zoo for many years after he retired.

Here are a few websites to help you locate volunteer opportunities:

1. "Volunteer Match" (website: volunteermatch.org): this website helps you find out about nonprofit organizations looking for volunteers.

2. "Global Volunteers" (website: globalvolunteers.org): this website lists volunteer vacation opportunities throughout the world.

3. "iCouldBe" (website: icouldbe.org): this website specializes in pairing volunteer mentors with at-risk middle and high school students.

4. "Create the Good" (website: createthegood.aarp.org): this is an AARP sponsored website where you can post your profile including your skills and interests, and others can contact you for a volunteer opportunity matching your profile.

5. "Senior Corps" (website: nationalservice.gov/programs /senior-corps): this website matches volunteers 55+ to act as foster grandparents to children of all ages, be senior companions to adults so they can live independently in their own homes, and several other volunteer opportunities.

6. "Big Brother/Big Sisters of America" (website: bbbs. org): this organization matches mentor adults with mentee children to provide friendship, emotional support, and guidance to youth through their involvement with positive, adult role models.

CHAPTER 9

Employment

———

Some people return to work because they're bored in their retirement and had always found their employment years stimulating. Some never retire because they can't imagine doing anything else. Warren Buffett is an American business magnate, investor, and philanthropist. At age 90, he is still the head of Berkshire Hathaway, a multinational company he has been running for over 50 years. His partner and the company vice president, Charlie Munger, is 96.

Usually, the more compelling reason people seek a job in their senior years is because they don't have enough income and need to work. Regardless of the reason, according to AARP Magazine and the Bureau of Labor Statistics, the percentage of older workers is climbing including those working into their seventies, eighties, and beyond. For many who continue to work in their later years, they feel a sense of purpose which helps with their psychological well-being.

My friend, Rosie, got a job in her eighties working part-time as a salesclerk in a clothing store geared to senior women. Rosie is a people-person and loves chatting with others. She took the job, not for the money as she was already financially stable, but to interact with her customers. She was perfectly suited to that niche. During the years she was employed there, she advised clients on which styles and colors looked good on them, whether a particular outfit was appropriate for their needs, and accessories that would match. Rosie's job stimulated, excited, and uplifted her. She passed that spark along to the store's patrons.

The reality is that for most older workers, they probably won't ever be able to earn what they did in their younger years. Perhaps you can only supplement your current income from a pension, Social Security, savings, investments, family, or other sources. Nevertheless, jobs do exist for the over-fifty crowd. You will want to assess whether you only need a small amount of additional income and can work part-time, or if you must work full time.

You might have to make some changes in your life if money is a pressing issue. Maybe you can live in a less expensive abode or share housing with others in order to cut expenses.

If you reside in your own home, you might rent out a room. Or, you might opt for a temporary rental to people vacationing or on limited business trips to your area. Check websites such as Airbnb.com to help you connect with folks looking for short-term rentals. A friend has been doing this for years to help her generate income toward paying the mortgage on her house. Short-term renters enable her to not rent for a while if she wants a break, wants her vacant room for her own guests, or plans to take a vacation herself.

If you're thinking about full time work, you might retrain for a new career. I went from probation officer to actress, author, public speaker and blogger. You don't have to do what I did. It's just an example.

You can find training programs for free or low cost at most colleges or high school adult education programs. Try to choose something that seems satisfying—something that excites you.

Identify a job that appeals to your interests, abilities, and physical and mental condition. Google it to see where it might exist in your area. Call your local senior center to find out if they have job listings for their members. Check local employment agencies to see if they can refer you to an appropriate job. Your local State Department of Employment office may have what you're looking for. Network: ask friends, neighbors, and acquaintances for job leads. Check bulletin boards at the library, senior center, market, gym, and anywhere else you encounter them.

Here are some examples of paid jobs many seniors do:

ACTOR

I get paid for acting in theatrical and commercial productions. They have many spots for older or senior actors. You can sign up yourself on CastingNetworks.com or seek a commercial or theatrical agent who will refer you to auditions. If this interests you, I would suggest that you enroll in an acting class for seniors to learn how to be successful at this endeavor.

APARTMENT MANAGER

Owners of apartment buildings are looking for on-site managers. You get a discount on the rent if your chores are minimal and the size of the building is small. You might get a free apartment and possibly a salary as the responsibilities and/or the number of apartments increases. You can contact apartment management companies to offer your services. Google "apartment manager positions" and include the name of your city and state to find appropriate job postings.

BABY SITTER

If you're good with children, put the word out to family members, friends, acquaintances and neighbors that you're available for babysitting. You might just have a child stay at your home for a while after school until his parent can pick him up. Or, you might work at the child's home watching him for a few hours or even days if the parents go on vacation. You might even accompany the family on their vacation to watch the children while the parents are sightseeing. Of course, that offers you a free vacation, too.

BACKGROUND PLAYER (FORMERLY CALLED "EXTRA")

Film, television and video projects need people to appear in the background of a scene. You usually wear your own clothes. If you live in a location where filming is done, research how to be a background player. Senior acting classes can direct you. Sign up online with CentralCasting.com, NowCasting.com, or Castingnetworks.com.

BAGGERS

Older workers are often hired by markets and stores to bag groceries or other purchases. Hours are usually flexible.

BANQUET WORKER

This type of service job can yield part-time income and has flexible hours which can be worked into your regular schedule. Google "catering services" along with the name of your city or location. They are seeking servers, drivers, cooks, kitchen managers, and event staff.

BARTENDER

Look into getting a bartender's license. You can work part time in a bar, restaurant, or at banquets or events.

CASHIER

I've seen seniors in markets, drug stores, hardware stores, and other retail establishments ringing up sales. Ask the store manager if they are hiring. Fill out an application. Stores like seniors because they are reliable employees.

COMPANION JOBS

Some elderly, sickly or disabled people want companionship. There are jobs visiting them, taking them on short outings, or maybe doing small chores. Some agencies handle these type of jobs. Look for ads in the newspaper or online. Sometimes, just contacting an assisted living or nursing home will yield you information about their residents who are seeking a companion. Or, contact professional gerontologists who might want to hire a companion for their clients. Find these resources online.

CRAFT FAIRS

Sell at craft fairs your own handmade items or merchandise

you purchase. These events are held outside in parks and parking lots or inside at various venues. You will have to pay a fee for your space. Then, you'll have to set up your own table, tent top (optional), and stock it with the items you are selling. You are responsible for dealing with how you accept payment (cash, check, credit card), how you make change, wrapping the item, paying tax on sales, obtaining a business license if required, etc. When you visit a craft fair, ask the venders how they do it and where fairs are held. Talk to the promoter to find out how you should proceed. Check online for more information.

CRUISE SHIP WORKER

You could work as a housekeeper, server or retail assistant while being paid and cruising for free to interesting places. Check "cruise line jobs" on the Internet. I remember hearing years ago about a famous author (I think it was James Michener) who took a cruise when he was in his late eighties. He thought he would be the oldest person on the ship only to discover that there was a crew member in his nineties.

DAYCARE

Seek out a job at a child, adult, or disabled day care program. Or, start one of your own in your home or a rented facility. That, of course, would require special licensing.

HOTEL WORKER

Hotels need various types of service employees including desk clerks, bell hops, maintenance workers, housekeepers, office workers, and more. I've seen some seniors working in these positions.

HOUSE SITTER

There are jobs staying at people's houses overnight when they're away just so the house is occupied. It might also involve watering the grass and indoor plants, taking in the mail and newspapers, and the like. Maybe it's combined with pet sitting for Fido or Fluffy. To find house sitter jobs, check local bulletin boards or help wanted columns in local newspapers. Make up business cards and/or flyers with the services you offer, distribute them door-to-door, and post them on bulletin boards around your area. Ask your children, family members, friends and neighbors to tell or email their friends about your new endeavor. Email everyone on your own email list about it, and ask them to forward your email to those on their own email list.

INTERNET JOB RESOURCES

Online websites such as "Rent A Grandma" (website: rentagrandma.com) and "Rent A Grandpa" (website: rentagrandpa.com) match seniors with those seeking to hire someone in that age range for simple, temporary jobs such as babysitting, gardening, and the like. I once worked as an actress for one of their online, promotional videos. Google to see if there are other websites offering similar services.

INTERNET SALES

Sell your crafts online. Etsy.com is a website devoted to crafters selling their wares. Buy garage sale items or discounted new items and resell them online at websites such as: Craigslist.org, eBay.com, or Amazon.com.

MARKET RESEARCH

Some market research companies pay people to test a product or provide their opinions about a targeted product, business, or service. This may be done at a designated location or from your own home. Google "Market Research Companies."

MOVIE THEATER WORKER

You can work part-time for a salary at a local movie theater and see the current attractions for free.

PERSONAL SHOPPER

Some Internet companies such as Instacart.com hire people to shop at grocery stores and purchase food and other items for the requesting customer. The personal shopper is given a list that the customer has entered on the company website. After the purchase is completed, the personal shopper delivers the bags of groceries to the home of the customer.

PET SITTER

Many people are looking for someone to care for their pet(s) while they're away. It may involve going to the person's home, feeding the pet, walking a dog, giving the pet its medicine, changing cat litter, and so on. Or, you might keep the pet at your residence while its owner is away.

Sometimes the job involves actually sleeping at the owner's home to care for the pet. You would earn more that way and have lots of free time because you are able to come and go as you please as long as you take care of your pet duties.

Some people hire dog walkers strictly to come to their house and take their dog for a walk. They may just be too busy to do so themselves, and they want Woofie to have his daily exercise.

I have two friends who were pet sitters. One had quite a clientele and often had to turn down requests as she was booked long in advance. She built up her business by getting referrals from other clients.

Other sources of clients are: leave your business cards at the local veterinarian's office; visit local dog parks and hand out your business cards to the dog owners you encounter there; distribute flyers in mailboxes or door handles in your neighborhood; post flyers on local bulletin boards; place a small ad in your local throw-away newspaper; or place a free ad on Craigslist.org or other similar websites. Never forget to network: ask friends, family members, acquaintances, and strangers to spread the word. Give them several of your business cards to hand out to others.

PRODUCT DEMONSTRATOR (AKA DISPLAYER)

These are the folks handing out free samples of products at supermarkets and other places where food is sold. I'm sure you've seen these workers and probably tasted their offerings; we all stop to get our free snack. My friend, Rosie, whom I've mentioned before, worked part-time for a while as a product demonstrator at her local market before going on to work as a clothing store salesclerk. It meshed well with her outgoing personality as she got to chat with customers as they tasted their tidbit.

RECYCLING

Collect old items or buy them at garage sales. Refurbish them and sell them at your own garage sale or online at sites such as Craigslist.org, eBay.com, or Amazon.com. For online sales, write a description of the item and post it on the website along with a photograph and a price. All inquiries and bids are handled by the website which acts as a middleman. It collects the money, takes a small percentage for their fee, and sends you the rest as well as notifying you of the winning bidder. Then, you mail that person the item.

RESTAURANT WORKERS

Many workers over age fifty are employed in restaurants as waiters, waitresses, or bussers. They may also work at other jobs such as preparing the restaurant to open (filling holders for napkins or condiments, wiping tables and booths, and cleaning the food display) or at closing time such as cleanup and janitorial services.

RIDE SHARE DRIVER

Do you have a newer, clean car, a driver's license and a good driving record? Sign up as a ride share driver with companies such as Uber or Lyft. You can set your own hours and work or not work whenever you like. You will have to carry the appropriate car insurance. Google them and apply online.

SALESCLERK

There are a lot of store sales jobs available. My innovative friend, Rosie, began modeling in the periodic fashion show a local store held to attract senior customers. There wasn't a salary, but she got a discount on clothing she purchased. While looking through the racks, Rosie often chatted with other customers offering advice on clothes that would look good on them. The manager saw how well she related to the clients and offered her a part-time job as a salesperson during peak seasons and store sales. So, when you see an opportunity, create your own job.

SECRET SHOPPER (AKA MYSTERY SHOPPER)
You can work posing as a customer in a store to help assess how the employees are handling customers or other facts that management wants to know about the store. Secret Shoppers make purchases and then write an evaluation of their experience in that store. Google "Secret Shopper" or "Mystery Shopper" jobs.

START YOUR OWN BUSINESS
According to AARP, twenty-six percent of all new businesses in 2015 were started by someone age 55 to 64. If you have a skill of some sort, start your own business. For example, do you like to fix things? Start your own handyman service. Put an ad about it in the local newspaper or post on bulletin boards. Post it on online websites such as Craigslist.org. Pass out flyers and business cards in your area. Ask others to spread the word.

I know a woman who, at the age of 75, started a senior, online newsletter about activities for seniors in her neighborhood. Now, some years later, she has sponsors who pay to put their ads in her newsletter. I know someone else who gives classes of various types held at her home. She has gone on to produce theatrical talent shows starring only senior talent.

TEACHER

Many people retire and then begin teaching, using the skills they had learned for their former jobs. If you have a skill needed in schools such as mathematics, think about teaching it to the younger generation. You might also teach your art or dance skills in schools specializing in them.

TOUR GUIDE

This can be a volunteer position as listed previously. However, it also might be a paid job. There are professional tour companies that operate day tours for out-of-town visitors, and they hire tour guides to lead their customers on local walking or bus tours. Tour companies also are seeking guides to travel for days or weeks with an organized tour. Besides a salary, your expenses are paid and you get a free trip. Some companies are looking for people to meet arriving tourists at airports and transport stations to drive them to their hotels.

Do you have knowledge about a certain subject or location? Check online or the library for tour companies specializing in your area of expertise. You may not even need experience as some companies will train you to lead tours.

TUTOR

If you have an academic skill, and teaching a whole classroom full of students is too much for you or not appealing, think about tutoring one-on-one or to just a few at a time. Your clients can be children or adults. Call schools to list your services or private tutoring companies to apply. Post yourself and your skills online at social networking sites such as LinkedIn.com or Craigslist.org.

USHER

Although I listed this earlier as a volunteer opportunity, some usher positions are paid such as the one I referenced at Dodger Stadium in Los Angeles, California.

There are many more opportunities for activities, pursuits, and jobs. These are just examples of what I've heard about, what I've done myself, and what friends and acquaintances have done. Be proactive in searching for your ideal niche. It exists and is waiting for you to find. Reinvent yourself! If I and so many others have done it, so can you.

CHAPTER 10

Posts from My Blog

———

I have been writing a free, online (Internet) blog since 2013 titled "Reinventing Yourself in Your Retirement Years," which can be accessed at: LeeGaleGruen.wordpress.com. A blog is similar to a newspaper column where the columnist usually writes about different subjects under an umbrella theme. I started my blog to identify and write about my thoughts, observations, experiences, discussions and the influences in my own life that I felt were universal to my age demographic—retiree and senior. My goal is to help others find more joy, excitement, and purpose after they retire whether from a job, career, profession, parenting, or whatever their main activity was in their younger years. I view it as an opportunity to help someone else who may be struggling as I struggled when I retired.

My blog is aimed at retirees, those contemplating retirement, baby boomers and seniors just like this book and my public talks. Please excuse me if some of the things mentioned in my blogs were already covered in earlier parts of this book. My book, blogs, and public talks overlap as they are all directed toward the same purpose.

The blog entries span from June, 2013 to December, 2019, starting from the most recent and continuing in descending order. The topics are random and not in any particular sequence. They focus on matters I'm sure most people have thought about or encountered in their own lives but perhaps with a fresh twist not considered before. They tend to end in a teachable moment. You may not always agree with my thoughts or perspective, but I hope my writings will motivate you to take action to change your own life for the better in your retirement and senior years.

You can check out my free blog at:

LeeGaleGruen.wordpress.com and sign up to "follow me" so you will be notified by email when I post a new blog every two weeks.

BLOG POSTS FROM 2019

Holiday Letters (December 23, 2019)

This time of year, I usually receive a plethora of holiday letters via email or snail mail from various family members, friends, or even acquaintances. The contents usually follow a formula: recapping the sender's year with snippets of what they and their loved ones have done during that time. I don't know how or when this practice started, but I don't remember it in the first half of my life.

I usually hate those missives because, more often than not, they're filled with fairy-tale wonderfulness making my life pale in comparison. Everything seems to have a positive spin. It might read: "Hyacinth is loving her new college." Of course, I know that Hyacinth was expelled from her old college for having drugs in her dorm room, and that she did a short stint in the local jail with some follow-up community service as a result. Maybe it informs us: "Maxwell finally fulfilled his longtime dream of leaving his old firm of Smith, Jones, and McGillicuddy and starting his own company." Unwritten is that Maxwell was booted out from SJ&M for shoddy work, and his new company headquarters is located behind the house in a 6×8 metal shed furnished with a card table and cinder block bookcase.

We all have our ups and downs–our positives and negatives. A full dose launched in our direction of just one or the other is a turnoff, no matter in what form it is delivered. We all compare ourselves to each other, and when one constantly presents as wonderful, blessed, and fortunate, it becomes tiresome and boring. Conversely, when one bemoans and whines about most things, it becomes tiresome and boring.

Those two extremes, everything is wonderful or everything is terrible, are usually performed with a hidden motive. The former is a type of one-upmanship. At its essence, it is bragging–mine is better than yours. The latter is a form of victimhood to suck more than the practitioner's share from the attention pool.

If you must send or email a holiday letter, tell us what really happened, not just the Pollyanna version, but be careful not to overload it with poor-me isms. We can see through it all, and we may repay you in kind.

Remember to enjoy your holiday season like a guileless child without an agenda and not use it as a tool to manipulate. With that, I leave you with my holiday letter:

****LEE GALE GRUEN'S 2019 HOLIDAY LETTER****
Happy and Merry Christmas, Hanukkah, Kwanzaa, Posadas Navidenas, Solstice, or (fill in the holiday of your choice.) Just want to bring you up-to-speed on how wonderful, terrific, amazing, incredible, and (fill in any positive adjective) my life has been this past year.

In January, I completed blah, blah, blah!
In February, my son was elected blah, blah, blah!
In March, my oldest grandchild started blah, blah, blah!
In April, my dog learned blah, blah, blah!
In May, I was awarded blah, blah, blah!
In June, my youngest grandchild was chosen blah, blah, blah!
In July, my daughter finished blah, blah, blah!
In August, I traveled to blah, blah, blah!
In September, my middle grandchild mastered blah, blah, blah!
In October, my friends threw me a blah, blah, blah!
In November, I bought a blah, blah, blah!
And this month, December, I'm finally able to tell you all about it and make you drool.

HAVE A STUPENDOUS HOLIDAY SEASON,
BUT NOT AS GOOD AS MINE, OF COURSE!

The Day I Became Ma'am (December 12, 2019)

Some events make an immediate and abrupt change in our lives. When you have a baby, one moment you're not the parent of (insert the long pondered name you gave your adorable offspring), and the next moment you are, and your life is never the same. When you're involved in a major accident, one moment you don't have four broken limbs and a fractured skull, and the next moment you do, and your life is never the same.

Most transformations to our lives, however, come on minutely with the aging process. We don't notice it as the progression is so gradual. It's only over months or more likely years that we clock the transformations.

Of course, you evolve from instant to instant. But, what is the exact moment that you morphed from one major phase of your life to the next? I remember the day someone first called me ma'am. I was in my late teens and still felt like a kid. I was crossing a busy intersection directed by a police officer who was hurrying people along.

"Move it, ma'am," he yelled in an irritated voice.

I didn't even know who he was talking to, but I was sure it wasn't me. After all, I certainly wasn't old enough to be a ma'am. I glanced at him and saw that he was glaring at me impatiently as he waved his arms directing the traffic. It shocked me; I'd never been called ma'am before. When did I go from being a miss to a ma'am?

I'm now asking that question in my senior years. When was the day, the hour, the minute, the second that I actually became a senior? I'm not sure? I look in the mirror and wonder who that is gazing back at me pondering the same question.

It's hard passing through the stages of our lives. However, we have no choice. If we're alive, we can only move forward toward the inescapable, like it or not. The takeaway here is that our mental thoughts and emotional identity often lag behind our physical strength and appearance. What we think of ourselves is not necessarily how the world views us. We must be aware of the difference between the two. That leaves the only consideration: how we deal with it.

Some rail against aging, trying as hard as they can to avoid it, reject it, disguise it. You may convince yourself that you've done so, but it's not true. Others can see through your little guise even if you can't or choose not to.

Being a ma'am didn't make me any different than I was the day before. It's just a word, not a description of my character, personality, lifestyle, and beliefs. I'm no longer the immature young woman I was then having transformed ever so slowly into the mature senior I am now. That process was going to happen no matter my machinations along the journey.

So, one alternative is to accept and embrace your age whatever it may be at any moment. Stop fighting the process and go with the flow as the kids say. It will make your life easier, richer, and more enjoyable as you amble along that inevitable path.

Up High (November 28, 2019)

We all want to be up high. As young children at a parade, we tell our parents to lift us up high. As adults, we strive to climb the social or corporate ladder to raise ourselves up high.

What's the big deal with being so high? Does it make us happier or more content? The race to the top is fraught with victims trying and failing to claw and scratch their way to the apex of the mountain. We are competitive beings. We grow up with emphasis on besting another no matter who that other might be: friend, acquaintance, co-worker, parent, sibling, even our own offspring. And, the besting portion comes in any form that stratifies folks—someone always higher by some arbitrary measurement than someone else.

Everyone seems to want to surround themselves with the good life which so many identify as material possessions. However, according to the Hedonic Treadmill, it never satisfies, it only makes its practitioners crave ever more of that same stuff.

Is it possible to just be satisfied? Can we be okay with where we are in life, even though that guy over there has more money, a bigger house, more successful children, or a later model car? It's hard because that's not what we were taught in our families, at school, and in our society. However, that constant dissatisfaction and competition grows tiresome. Manifesting in the form of jealousy, anxiety, nervousness, sleeplessness and similar outcomes, it takes a huge toll on our physical and mental well-being.

How do you walk away from always wanting to be up high, up higher, up highest? First, you have to recognize you have that affliction. It may be so ingrained that it's hard to spot. Then, you have to want to cut it free—really, really want to. You will have to formulate a plan of action on how to go about it—steps to take. This is different for everyone, but with some honest thought, you can arrive at your own customized list.

It could involve minor changes such as volunteering to help those less fortunate or giving away certain possessions.

It could be as drastic as quitting a job, moving away from a neighborhood, or even cutting certain family members and friends loose.

Finally, you must work at it daily as you must for any change of long-term habits. It may take the same length of time to defeat as it took to become entrenched—years probably. Yet, if you want it badly enough...

Buddha was thought to have been born into a privileged life which he renounced to become an ascetic and pauper. Hey, if Buddha can give it all up in pursuit of enlightenment, maybe there's a chance for us.

Our Gang (November 13, 2019)

We all need good friends to hang out with. There's a comfort level about being around people we like, we've known for a while, and with whom we share common interests. Humans are not solitary beings. We are social beings who enjoy the camaraderie of like-minded folks. They are our support system, our cheering squad, our comforters.

Some people, however, refuse to open themselves up to making new friends. They stick to those they know to the exclusion of anyone who tries to break into their tight clique. Sometimes, it's to the point of being rude.

I remember a situation where I was sitting in a huge, noisy room at a large, round banquet table. It was my first time attending that organization, and I didn't know anyone there. The person seated on my right physically turned her back in my direction as she chatted up the person on the other side of her. There was a bookend effect from my left. Together, they served to isolate me. Perhaps you've had a similar experience.

Why do people behave like that?

Rather than thinking it is a fault in yourself, maybe it's a fault in the back turner. Perhaps they are so uncomfortable with new situations that they have to form a blockade to keep intruders out. How sad for them. They might miss an opportunity for a new point of view, of learning something they didn't know, or of interacting with a charming personality.

I have a group of friends who are very open and agreeable with any in the group inviting newcomers to our outings. We never give it a second thought. So, I did the same thing with a different group of friends without asking if it was okay with everyone. It just didn't dawn on me that it would be a problem. Wrong!

Another in that group became very huffy and cold to both me and my invited guest. I noticed how visibly upset she seemed. I couldn't figure out why she was acting that way, so I asked her when we were alone for a moment.

"I thought it was just going to be the four of us. I didn't know that there was going to be a stranger here, too. It just changes the character of the get-together."

In truth, she's right; it does. To me, it was just a few friends joining each other for lunch. However, I had spoiled it for her. I should have asked permission of the others before inviting an outsider.

We are not all alike. I enjoy meeting and getting to know new people. I find it interesting and stimulating. However, not everyone feels that way, and I must remember that.

Old relationships are precious. Treat them accordingly. But, try to open yourself up to new ones. It might just expand you.

OMG I Just Got Younger (October 30, 2019)

Take off one candle from the birthday cake. I'm a year younger than I thought!

When the subject comes up, I've been telling people my age or at least what I thought was my age. I've never short-changed my years, trying to drop five or ten of them to represent myself as being younger. I am what I am, and I have never bought into presenting myself otherwise.

Last week at my gym class, I got into a discussion with another member about how old we were going to be on our next birthday. She thought she was the oldest person there and was so excited to find someone older—by one year. As we continued talking, we discovered we had been born in the same year, she in March and I in December.

Wait a minute, something didn't compute. It seemed that either I was a year younger than I was claiming, or she was a year older. I was sure I was right. After all, I'm pretty sharp and don't usually make significant mistakes like that.

I rushed home and grabbed my cheapo calculator. It seemed to tell me that she was right. Naw, it must be defective. How long had it been since I changed the batteries? I took to google and typed "age calculator" into the search box. After inputting my date of birth, up came a number that agreed with cheapo and my gym mate. But, how was that possible? I had been claiming the wrong age, even on written forms where it was requested, upping it by a year.

The only thing I can figure out is that I went to my high school class reunion a few months ago, and many attendees were a year older as I had been among the youngest in that class having been born nearly at year's end. So, hearing them talk about their age, I guess I started saying the same thing.

The silver lining to my faulty memory is that I just got a year younger! Now, how often do we get that, folks?

Funny, though; I don't feel any different. Yes, it's the same old me. Being a year younger doesn't make any difference. My takeaway: calculations of ages and birth dates are just numbers games. It's what you do with those precious years, days, hours, minutes, and seconds that matter.

Earlobes and Such (October 16, 2019)

We use our bodily parts in various ways to hold the objects necessary in our daily life. We balance glasses on the bridge of our nose and the tops of our ears. We hold up our pants by cinching belts around our waists. We strap watches around our wrists. We tie young babies to our backs. As the child grows larger, we hoist it on our hip bone to straddle our body for balance as we carry it.

I came upon a young woman who took the concept to a whole new level. She had stretchers in her earlobes. (See my blog of June 5, 2017: "Generational Differences," which features "gauges" as earlobe stretchers are called.) That is a style now among many of the younger generation.

The stereotypical waitress' answer to always looking for a pen or pencil is to shove it through her hair to rest on the top of her ear. However, this young woman's innovative answer was to push it through the large hole in her earlobe.

Adaptability can be brought into all aspects of our lives: our jobs, our studies, our relationships, our parenting... Always doing things the tried-and-true way doesn't allow for expansion.

Think about things you'd like to change about yourself or do differently. Focus on how you might morph to enhance your life. Make a conscious effort to imagine the steps you can take. Compile a to-do list using a computer or even the old-fashioned method of pen and paper, even if you don't keep your writing implement as handy as the appendage dangling from your ear.

Strive to make your life fuller and more satisfying. Create ways to stretch yourself in lots of areas, not just your earlobes.

Touching a Giraffe (October 1, 2019)

I was on an amazing trip to Africa a few months ago. One day, we stopped at a giraffe rescue compound. Up close and personal was their philosophy. The staff even gave us food pellets to feed to our long-necked friends. What a privilege to be able to touch such a beast.

Touch is one of our five senses which gets less than its fair share of credit. We're so focused on vision and hearing, that we forget the importance of touch in the quality of life.

Animals love to be petted. Touch yields purring from our cats and contented sighs from our dogs. But, what does touching an animal do for us? Is it like an electrical charge of mutual joy between the human touchor and the animal touchee?

To me it is. There is something about touching an animal that immediately calms me. It could be I am so focused on the task that I'm not thinking about anything else. However, I suspect it's more than that. It's a tactile sharing with a sentient being of this earth—a non-judgmental one without an agenda.

I feel their touch as much as they feel mine. And it just plain feels good! I have written on the importance of touch in this blog before. (See my blogs of February 17, 2018: "Hugs," and February 4, 2016: "The Power of Touch.")

Some people seem wary of touch or even averse to it. I can understand that; it's a kinetic interaction which can be perceived as uncomfortable to them. When you plan on touching another, whether human or otherwise, be sensitive to whether they enjoy that sensation or not.

If you are one who has never liked being touched too much, you might try to accustom yourself to it. Start by taking baby steps, maybe with gentle, domestic animals. Slowly move up from there as touch becomes more palatable. You may discover a contentment you've been missing.

Don't forget to include touch in your interaction with folks. Touch your children, grandchildren, and those you love. Touch a stranger when appropriate. A handshake, a pat on the hand, or linking arms can melt even the iciest, most standoffish opponent.

Life Is a Pinball Machine (September 16, 2019)

A pinball machine is an apt metaphor for life. From our birth, we are propelled down a jagged, unpredictable path strewn with obstacles. When we hit one, it bounces us in a different direction until we meet up with a new impediment. From there, we are pushed along yet another route and on and on. As we weave our way along, we encounter experiences which we would not have had but for the random jumping between points.

Think of various examples in your life and how they occurred. So often, they were simply a shot in the dark—you were just at the right place at the right time or the wrong place at the wrong time. Had arbitrary, proceeding events not occurred to put you there, you would not have encountered those particular circumstances.

Such an unplanned stumbling from one destination to the next is what constitutes life. Ponder this for a moment: what events led to your attending the school you did, making the friendships you have, settling on living in a particular city, obtaining your job, meeting your partner, and everything else in your life?

Toward the end of college, I signed up for interviews with a host of recruiters who had come to the campus seeking potential employees. When I graduated, I accepted a job as a probation officer simply because that was the first one offered to me. I didn't even know what a probation officer did. I remained at that career for thirty-seven years. Many of my closest friends were co-workers I met there.

After I retired, I mentioned to a friend that I was bored and directionless. She told me about a local school with classes for seniors. I perused the Schedule of Classes and mistakenly signed up for an acting class, thinking it was just a play discussion course. Never having acted in my life, I was hooked that first day after reading a scene with another class member. That experience changed my life, and I went on to become a professional actress as a senior.

So, life is simply a crapshoot. We make our way along, careening and readjusting as we go, hoping that it will turn out well. The only fleeting control we have is what we do with the situation once we land at any given spot. Be flexible and prepared to deal with whatever the pinball machine of life hands you.

Cool Your Jets (September 2, 2019)

We are all impatient, some more than others. We are concerned about how future events will unfold. We want our agendas to be realized immediately. However, living in a world of billions, that's usually impossible. We must wait our turn in the queue. We must rein in our impatience. We must plan our activities in advance to allow plenty of time to reach the goal or outcome we seek.

Trying to be patient can create anxiety, sleep problems, distraction, and all types of other behaviors which interfere with our everyday lives. However, we have no choice; we must learn to grapple with delayed gratification.

How can you do so if you are a personality type with substantial difficulty in that arena? It's hard, but it can and must be done for your well-being. Here are some ideas:

1. You can participate in a soothing activity that redirects your mind and thoughts. I know someone who takes to her piano whenever she feels anxious.
2. You can schedule activities that divert your attention such as watching a movie, playing cards, or attending an interesting function.
3. You can engage in physical exercise such as sports or attendance at your local gym to help channel your nervous energy.
4. You can discuss your feelings with a friend as a sound-

ing board to get a better perspective on the particular situation.

5. Or, you can make the decision to change your modus operandi.

Your modus operandi is simply your normal way of behaving. Changing your M.O. is the hardest choice of all. It takes constant attention and self-assessment to be aware of how you are acting, to settle your mind, and to choose to move on to something else.

Unlike the aforementioned, short-term fixes, a significant change of behavior may take years to accomplish and possibly therapeutic intervention. Success at that endeavor depends heavily on the depth of your desire to discard old habits for new. If you are able to accomplish such a feat, however, it will be the most rewarding and helpful to you.

I Signed Up to Be an Uber Driver (August 17, 2019)

I was trying to download the Uber app onto my cell phone. It was a new learning curve for me, but I wanted to be hip like everyone else and try out the popular ride sharing concept.

I followed all the correct prompts on the Uber website, or so I thought. After completing my efforts, I received an immediate email from Uber welcoming me to their pool of drivers. They wanted all sorts of personal information such as my driver's license number, insurance, and the like.

I have no idea what I did to become part of the Uber Drivers Club. Truth be told, I'd probably be the worst sort of Uber driver. My driving skills are okay but nothing to brag about. My patience with the full range of personalities an

Uber driver might encounter is limited. And, my sense of direction stinks.

After I was enrolled as an Uber driver, the problem became how to unenroll. Apparently, Uber doesn't want their drivers to drop out, especially before they even begin. No matter how hard I tried, I couldn't quit my new job. I finally gave up and figured I'd just remain on their roster.

Well, Uber didn't like that either. They were not about to brook a driver who didn't provide her driving information, and certainly not one who didn't drive. I continued receiving emails from Uber insisting upon the sacred data. I ignored them, but they persisted—Uber can be very persistent.

They finally got the idea and stopped pestering me. However, I don't know if I'm still buried somewhere in their data bank of drivers. I can't help wondering if this type of snafu befalls others, too? Does it happen to younger people, or is it just us older folk? What did Uber say on its end after I bailed? *Oh, another ditzy senior.*

Never mind, I do know that I went on to become a successful Uber passenger after a few upsetting mishaps. (See my blog of March 4, 2018: "Uber et al.") I have even learned a couple of things from my Uber rider experiences. For example, I bought one of those handy dandy devices that holds a cell phone near the dashboard at close viewing range used by all Uber drivers while their phone's GPS navigates the route. Now, if I ever do decide to activate my Uber driver status, I'm all set!

Always be willing to learn from your experiences. When you encounter a good idea, borrow it, steal it, claim it for yourself. Good ideas are good ideas, no matter where they come from, even Uber.

Feeling Out of Place (August 4, 2019)

Sometimes we find ourselves in situations where we feel out of place–you know, that awkward, uncomfortable sensation because we don't quite fit in. We try to adapt, but all we can think of is, *how do I get out of here?* It's particularly hard in a situation where everyone else seems to know each other, to interact comfortably, and we are the odd man out.

I think most folks have found themselves in such a predicament at some time in their lives. We dread it and often avoid participating in a potentially interesting activity because we fear we may experience that distasteful feeling yet again. The one thing we forget is that everybody was in the same dilemma in some venue somewhere when they first attended, and they were the odd man out. They felt uneasy and thought of bolting.

As I've previously discussed in this blog, I moved to a large, active retirement community three years ago knowing no one. I was intimidated and uncomfortable everywhere I went. The community offers a plethora of clubs, events, sports, and activities of all kinds.

Each thing I attended, I had to go alone. Of course, it seemed like everyone else there was with lots of friends. It was hard, and I often debated whether to even make the effort. However, the thought of isolating myself inside my four walls was worse. Slowly, I found my own friends, became comfortable, and now I'm very happy.

You must push yourself and bear up under the discomfort in order to reap the rewards, just like you've had to do all your life at school, in your job, dating, raising children, and so on. Like all skills, the more you do it, the more adept you become.

It seems we must wade through the sludge to get to the gold. So, hang in there, continue going back, keep starting conversations with other participants. It will slowly get better. It makes it easier realizing that it doesn't just happen to you, it happens to all people no matter how rich, attractive, successful, or accomplished.

Monet and Me (July 23, 2019)

Ah, Monet. We hung out together recently. That is, Monet did the hanging–on a wall at the de Young Museum in San Francisco, California, with me in attendance and in awe. To my chagrin, I failed to dress for the occasion–a faux pas as Monet would say in the French of his origin. Yes, I stressed primary colors that day forgetting that my pal Monet is definitely a secondary colors kind of guy.

No matter; we were both gobsmacked (I've been dying to use that trendy word) by the beauty of his garden and his ability to render it on a flat surface. Yes, two of totally different interests and viewpoints can come together over a shared commonality.

Monet and I were born 100 years and 4,000 miles apart. What would we have talked about if we hadn't had such distances between us? We would certainly have discussed the beauty of nature. We might have marveled at the intricacy of a leaf, the color of a flower, the soothing ripple of water.

It's not always easy to find something in common with another. But, more often than not, there will be a little nugget if you dig deep enough.

I attended a banquet dinner last year and was sitting at a table with some folks I didn't know. One man tried to engage me in conversation, but each thing he mentioned didn't hit a cord. Finally, in response to yet another of his queries, I revealed that I had graduated college in 1964 from UCLA. Voilà (to continue in a Francophile mode), my table mate began discussing Kareem Abdul Jabbar who was a student at UCLA around that time and became a top ranked player on the university basketball team. I know very little about sports, but I was able to contribute that Kareem was known then by his birth name of Lew Alcindor. That opened up a lengthy conversation which segued into different topics.

Find common interests with those you encounter. Keep bringing up different subjects until you hit upon something that excites you both. It's there; you just have to keep searching for it. Even the dullest, most withdrawn human will shine when you strike upon their passion. That's the way to make friends!

Drumming (July 9, 2019)

I spotted a guy on a subway train with a huge drum. I guess he subscribes to the old adage: you never know when you might need a drum.

Drums, those wonderful creations by humans, are of the percussion persuasion. They can be played using sticks, palms, elbows, whatever. They can be professionally made or cheaply crafted out of materials at hand.

I've seen street drummers banging out wonderful rhythms on an assemblage of pots, pans, plastic pails, and other assorted items that make a resonating noise when struck. Some of those drummers have even turned to the curb of the sidewalk to continue tapping out their message. The wonderful steel drums played in the Caribbean were originally made from 55-gallon oil barrels.

Drums let us beat out the rhythms in our head. Drums are cathartic, enabling us to pour out not only our joy, but our rage, anger, upset, disappointment, and all other sorts of negative emotions. The drumming member of the band is the guy/gal who gets to flail, gyrate, posture, and genuflect as he pounds those skins. What a workout, and what a release, physically and emotionally.

A popular pastime in recent years is the advent of drumming circles. They are a grass-roots endeavor and promote community camaraderie among its members. Groups get together with each participant bringing their own drum. The particular type or style is unimportant. All that is required is a drum of some sort to receive the pounding of each player as they belt out their collective message to the world.

Drumming is a form of amplification of the body's expression of rhythm: finger tapping/snapping, dancing, singing, scatting, body twisting, etc. Humans today and down through the ages all the way from sophisticated societies to the simplest of tribal people have felt the need for bodily expression through sound and movement. Drums are enablers to that end. And best of all, they are portable and attract others in an upbeat (pun intended) gathering. So, acquire your own drum and get to it; bang your woes away!

Bailing Out at the Last Minute (June 24, 2019)

How important is it to stick to your word? I mean, what's the big deal if you back out of a promise or commitment? I've addressed this subject before. (See my blog of May 14, 2018: "Keep Your Promises"), but this is a different slant.

To most people, it can be irritating, upsetting, or even painful when someone reneges on plans with very little notice. The one depending upon your acting toward a specific end may have staked a lot on that promise. They may have switched around other obligations, refused new invitations, or generally rearranged things in their life with your agreement as the catalyst.

We all have to change our arrangements from time to time; we're human. However, try to give lots of advance notice. Backing out of a commitment at the last minute is fraught with all types of fallout.

The practitioners of short notice bailing-out may do so for acceptable reasons. Something seriously urgent may have come up, they may legitimately have been delayed, or they may have had an accident. But often, it's something as simple as: they don't feel like it, they expended their energy on other activities that day, or they got a better deal. I've been at the receiving end of such behavior from time to time. What I'd like to ask those actors is, "How do you feel when someone backs out on you late-term?"

I remember once a friend who was divorced telling me that her young son had waited for hours in front of the house for his father to pick him up for their planned excursion, but the father never arrived. The son was devastated. The father's subsequent excuse was lame and selfish.

I have been involved in relationships where the other party became angry and spontaneously backed out of a promise or commitment as a means of control or to inflict hurt. Of course, I learned never to trust their promises, and I proceeded accordingly.

Here's a variation on a theme: Years ago, I had a friend who, when I'd suggest a particular date to meet, would check her calendar and tell me, "I don't have any plans for that day, yet." I couldn't figure out if that was a yes or a no. What exactly does "yet" mean in that context? It became clear that her pattern was to hold me off to see if she got a more exciting opportunity. She probably practiced that technique with most in her sphere, placing herself in a position to wiggle out if she desired. Needless to say, she is now a former friend.

When others rely on your word, and it soon becomes clear that said word is unreliable or of a waffling nature, the blowback to you will be a loss of trust and a rift in the relationship. Go ahead, take the plunge–commit. Then, do your utmost to follow through, even if you're pissed off or get a better, last-minute offer. If you can't seem to do that, don't be surprised as one friendship after another melts away

Fixations (June 10, 2019)
I have written often on this subject, yet it keeps calling me back. I hear chatter, see ads, discover new offerings in this field. Yes, we humans fixate on our bodies. We find the parts that are not considered attractive in the time, age, and location

in which we live, and we obsess about them. I'm too tall/short/ scrawny/corpulent, my nose is too big, my hair is too limp, my eyelids are slanted, my ears stick out, my biceps aren't muscular, my breasts are too small/large, and on and on.

Of course, styles in beauty and attractiveness change with the times. Peter Paul Rubens, late 16th century artist, painted very full figured women as that was considered beautiful when he lived. Today we call them fat. Ancient statues from Rome sport large Roman noses as it was considered good-looking at that time. Today, we seek rhinoplasty for such a protuberance.

Even though I am of average height now, I matured very quickly and was the second tallest kid in my sixth grade class. The tallest was also a girl. I hated it and wished I could be little, cute and popular like Bunnie. I remember that we had ballroom dancing classes in school every week, and they would line us up by height, the boys in one line and the girls in another side by side. I was always second to the last in the girl's line or last if the aforementioned tallest was absent. Chances are I would get one particular boy as my partner who was wimpy and had an underbite. I'm sure he wasn't any happier drawing me to dance with during the "ordeal," either. I despised the whole thing.

We run to our idols: doctors, surgeons, hairstylists, personal trainers, fashionistas, anyone who can disguise or change that horrible feature about ourselves that we abhor. Once we do away with one, we find another to fixate on. Okay, the bump in my nose was removed, but how about my big hips? Okay, I got rid of my wrinkles, but I hate my thinning hair. Let me run to the gym and work out, let me get liposuction, let me stuff myself into girdles, slimming pants, A-shaped skirts, Hawaiian shirts, let me starve myself–anything to hide my awfulness from the eyes of others.

How sad we humans are. How funny we would seem to alien beings arriving on our planet. How strange we must seem to the animals of the world.

Does a horse fixate on its mane being shorter than another's–darker, lighter, thicker, thinner? Yes, certain traits in the animal world attract a mate: longer tusks, larger chests, more colorful feathers, etc. However, we humans have taken it to an extreme as we are wont to do. If it doesn't come naturally, we spend our time, energy, and money scurrying to the fixers of our fixations.

Watson (May 27, 2019)

Life can be such an adventure. Simple day-to-day activities can yield gold–unexpected finds and excitement.

I went to Home Depot a few weeks ago for the usual reasons people go there; it was just one of my chores for the day. I was ambling around pushing one of their larger-than-I-am shopping carts when I turned down a random aisle. In front of me was Watson, a beautiful English setter as his owner informed me. I had never met an English setter before.

Watson was as sweet and gentle as he was beautiful. He was also like flypaper, attracting practically every shopper who was lucky enough to turn down that enchanted aisle where he was holding court. Watson brought strangers together as they oohed and aahed over him, petted him, asked questions about him, and interacted with each other over their shared experience.

Watson's owner, or should I say the fortunate person allowed to accompany him on the other end of the leash, told the gathering crowd that Watson was a therapy dog, visiting inhabitants at places such as senior homes and hospitals to bestow his calm and magnificence upon them.

Watson accepted the adoration of all of us gathered around him in the Home Depot aisle that day without changing his demeanor in the slightest. He inhabited his purpose in life: bringing joy to those he encountered. He didn't become puffed up with his own importance, demanding of rewards or social position, manipulative, or any of the other things humans in such a position might have done. No, Watson simply remained Watson–a uniter, not a divider.

We need more human Watsons in the world who will bring people together and unite them. We need less division and derision. We need more calm, gentleness—more Watsonness. Are we humans fated to encounter that only in other animal forms?

Fragile (May 14, 2019)

Throughout my life, I've encountered people who are described as "fragile" both by themselves and by others. These people have been co-workers, family members, friends, acquaintances, and more. Fragile seems to mean that they can't tolerate too much pressure, stress, responsibility, expectations, etc., or they "fall apart."

I'm not the fragile type. I come across as responsible, capable, reliable, tough. Therefore, others have high expectations of me and are upset if I fail to live up to them. I am expected to show up on time, not complain, do the job assigned to me, and produce results, not excuses. However, fragile people are not held to this standard. They are given a pass because, after all, they are fragile.

I've never been sure if fragility is actual or a successful protective shield which is carefully honed during a lifetime. Certainly, it yields high payoffs to some practitioners. A co-worker years ago earned the same salary as I and had the same job description, but expectations for her were far less than for me. When extra work needed to be done, it was usually me who was tapped. And my reward? More work, of course. When I was lamenting the situation to another co-worker, his response was, "Well, she's fragile." That was my introduction to that descriptor of ineptitude, a very manipulative behavior in this case.

I've pondered over the years how to jump on the fragile train. I'm not a natural at it, and it doesn't fit my personality. However, I've tried to acquire the skill. Usually, however, my true nature shows through, and others don't let me get away with it.

So, I'm putting it out to the world. I want to be fragile. If you encounter me or deal with me, take your expectations elsewhere and let me screw up over and over with minimal consequences, at the same salary, of course.

Hiding (April 29, 2019)

We all hide in one way or another. It can be deliberately or subconsciously. We hide the traits, aspects, and details of ourselves that we think are undesirable or a turnoff to others.

Hiding can take the form of outright lying or simply omission. Hiding can involve deception from small, socially acceptable behavior to a major ruse.

Commerce encourages us to hide our appearance and age by hawking products such as hair dye, wigs, cosmetics, plastic surgery, and the rest of that ilk. They couple that with propaganda which convinces us that our altered presentation to the world is okay, appropriate, no big deal, "everyone does it." Entertainment idols help sell that lie by partaking and flaunting it to the public. Seventy-something actresses look forty, parading their deception and bragging about it. Ordinary folks seeing this in the media comment on "how wonderful she looked on TV the other night."

There was a time when women who wore makeup were considered "painted ladies" and scorned by polite society. Now, it's just the opposite. Both sexes spend multi-billions of dollars worldwide on cosmetics, procedures, and the like to alter their appearances to something they think will be more pleasing to others. They put their health and even their life in danger with elective surgical procedures, again to try to present a different self to the world than what they consider the ugly one they wear naturally.

Behaviors such as anorexia and bulimia have to do with poor body image. Where does that come from? Why are we telling people that "you can never be too rich or too thin"? Why don't fashion models look like the majority of people?

We teach this self-assessment to our children who want to emulate what they consider "grown-up" behavior. They quickly learn by their teenage years which of their bodily attributes are unattractive: nose, hair, height, weight, voice, skin color, and on and on. Too many obsess about it. Commerce, always on the lookout for new grist for its ever churning mill, panders to this market, too.

There's nothing wrong with trying to look nice. However, when it impacts your view of yourself and the world and tends toward the pathological, dangerous, or even life threatening, it is a major problem.

Fred Rogers of "Mr. Rogers' Neighborhood" fame used to make his young TV listeners feel special by affirming he liked them no matter how they looked or acted. Where are the Mr. Rogerses of today? Who is telling our children now? Who is telling our grandchildren? Who is telling us?

Outfoxed by a Plant (April 15, 2019)

Ah, the things we do for our loved ones. We go to great lengths and expend enormous amounts of time, energy, and money when the motivation is right. What greater impetus than when the object is someone/something we love. Wouldn't you do just about anything for your children, parents, spouse, significant other, pet…?

How about our plants? Well, maybe they don't have quite the impact on us as the aforementioned categories. However, I have a plant that is holding me hostage. It's my Dieffenbachia, also called in plant tomes: dumb cane. Believe me, mine is not dumb.

I bought the plant when it was a wee sprout, under a foot tall. I knew it would grow to have large, glorious leaves to brag about, just like its kith and kin. When I moved to my current digs almost three years ago, Dieff accompanied me in the back seat, drop-dead gorgeous leaves swaying with the movement of the car. I'd glance at him/her from time to time in my rear view mirror, feeling his calming influence.

Dieff has grown since he came to live with me and now stands proudly about four feet tall. He loves his new location, bright light but not too sunny.

I've always watered Dieff and my other plants regularly and carefully, using a water meter to check the soil moisture so as to give them just enough nourishment. When I travel, a neighbor takes over that chore, dutifully following my detailed, written instructions. Yes, I nurture my green darlings.

About three months ago, Dieff had an attack of some terrible ailment. His leaves started curling under like he had been punched in the stomach. (Do plants have stomachs?) I called garden stores seeking advice. I took to Google, reading everything I could. It seems that the fertilizer-laced water I'd been giving Dieff for five years had become too toxic for him in his dotage, and salts were building up in his soil. Actually, that doesn't sound too different from me as I've aged.

According to Google, I must flush Dieff with a gallon of distilled water. I rolled Dieff outside on his wheeled platform, struggling to keep the heavy pot upright. I almost blew out my back, but this was an emergency.

The flushing worked! Within two days, Dieff was back to his old self. Things went well for the next few months as I eliminated all fertilizer and fed him only tap water. His rebellion happened yesterday. He screamed at me, "I don't want that tap crap! GIVE ME DISTILLED." He emphasized his point by curling his leaves under as only he can. I may have heard a few coughs, too, but I'm not sure.

I ran to the store and stocked up on ten dollars' worth

of distilled water. (I don't even buy bottled water for myself.) After another flushing, Dieff perked up and has stopped harassing me, but he definitely has me twisted around his little finger–ah, stem.

Yes, we go through all sorts of machinations for those we love, no matter what their DNA. (Do plants have DN–oh never mind?)

Put-Down Humor (April 1, 2019)

Why are so many jokes based on putting someone else down? A roast (ceremonious public ridiculing) is filled with anecdotes, jabs, stabs, and emphasis on the failings and negative aspects of the roastee. He/she must suffer through the ordeal with a smile-plastered-on-face look to prove that he can take it.

If someone has a weight problem, no matter how accomplished he might be, there is always a fat joke lurking. There are the jokes about ethnicity, sexual orientation, intellectual challenges, country of origin, frugality, and on and on. What does the joke teller or the passer-along of the denigrating email get out of his act? What do the bystanders who laugh thereby encouraging this behavior get out of it? Why is this type of "humor" so pervasive starting from childhood?

Maybe it makes the offender feel superior. That, of course, means that they must feel inferior. Yes, we all have feelings of inferiority no matter how attractive, skillful, intelligent, or wealthy we are. We have a tendency to focus on the parts of us that aren't as desirable as those of some arbitrary standard that has been set by others: parents, peers, authority figures, media, big business, etc., and to feel inferior as a result. Oh, we may be very good at hiding those feelings from the world and even from ourselves, but we sure love a good joke at the expense of another.

A put-down comedian who rose in the ranks in the 1960s and persisted into the 2000s, commanded a high salary, and booked lots of appearances was Don Rickles (now deceased). He was lauded as "one of the best insult comics of all time," and was sarcastically dubbed "Mr. Warmth" due to his being the polar opposite.

As a young woman, I somehow found myself at a night club attending a live performance of Don Rickles. His whole delivery consisted of finding people in the audience and ridiculing some aspect of them–brutally, in my opinion. I was a nervous wreck during his entire act fearing that he'd pick on me. Although I never found his brand of humor appealing, so many did. You should have heard the laughter in that night club. Don Rickles himself was a small, unattractive man with a loud mouth that spewed venom. One can only wonder what he endured growing up as a child. To me, he is a spot-on example of "the best defense is a good offense."

Must we boost ourselves up at the expense of others? Do we really go home feeling better having put someone else down? Is there another way to improve our own self-esteem?

Economics of Condolences (March 19, 2019)

A friend recently wrote me that her beloved cat of almost twenty years had died. She commented that more than 125 people wrote her condolences on her Facebook page, a significantly greater number than when her parents died.

Why is it that people can give sympathy so much more easily at the loss of a pet in someone's life rather than a human? Is it too personal when the loss is perceived to be so enormous—too close to home? Does the potential offerer fear getting into a long, emotional discussion with the aggrieved which might delay the former from a busy schedule? Pets are considered lower on the scale of importance, and perhaps that allows us to spend less time at the task of offering our regrets.

How many times have we uttered that casual opener, "Hi, how are you?" expecting the answer to be the standard, "Fine"? However, when the answer is something like, "Awful, my (fill in the blank) just died," we're stuck. If it's an in-person encounter, how can you just respond, "Oh, sorry about that. Ah, I have to go now"? If it's a telephone conversation, is it okay to say, "Hold on, I have another call coming in"? Such behavior would cast you as uncaring, insensitive, selfish, and more. So, to be socially acceptable, we must immediately stop everything to offer comforting words, mentally calculating how long before we can slither away.

I wonder if my friend would have gotten such an abundance of responses by the same people in person. With Internet platforms, we can be quick and go on our way while still getting brownie points for our thoughtfulness. It's that old economic principle: seek the maximum amount of gain for the minimum amount of effort or, stated in more economic terms, when making decisions that are in your own self-interest, strive to achieve the highest benefits at the lowest costs.

The operative words are "decisions that are in your own self-interest." Are we only going through the motions of caring with thoughts of "what's best for me" playing in the background? Human nature dictates self-interest responses to stimuli. However, can we stop for an instant and truly feel for another human being? Can we be genuine in our outpouring of concern for another human being? Can we put our busy lives on pause for just a bit to sincerely comfort another human being?

Forgiving Yourself (March 5, 2019)

We all screw up sometimes. No matter how hard we try, plan, or manipulate, circumstances may alter "the best laid plans of mice and men." There's another wonderful image in that vein about the deities finding great humor in the feeble efforts of mere mortals.

A while ago, my son was entrusted with an artistic piece made by a family member who had expended many hours of labor in its creation. My son was to bring the object back home to be a centerpiece in his family's household. He carefully carried and stowed the coveted, bulky item in the airplane overhead compartment. Upon landing and disembarking, he then hand-carried it to the baggage claim area where he set it down briefly so he could retrieve his suitcase from the carousel. That's when the deities let out a full belly laugh.

Upon returning, the wrapped object was nowhere to be found. Panicky, my son searched and searched to no avail. He filed a claim with lost and found, but it never turned up. He was devastated and felt he had betrayed a confidence.

This is just a small example of when forgiveness should enter the equation. Sometimes, the hardest form of forgiveness is to forgive yourself. Why do we hold ourselves to such high standards, fearing to admit that we're only human? I'm sure you can contribute such a war story of your own. We've all been there-done that, and it's usually painful and racks us with guilt.

If an offender committed an act against you which caused you pain, discomfort, inconvenience, or upset, look at his/her motive. Was the act done without guile? If so and he is contrite and usually trustworthy, you must forgive him. If the act was done deliberately, and that is his usual modus operandi, then he must live with such a flawed character trait and suffer the ramifications: frequent loss of friendships and relationships, ongoing conflict and tumult, others always on guard around him, and eventual disappointment and loneliness as all close contacts distance themselves or bail out altogether

If you are an example of the deliberate, conniving, the-end-justifies-the-means type, then be prepared to live with the consequences and stop being so surprised when they finally happen. If your act was committed without such duplicity, you must forgive yourself. One final saying to make the point: "To err is human, to forgive divine," and that includes forgiving yourself.

Outliers (February 18, 2019)

What is an outlier? It is an extreme example of something—the farther ends of the spectrum or uncommon within a distinctive category or group.

So what happens if you or someone close to you is an outlier? Are you or yours the fattest, skinniest, most painfully shy, overly high strung, too-smart-for-your-own-good, developmentally disabled, and the like?

For example, a hyperactive child always seems to be the one creating chaos. He/she is soon identified by the group as the troublemaker and becomes shunned, causing distress to the child and its parents. Such behavior to get attention is the only way that child understands. The situation escalates resulting in them being ostracized even more, thus setting up a perpetuating cycle.

Being an outlier is particularly hard while growing up. One can be stamped with derogatory terms that stick for a lifetime such as: geek, wimp, fatso, beanpole, homo, crazy, ugly, stupid, weird and on and on. The medical profession is complicit in the labeling game. Although done for "scientific" reasons, diagnoses like: schizophrenic, paranoid, autistic and so forth categorize their recipients and put them in pigeonholes from which it is hard to escape. These terms affect future treatment, funding, jobs, eligibilities, etc., and follow said recipient throughout their lifetime.

How do you fit into a society that skews toward the middle when you don't? It's hard. You never feel like you belong. You are rejected by the main body of the group. You feel unwelcome, unwanted, unacceptable. Is there a place for you?

It's not easy to find one's niche in life. However, there is usually a community for everyone. You must look for like-minded souls and situations where you feel comfortable. You must seek out your tribe.

How do you go about it? The first step is to figure out what it is about you or yours that makes you or them an outcast from the mainstream. Then, search for people and places where your "thing" is acceptable.

I have always had a loud, projecting voice. All my life, people have told me to speak more quietly, and the rude ones just show irritation as they bark at me to "shush" while holding their index finger over their lips lest I don't understand. The truth is that I don't even realize when my voice gets loud. It does so when I'm tense, over-stressed, or tired. It has become worse as my hearing has deteriorated. People don't understand that. Many just think that I don't care about their admonition.

I discovered acting eighteen years ago. Now, I'm lauded for my loud, projecting voice. Yes, I fit in; my acting group admires my vocal abilities.

To find your kindred folks, you will need terminology to help you navigate. Is your child ADHD? Is your brother morbidly obese? Are you depressed? Is your mother an addictive personality? Yes, these and other painful labels have been thrust upon many, but they are also communication tools to help ferret out and find those who are similar and supportive.

Networking with others helps you learn about opportunities. The library can be a great resource as can the Internet. Use those labels you've always hated to your advantage, and find your clan.

Default Position (February 4, 2019)
A friend recently told me that my default position is positive. I'd never thought of it like that. Yes, our natural inclination as well as our life experiences do give us a default position. It's that mode we always return to no matter what happens to us.

Default positions range on a scale from positive to negative, and there are infinite degrees in between. What is your default position? Is it satisfying to you?

In my case, when something upsetting or unsettling happens in my life, I may get bummed out. However, I don't seem to be able to stay down for very long. It doesn't mean I don't feel bad or never get depressed. However, I automatically boomerang back toward the positive end of the spectrum. It comes naturally, and I don't think about it. I don't know why I'm like that.

Those whose default position tends toward the ill-natured extreme may long to move their needle closer to the other end. When such a tendency doesn't come naturally, can you do anything to change it, or are you forever stuck defaulting toward that negative boundary? My take is that you can change a long ingrained tendency, but only if you want it enough and are willing to work long and hard to achieve it.

I have had experiences in my life where my natural inclination was toward a position I hated. I'm thinking of my decades-long worry of incurring the disapproval of others. In my younger years, it was always so hard for me to stand up to people—to rock the boat. If called upon to do something I didn't want to, I'd often go along with it (nothing ever destructive) so people wouldn't dislike me. It took years and a lot of internal struggle to reach a more satisfying position. Probably the seeds of my original tendencies will always exist within me. However, I'm in control now, and I no longer put up with bossy, bullying, or over-bearing humans.

So, yes, it is possible to change. Figure out how badly you want to do so, the steps you need to take, and go to it. It may be daunting, scary, intimidating, overwhelming, and on and on. Nevertheless, DO IT ANYWAY! It could change your life.

Dwelling Decisions (January 21, 2019)

While working, how and where you reside are often dictated by considerations of employment, family, cost, and the like. Once you retire, the options widen. Many stay put in the tried and true–their comfort level. The idea of moving from the family home is too distressing, and they may remodel to suit their aging needs: a mechanical staircase lift, lowered counters, raised cabinets and dishwashers, walk-in (or roll-in) showers, and more. Others who possess nagging wanderlust may venture out to explore different alternatives.

I recently heard from a friend of a friend about her choice. She has become a nomad. She sold her house of thirty years and now moves between the West Coast of the United States, Mexico, and Europe, staying at each for long stints with travel interspersed. When she alights, she finds a short-term rental or stays with friends. She has carved out an interesting lifestyle. Her retirement may seem scary to some and exciting to others. I've heard (though it might not be correct) that the same Chinese character designates both danger and opportunity. Regardless of the Chinese alphabet, the metaphor holds.

I know of others who become minimalists, opting for the human version of turtles carrying their home on their back. These folks give up most worldly possessions, buy an RV, and continuously move about as the whim takes them.

Many downsize and find a like-minded demographic in which to settle such as an active senior retirement community. That was my decision. Still others strike out for distant and exotic lands, domestic or international, to pursue a passion–think Paul Gauguin.

A few friends have mentioned the idea of living with their children or other family members. They would have their own room in the main house. Or, they would occupy a small dwelling in the backyard, thereby creating a family compound. Many years ago, one of my cousins and her husband bought an apartment building with other family members, and each family unit lived in a different apartment. You have to like your relatives an awful lot to make this work.

There's the story, true or not, of some people living permanently on cruise ships. They have a room, all meals, housekeeping services, a doctor available, and they get to explore exciting destinations.

There is no right or wrong choice. There is just the choice for you. The important thing is that you make it when you can instead of someone else doing it for you when you can't.

Armful of Dogs (January 7, 2019)

Recently, I visited my friend, Janet, who is a Chihuahua person (a special breed of people). I spent a lot of time chilling with her two Chihuahua mixes. As soon as I started holding Pepe, Holly jumped up on the bench. I thought she would just sit next to me as is her style. However, she briefly climbed into my lap, not to be outdone by Pepe.

Pepe, a love–easy-going and friendly to all, is the sweet, cuddly type who adores being held and petted. Holly is a lot more skittish–a high strung presence; it takes patience to become her friend. I had to go through her barking and reluctant acceptance each time I entered the house for the duration of my stay. Once Holly gave me the okay, however, she couldn't get enough of me. Although she didn't like being held, after a few test sniffs, she tolerated petting. Of course, that required me to bend way down due to her low-slung stature, but I thought of it is good exercise.

Next, I moved on and stayed with my cousin, Gail, where I hung out with her mini-pincher mix, Sarge. Although his appearance matched his name, his personality was the polar opposite. Sarge was loving and licky, frequently jumping onto my lap and hunkering down. So many times when I walked into my bedroom, there was Sarge on my bed, proprietary and anxious to hang out some more.

Why do I love dogs so much? It started in childhood. I begin to notice something special about them that I didn't notice in human beings. I'll use dogs as my example, but the same applies to so many animals other than humans.

Dogs are loyal, dependable, faithful. With dogs, there is no agenda–what you see is what you get. They are never artificial, duplicitous, political, and will never stab you in the back. Dogs are always happy to see you no matter how crummy you are, how angry, smelly, miserable, or pissy. Dogs love you whether you're up or you're down. They never get mad at you, tell you off, ignore you, ostracize you, or pay you back. The only human who even comes close is Mommy, and even she fails the dog test.

The moment I get around a dog, I feel comfortable, relaxed. Dogs' needs are simple. They don't require the latest designer clothes, the newest luxury automobile, the trendiest (fill in the blank). They are not into status. Mankind would be well advised to emulate the canines among us.

On the other hand, people are like Pepe, Holly, and Sarge–each has their own personality. Some are warm and seek close contact, while others are nervous and don't like too much handling. I have great respect for dogs, and I'm always careful never to cause them distress to the best of my ability.

Can we be that way with the wide range of humans we encounter? Can we respect their individual personalities and alter our behavior so as not to cause them distress? Don't we wish people would treat us that way?

There's no need to come on like gangbusters when you perceive someone is highly uncomfortable with your usual modus operandi. Respect each individual's personality, and interact with them appropriately so as to maintain their comfort level. You will be much more likely to have a successful encounter than if you treat everyone with a cookie-cutter approach.

BLOG POSTS FROM 2018

Snowball (December 23, 2018)

I met Snowball some years ago at an EcoFest held on the lawn of the La Brea Tar Pits in Los Angeles, California where I was a docent. Snowball was part of the attractions at the booth of the Los Angeles chapter of the Southwestern Herpetologists Society.

Snowball's owner, Jarron, adored him/her, just as you or I might adore our child, dog, cat, parrot, monkey, or lemur. He was full of information about Snowball and couldn't wait to share it with me after I expressed interest. However, he failed to tell me how his pet got its name. I like to imagine Snowball was born or adopted during the winter holiday season.

Jarred explained that monitor lizards are usually aggressive and dangerous in the wild, but Snowball had been bred in captivity and gentled by humans from the time of wee lizardhood. So, he/she was docile and not dangerous. Jarred encouraged me to pet Snowball. Its skin felt dry and bumpy under my fingertips.

FYI (courtesy of Jarred and the Internet): Crocodile monitor lizards, a relative of the Komodo dragon, are native to the jungles of New Guinea. They are thought to be the longest known lizard species in the world, usually growing to five to seven feet in length but sometimes reaching over ten feet long. Two-thirds of their length is in their slender tails which they whip around like a weapon. They have sharp, curved claws to aid in climbing trees. In captivity, they can live eight to twelve years.

I saw other reptile owners cradling and cuddling their pet snakes, lizards, and assorted others of the reptilian persuasion. One guy was walking around with his own large lizard clinging vertically to the front of his sweater like an armor breastplate.

Later, a herpetologist club member approached me while I was manning the La Brea Tar Pits Museum booth. She was extremely distraught and crying.

"Do you know anyone in the museum who would like a dead snake," she wanted to know.

I had never been asked such a question before nor anything remotely similar. It seems that when she had taken her pet snake out of its cage, it was dead. She had owned and adored it for over twenty-five years. She wanted to donate it to a good cause. Amazingly, after a few inquiries, I was able to find a potential recipient of her prize. He was a young, part-time employee of the museum. He planned to use the snake in practicing to build scaffolds for disarticulated, ancient animal bones to display in natural history museums, a pursuit he hoped to make his career. Snake giver and snake receiver conversed and struck a deal.

Beauty is definitely in the eyes of the beholder. We each see beauty in our love objects regardless if they are ugly, strange, weird, or off-putting to others. Be grateful for those who love you. You may seem ugly, strange, weird, or off-putting to some, too.

A Tandakoan's Reflection on an Obituary (December 9, 2018)

I opened an email from my longtime, high school girlfriend, Sheila. Part of it read, "this was surprising in today's newspaper." There was an attachment, so I clicked on it to find an obituary with a photograph of a woman I didn't recognize.

As I read further, I realized she had been a classmate of ours, and we had all graduated high school together. I've saved the patch from my class sweater of the emblem of our senior class: the Tandakoans, for fifty-nine years.

Why do we keep such trivial objects? Probably because they are symbols of passage. Passages are events that mark major turning points in our lives. Among all the minutiae of our existence that are quickly forgotten, these are the happenings that we remember year after year. We might celebrate or bemoan them in a ceremonial manner on special anniversaries.

I remember when I turned fifty, Sheila organized a Brownie Troop reunion. Those attending showed up with photographs of our troop members, Brownie and Girl Scout badges, and other nostalgic items they had kept for decades. Our lives are filled with passages. An obituary marks the final one.

I hadn't seen Judy since graduation, but I remembered her as a bouncy girl with a quick smile and a ponytail. The obituary said she had died following a long battle with ovarian cancer. One by one, our ranks are thinning. Reading about Judy, I couldn't stave off thoughts of: when will it be my turn?

Does that frighten me; does that concern me? Yes and no. I'm frightened of the unknown, but not of the finality of it, maybe because I don't even understand what that means.

Can I choose how to make my final passage? I certainly don't want the path that Judy took or anything like it. Living my life to the fullest and going suddenly in my sleep is my preferred choice. But, all I can do is hope for that and do the living-my-life-to-the-fullest part in the meantime.

Waiting for Upcycle Days (November 28, 2018)

Life is cyclical. It's like a wave with peaks and valleys. The peaks–the good times–are exciting and exhilarating. But they can never be sustained. Life intervenes to drop us into the valleys–the bad times. It happens to all of us.

No, that guy at work, the neighbor down the block, the classmate at school for whom things always seem to go right are not imbued with some fairy godmother granting their every wish. They just do a better job of covering up their valleys than others do. Don't ever think that only your life sucks and everyone else's is wonderful. It doesn't work like that. We all ride the cycles of life.

So, how do we weather those valleys; how do we survive? One way is to keep looking toward that metaphorical horizon for signs of the next peak peeking over as you slog your way through. It's hard and takes constant vigilance to maintain a positive attitude.

It is easy to become discouraged and impatient hoping for things to turn around. There is not an assured time line. We can't know when the peaks will happen, when the valleys will happen, and how long the span between them. We have no choice but to wait it out. How we do the waiting is up to us.

We can become depressed, we can rail, we can act out. Or, we can try to use the lull positively as we wait for it to pass. Get to work on that story you always wanted to write. Learn that new skill you always wanted to master. Reach out and connect with those people and places you never had the time to do before. Take up jogging, walking, gardening, tennis, knitting, gourd carving, whatever. Even the down spells can have little seeds of positivity embedded in them.

Remember, without the valleys, you can't appreciate the peaks.

The Boot (November 11, 2018)

Almost forty years ago, a wartime drama film, "Das Boot," was released to movie theaters. It took place on a German submarine during WWII. Das Boot actually translates from German as: the boat. However, in my case, I am interpreting the literal English meaning: the boot—you know, for a foot.

Yes, the boot has come into my life. Although I don't anticipate a submarine attack from my particular one, its arrival has similarities. It was stealthy, unexpected, and out of nowhere.

It started a few weeks ago when I was returning a rental car at the airport. While walking to the pickup area to catch my Uber ride, I failed to see that my narrow sidewalk—with rental cars whizzing by on each side—took one step down. Yep, one step down is how I went—horizontally! Long story short, I broke my fifth metatarsal bone in not one but two places. Hence, "the boot."

That minor misstep has cut me down. The boot, upon which I am dependent to get around along with an attendant cane, has ruled my life for several weeks now. It dictates where I go, how fast I go, and how often I go. Lacing up the six, mean looking Velcro straps of the contraption alone wears me out. However, I must do so several times a day for foot icing, showering, and sleeping.

Friends from out of town visited for a get-together we had planned months earlier. I had to alter my plans to go out and about with them and to travel for a few days after they stayed in my home. I knew I couldn't do the walking, hiking, hill climbing, stair-stepping, metro riding, etc., so I begrudgingly opted to stay put as they departed.

So many unforeseen mishaps change our plans, routines, trajectories. Most people have had their own version of "the boot." It commands your undivided attention while everything else is put on hold.

How do we survive a case of "the boot"? It's not easy; it clips your wings. However, we must survive and carry on. I'm doing a lot of staying in/sitting down stuff: busy work that has been on hold for months, phone calling, clearing out my overloaded email box, mending clothes… Actually, it feels good to get a handle on mundane things that have been relegated to the back burner and gotten out of hand.

Try to make the best of your downtime. What other choice do you have? And remember, be careful—it's dangerous out there, folks—sigh!

Jangled on a Train (October 28, 2018)

I arrived some months ago at the San Diego train station ready to board an Amtrak Southern Coaster to travel up the coast of California on my way to my cousin's house. I had not taken the train in years, and I was pretty excited about the whole thing.

I explained to the ticket clerk that I had just flown into the airport, and my ears were clogged from the landing, so I probably wouldn't be able to hear the public announcement to board the train. She directed me to the handicapped section where an attendant personally retrieves those waiting there and accompanies them to the train.

When the time came, I walked next to a passenger in his motorized wheelchair who told me he took the train often. We were seated in a special car just for handicapped people.

Much of my ride was spent multitasking—conducting business on my cell phone while looking out the window at the vista as it flashed by. The combination of my clogged ears, the clickety-clack of the train wheels, and the periodic poor phone reception made it difficult to converse.

Apparently, my voice was getting progressively louder un-beknownst to me. Suddenly, a hand appeared from nowhere and dropped a note onto the fold-down table in front of me which held all my business correspondence. It read: *Seriously? (double underlined) Quiet!! Do we all "have to" listen to your conversation? Sh-sh-sh! Thank you*

Oops, I had offended someone, although I didn't realize that because one is handicapped one requires exceptional qui-et. Nevertheless, I turned around to identify my assailant and assumed it must be the woman sitting two rows behind me who was hiding behind a seatback.

I stated in a raised voice, "I apologize if I offended you, but you are always welcome to change your seat." She did not respond.

I continued my phone conversation but did ratchet it down several notches. A short while later, my assailant passed by holding a professionally printed sign which she held up briefly in front of me. It said something like: *Be quiet, this is a handicapped car.* She then made her way further down the car and showed it to other perceived offenders.

I thought to myself, *what a poor soul,* and said to her as she trailed past, "I'm so sorry that I disturbed you." Her re-sponse: "I don't care!"

Yes, it made me feel like shouting a retort at her back as

she continued down the aisle. I stopped myself realizing that this woman had enough aggravation in her life, and I could be charitable and not add to it.

If you are spending your brief time on this earth trying to modify the behavior of others to make yourself more comfortable, it won't work. Focus your efforts on modifying your own behavior. In this case, the woman could have simply inserted noise-control earplugs or earbuds attached to a music device.

If you are impacted by someone like the aforementioned passenger, remember to be charitable and understanding of their quirks. After all, your life is probably so much fuller than theirs, and I bet you have a few quirks of your own.

What's in the Stroller? (October 13, 2018)

I was sitting on a metro train a few weeks ago next to a woman with a Chihuahua in her lap. She kept stroking it and talking to it. The lady seemed a bit deranged. She had a knitted cap pulled over her hair, no teeth, and her clothing seemed mismatched. Parked in front of her was a baby stroller with a second Chihuahua in it. I'm sure both dogs occupied the stroller together when the woman was out and about on her daily routine.

Periodically, the dog owner attempted to make eye contact with people nearby as she chatted about her dogs. Most just ignored her or averted their gaze. A mother with a young child held it close to her, protectively, lest the child catch anything the woman might transmit such as a compromised mental state.

Over about a ten-minute period as I watched from my perch while trying not to be obvious about it, the owner pulled out a plush toy from the stroller, which she snuggled against the face of first one of the dogs and then the other. She also pulled out food and broke off little pieces which she fed to the dogs, occasionally popping a morsel into her own mouth.

After observing her for quite a while, I said, "You certainly take very good care of your dogs." Starved for conversation, she immediately began discussing the dogs with me. We chatted for the rest of the ride, about five minutes, on the subject of how much joy the dogs have brought to her life.

I looked at the dog on her lap and addressed it by the name she had called it: Mister. Mister immediately jumped into my lap and hunkered down. His owner was delighted and loved sharing one of her most precious possessions with me as I scratched Mister behind his ears.

When I departed the train, I again complemented my seat companion on what a good and caring owner she was. She beamed a beautiful, toothless smile at me.

Can we be willing to reach out to others who are not so cool, not so trendy, maybe a little socially offensive? Can we take that moment to connect with another fragile human being, toothless or not, smartly dressed or not? That encounter did as much for me as it did for her.

The Entitled (September 28, 2018)

Some people seem to think that they are more entitled to the goodies of life than others. They're the ones who fight to be first in selecting everything. Here are a few examples: they rush to the best seats, cut in line, cherry-pick the choicest portion of the communal food, maneuver themselves into the most advantageous spots, grab the… Well, you get the idea.

These are the same folks who think they can buy or manipulate their way in or out of anything. They may use different ploys to advance their agenda. "I'm rich, so I should have a more luxurious (fill in the blank)"; "I'm well-known, so I deserve a better (fill in the blank)"; "I'm sickly, so I merit a more advantageous (fill in the blank)"; "I'm elderly, so I require a more comfortable (fill in the blank)"; and on and on. Everyone can find a reason in their life why they should be more entitled than you, me, him, her, them, or whomever.

I was on a tour years ago in some exotic location, and we went out daily in a Land Rover to navigate the rough terrain. One woman always got there early and sat in the front passenger seat. She told us all that she had a bad knee, and the extra legroom allowed her to stretch out her leg. Coincidentally, that also happened to be the best seat in the house, offering the choicest view out of the panoramic front window as well as a prime location next to the driver/tour guide so every morsel of his spiel could be captured. One day, we arrived to see a man from our group in that coveted seat. The aforementioned woman was forced to sit in another spot.

"Would you mind changing seats with me so I can stretch out my sore knee," she said to him sweetly.

I loved his response which was no response at all. He didn't say a word and didn't budge. It was wonderful to see our entitled member confronted in such a silent manner, as we were all pretty sick of her uncanny need to always require the most desirable of everything on that trip.

It's a little unclear how these self-perceived, entitled beings got that way. Perhaps mommy and daddy enabled it as they were growing up. It could be a result of their feelings of deprivation. Maybe it's an adaptation to the natural competition among the seven billion plus of us on this planet. Of course, we all use our talents, skills, and abilities to get our "piece of the pie." But, the entitled of the world take it to another level altogether.

Are you among the always entitled, or do you know someone like that? Folks of such an attitude, position, or outlook are completely off-putting to everyone else. We are all human beings, and we live in close proximity to each other, jostling around like nervous atoms trying to get comfortable and find our place. One person is not more special or important than anyone else, although he/she would like to be.

Let's be grown up and fair about this. Let everybody in your sphere have a chance for the best this or the finest that. When it's always about you, you may find that you're no longer in competition because you no longer have anyone who is willing to be involved with you in any way. You will be left to enjoy your best this or finest that all by your best and finest lonesome self.

Come into the Modern World (September 12, 2018)
It's easy to get left behind with the rapid-fire changes that have happened in our lifetime: new ideas, new discoveries, new ways of living, new technology, and on and on. Each time something new happens, it presents us with a steep learning curve.

Now, in order to buy the latest car, some dealerships offer classes on how to operate the darn thing with all its technology components and gadgetry. Today's television sets come with a remote control reminiscent of a cockpit dashboard.

More and more people are shying away from the pressure and falling further and further behind. However, the alternative is worse as their world gets smaller and they become isolated.

When friends and groups I belong to plan events, email blasts are what notify the participants. It's sad when someone wants to be a part of the activity but defensively admits that they don't know how to use a computer. No one volunteers to call them for each update and chance playing the irritating game of telephone tag.

I remember my resistance to learning to use the Internet because of the difficulty in understanding it. I insisted that my life functioned just fine the way it was, and that if I didn't already know something, I wasn't interested. The turning point came well over a decade ago. After trying to convince me unsuccessfully for a few years, one day my son said the magic words: "Mom, come into the modern world."

Yes, I envied those who were able to use email to communicate instantaneously. Yes, I too wanted to access the knowledge of the ages with a few keystrokes. And, most of all, I wanted to make my son proud of me.

I took the plunge and enrolled in a school. I signed up for one course in word processing and another course in the Internet. The latter was so difficult to grasp that I continued to attend it over and over for an entire year until I finally got it.

The truth is, the Internet has opened my life in ways I never imagined. Writing this blog is one of them. The best of all, however, is that I can email with my son, and it blows his mind when I talk tech-speak with him. Yes, he is proud of mom.

Life Is a Labyrinth (August 28, 2018)

Some months ago, I strolled a lovely community labyrinth. Some anonymous person or persons had searched for the stones, gathered them, hauled them to the site, and laid them out in an intricate maze, all so I could enjoy it and discover its message. Labyrinths date back more than 4000 years and have been found all over the world. Although many dead ends abound for the labyrinth voyager, there is only one pathway which leads to the center—the goal.

As I made my way around the contortions of this ancient puzzle, it set the stage for quiet, contemplation, solitude, and peace. I felt relaxed and had these thoughts:

Life is a labyrinth. We go around in circles seeking our goal but often hit one barrier after the next. When we reach a dead end, we are forced to retrace our steps and try a new direction. We can visualize what we seek, even see it. Sometimes, it seems so close, and yet we are quite far. At other times, it seems so far, yet we are actually very close.

We each travel on our own personal quest. We are surrounded by the same environment as our neighbors, but we view it differently, experience it differently, interact with it differently, each in our own reality bubble.

Yes, we can take shortcuts. We can step over the boundaries of the labyrinth and rush to the end. But, we've shortchanged ourselves. We've forgotten the importance of the process which is how we learn about life so we can appreciate and benefit from the eventual attainment of our objective. Otherwise, we have no understanding of what we have reached, and we may destroy it with our ignorance.

Don't fight the labyrinth. Embrace it. Follow it. Grab it. Don't rush things—focus, go with the flow as they say. This is not a contest–no winners and losers. Discover the pace that works for you; discover which path works for you. It's different for everyone. The wealth is attained from the journey, not the completion.

Half-Assed vs. Whole-Assed (August 13, 2018)

Some people put a tremendous amount of effort into what they do: jobs, leisure time, parenting, helping others, and so forth. Other people do as little as possible on such activities. Why is that?

Let's look at the workplace for example. When I was working at my career as a probation officer, it was obvious to all my co-workers who the people were who really did a good job and who did as little as they could to just get by. The latter group was not bad enough to be fired; they managed to produce to the level of being barely competent. I could never understand their motivation or lack thereof.

The way I see it, even if you don't particularly like your job or work, you still have to devote a significant number of hours to it. It's just too boring not to tackle your task with effort and enthusiasm. If you must do the time, do so in a way that brings reward to yourself.

Performing a half-assed job is fraught with negativity, yields feelings of inadequacy, and produces minimal reward.

Doing a whole-assed job gives you a sense of accomplishment, esteem from peers and superiors, and pride in yourself. This dichotomy can be extrapolated to all areas of your life: your home, your work, your relationships, and your leisure time.

Even the great Albert Einstein worked a day job for seven years in a patent office before leaving to take over the chair in theoretical physics at the University of Zurich. Purportedly, he was well-liked and even received a promotion at that earlier, survival job which he referred to as his "cobbler's trade."

If you must be a waiter while trying to bag that great acting role, why not be the best waiter you can be? Those seconds, minutes, hours, and so forth spent at the job are the same amounts of time deducted from your lifespan. So why not make them as rewarding to yourself as possible?

Clowny (July 26, 2018)
I'm guessing that most people have experienced a devastating incident or many during the difficult time of growing up. Dragging childhood pain through the decades shapes our adulthood. The memory of one in my life remains fresh and clear sixty-two years later.

I was about fourteen, shy, scrawny, and very concerned about what others thought of me. Girls were just starting to wear lipstick, and I coveted jumping into the adult world with such a daring step.

At that time, there was a company called Ponds which featured as its main product a cold cream, the equivalent of today's facial moisturizer; the company is still in business. Ponds was testing a possible expansion into the makeup field and was giving out free samples of lipstick in tiny tubes. My mother acquired a few and gave me one to inaugurate my foray into being a real woman.

I practiced applying my Ponds lipstick sampler until I got it just right. D-Day arrived for my first appearance at school as the new and sophisticated me. I've never forgotten that day so many decades ago because of one word.

I walked into my first period class which was girls' gym. The locker room was filled with my female classmates changing into their gym clothes. They all turned as I entered. One girl (I still remember her name) took a look at my bright, red lips contrasted with my remaining washed out complexion and pronounced, "You look like a clown. We should call you Clowny." Everyone laughed and immediately took up the chant: "Clowny, Clowny, Clowny."

My goal in life was to not call attention to myself, but I had managed to achieve the polar opposite only because I wanted to act grown-up like the rest of the girls. I was humiliated! Trying not to cry in front of my harassers, I ran to the bathroom, grabbed some toilet paper, and wiped off that stupid Ponds lipstick, not to be attempted again for at least two years.

That didn't stop the fun the others were having. Clowny remarks followed me for the next few weeks not only in the gym but in other classes I shared with some of them.

Memories such as these mold our grown-up selves. Some use such experiences to become compassionate adults, remembering the cruel rites of passage they encountered themselves. Others do the opposite by seeking victims to extract the revenge they were unable to mete out to their original tormentors. If your aim is to assuage your pain, choose the compassionate path as it will yield you a much higher return.

The Passive-Aggressive Jab (July 11, 2018)

What I've termed the "passive-aggressive jab" (PAJ) is definitely a one-two punch thrown when you aren't looking. It's that oh-so-subtle put down that you can't quite define, can't quite grasp. The PAJ is usually delivered when you're off-guard, and all of a sudden you sense that everything feels weird.

The jab thrower might be a friend, relative, boss, teacher, co-worker, acquaintance, stranger, or any other relationship description. He/she might have a pleasant smile on his face during the punch, so you doubt that it was really meant the way it made you feel. You wonder if you are wrong in your assessment, and you doubt your own sanity.

Am I crazy, or did he just say that?

The puncher's comment is usually structured so it can be interpreted in different ways. You wonder what kind of a person you are to attribute it in such a negative manner. Maybe he meant it in the best possible light, and you're the creep.

Over time, you begin to notice more such behavior on the part of the jabber. After a while, you begin to suspect that you were right all along. However, any confrontation will yield something like "What are you talking about? That's not what I meant."

You have been turned into the bad guy. He and anyone else he can enlist into his camp look at you askance and defend poor him.

Why do people behave that way? It doesn't matter. If

such behavior stokes his ego in some fashion, that is not your problem to figure out or fix. What is your problem is how to combat such conduct when it's aimed at you? It's hard, but it can be done.

First, you have to realize that you've been the victim of the passive-aggressive jab. Next, you have to swerve to avoid it, just like the boxer does to deflect the hit. In this case, it's an emotional swerve. Here are some countermeasures you might employ:

1. Refuse to engage!
2. Don't respond, even when you suspect that a grenade has just landed at your feet.
3. Resist retaliating in kind; that only becomes a pissing match of put-downs.
4. Stare him down.
5. Wait for an opportune moment where you can whisper privately to him, "I'm not playing that game."
6. Take your leave, either physically or emotionally.
7. Socialize with others present and avoid your attacker.
8. Maintain self-control.

Remember not to try to reason with him. That's what he wants so he can make himself look like an innocent. Instead, try some of the above suggested techniques. If one doesn't cut it, try another. Create some of your own. Make them work for you.

The Big Reveal (June 26, 2018)

We all want to put our proverbial best foot forward when trying to attract a mate (or even friends). In this highly competitive endeavor, many hedge their truths, puffing up their more desirable accomplishments or traits and downplaying the not-so-flattering aspects. After all, we don't want to drive someone away before they even get a chance to learn to adore wonderful us.

The grumpy, negative person plasters on a happy face. The older person chops a few years off their age. The not quite-wealthy enough person adds a zero or two to their net worth, presenting his/her Mercedes as paid in full when it is really leased. The not-quite-educated-enough person adds a degree or two. Makeup, hair dye, clothing, and surgical enhancements all play their part to this end. But, what happens when the sucker—ah, potential mate—learns the truth?

In lockstep with the above overt deceptions are the covert deceptions. These take the form of "failing to mention." If you murdered your mother and just got out of prison, don't mention it and the sucker—sorry, potential mate will never be the wiser, at least not in the beginning.

Many practitioners of the aforementioned arts eventually are forced into "the big reveal." After the sucker—ah, potential mate—is hooked and "in love," a circumstance may occur where the hidden fact seeps out. It could be something like guilt which propels the blurted-out truth or a situation where the practitioner is caught not knowing something he/she should in their purported position.

I remember many years ago where a co-worker told the others in the office that she had a PhD in anthropology. Everyone believed her; after all, who would lie about a thing like that? One day, the subject of Anthropologist Louis Leakey of Olduvai Gorge fame was the topic of conversation in the coffee room. Our resident anthropology PhD didn't know who he was, information that every student of that discipline learns in Anthropology 101. Well, that started the entire staff questioning anything she had ever claimed about herself, a despicable situation to be in.

What happens when you and (fill in the blank) are married or at least have been significant others for years, and your secret comes out? I know someone who was not quite as divorced as she had claimed to her live-in boyfriend of many years. She was outed by a casual remark from a guest at a party they attended. Their relationship began to unravel from there.

What about the stark check boxes on your online dating profile? In this age of connection via internet, you only have a photo and some brief text to catch your fish. It's almost a given that years are shaved off ages, photos are out-of-date, and other data is tweaked. There are even professional profile writers you can hire to help put that aforementioned best foot forward.

Eventually that shaving, tweaking, and other manners of deception will have its way. It may take years, but it will. I have one friend who did her "big reveal" of lying about her age after a few dates with a man she had met online. He became very angry and walked out in a huff complete with swirling dust clouds. This same friend subsequently met another man online, again lied about her age, eventually did the "big reveal," and he didn't care. They are now happily living together.

So, there you go. The big reveal can be malignant or benign. Ya pays yer money and ya takes yer chances.

Lying as a Lifestyle (June 13, 2018)
I guess we've all told lies of one sort or another, little white lies

and not so little white lies. We have different motives for doing so: to keep our personal information private, to keep from hurting another person's feelings because we're worried about the reaction of others, and so on. The right or wrong of such behavior is a matter of degree for each individual.

Some feel that telling little white lies to save the feelings of another is just a kindness. Pushing the envelope in how they present themselves, other folks might feel, is justified as it's nobody else's business. But, how about when lying becomes a lifestyle?

There are some people who lie about so many things just because they can. When found out, others wonder "why" since it seems so petty and unnecessary. For people engaged in such a lifestyle practice, lying feeds upon itself and becomes pathological. They lie to always put themselves in the most favorable light at any given moment. However, what they fail to understand is that once branded a liar, they remain forever in an unfavorable light.

Then there are those who deliberately withhold significant information under the guise of, "well, I didn't lie." I've had that experience a few times in my life with significant others who failed to mention very compelling facts about themselves and kept that deception going for years until I finally found out or they admitted it to me. Yes, it was information that might have defeated the relationship from the beginning, so I guess they sensed that and kept their secret so I wouldn't walk away. It just seems to me that that is no way to have a friendship or relationship—based on falsehoods. Yet, that behavior goes on with so many. I wonder if the perpetrators are really content or satisfied with what they have sown.

The trouble with lies is that you have to remember them and keep feeding them. To the practitioner, it must become an exhausting endeavor, like the juggler spinning plates on sticks, running from one end of the line to the other to stoke each twirling disc as it begins to slow down and threatens to crash. What an unenviable position. Consider carefully the possible consequences before telling a lie. Is it really worth it?

Tone It Down (May 30, 2018)

Why do some people feel that it is their place to tell others how to behave? I can understand if the person is in a position where that is expected such as a teacher, employer, parent, mentor. But, what about when the teller is simply a peer who has decided to take on that role?

I had an experience not too long ago where I was on a tour of an historical house with other people from a club I belong to. At one point, the entire group was crowded into the bathroom while the docent discussed various features. When I noticed an odd-looking metal tank over the bathtub, I put my fingertip on it and asked the docent, "What's this?"

One member of the assemblage who I barely knew stated in a loud, scolding voice, "Don't touch that; that's an antique!" Her manner and resonant baritone caused everyone in that room, about twenty people, to turn around and stare at the miscreant–me.

Technically, she was correct. I should not have touched it. I did so without even thinking. However, this woman's delivery and self-appointed authoritarianism was completely out of line. She treated me as though I were a misbehaved child.

What she might have done was take me aside privately after the fact and mention in a calm, nonjudgmental voice that it is not advisable to touch antiques as the oil from skin can be harmful to them. If someone behaves that way toward you, you might take them aside and, in a calm, nonjudgmental voice, notify them that you are not interested in their unsolicited opinion of your behavior.

If you position yourself as an uninvited arbiter of your peers, tone it down a notch or ten. No one is interested in being judged or dominated by you. If you find yourself being ostracized by others, and you have no idea why, perhaps that is the reason. How would you like it if somebody behaved that way toward you?

Keep Your Promises (May 14, 2018)

When we make a promise, it's a commitment to do what we pledged we would do. It can be something as simple as meeting someone at a specific time and date, or something as large as paying for someone's college education.

Because promises historically have been misunderstood or deliberately rescinded, society has created oath taking. In America, this usually involves raising your right hand and swearing, often on a revered object or person, to keep a promise be it telling the truth, fighting for your county, or matters of similar gravity.

Going further to insure keeping promises, the law created an instrument called a contract. Often, when we enter the complex and important promise relationship, we sign a document binding us to follow through on what we promised. If it doesn't go smoothly according to the plan, we have courts of law with judges who will hear evidence and decide on how the promise should be interpreted and what each party is obligated to do.

In our private lives, we don't have courts of law to force us to fulfill our promises, we only have our word. Others to whom we have made promises depend on them and might even make life altering plans according to the terms of our promise.

Are you a person who follows through with your promises, or are you one whose pattern is to break your promises when you want to manipulate the situation, when you get angry, when you're not in the mood, or for a myriad of other reasons that suit you at the moment? If you fall into the former category, those in your life most likely trust you and value their relationship with you. If, instead, the latter classification describes you, those in your life probably don't trust you and avoid ever depending upon you or making promises themselves that you might depend on. Worse yet, they might break promises made to you without a second thought as that has become the established modus operandi of your relationship.

Being pegged as one who can't be depended upon to keep your promises, you isolate yourself to a lonely cave. So, if you have no clue as to why people in your life have withdrawn from you, take a look at your own behavior, and see if part of it involves failing to keep your promises.

My Body Won't Cooperate with My Lifestyle (April 16, 2018)

My body is getting more and more uncooperative as it and I grow older together. Where is that gal who could ski all day and boogie into the night? Where is that woman who could travel the world, exploring other cultures from early morning to late in the evening? Where is that multitasking me who could work full time, raise children, run a household, and still squeeze in friends and fun—all at the same time?

These days, corpus meum seems to have a mind of its own independent of my thoughts and desires. Regardless of what I direct it to do, it does its own thing. It has cramped my style more than once. It's so hard to accept that I'm no longer in control; I want a divorce! I'll find a new body that is much more in sync with how I envision myself.

I'm in pretty good health, but small, irritating things are happening to my body. When I finally accept and cope with one, another springs up. When I think I've got everything pretty much under control, MB morphs and "wham," it's another change I have to incorporate.

Friends and acquaintances tell me the same thing is happening to them. What to do, what to do? Well, we can try railing to the wind and lamenting our lot. Dumping on anyone who will listen is another possibility. Hunkering down with the covers over our head is a third way to go. Unfortunately, those options only waste time and put off the inevitable of accepting and becoming comfortable with the new you.

New You doesn't have the energy level that Old You had. NY gets tired more easily. NY doesn't bounce back so fast from illnesses, upsets, or just about anything else that comes your way. NY can become a true PIA (pain in the ass). Nevertheless, NY is all you have, and you can't go back to OY no matter how much you wish it, how much you try, how much you rail.

So, you have two choices: accept NY, come to terms with your aging body, and embrace all the things you can still do, or reject NY and be miserable. And remember, if you're stuck in the latter, you can always switch to the former.

A Hitch in Your Gitalong (April 2, 2018)

Many of you may remember Gabby Hayes who was an actor in Western films in the 1930s and 1940s. He often played a wizened, cantankerous old coot who was the sidekick or cook on cattle drives. In one of those roles, he had a limp and explained when asked about it, "I got a hitch in my gitalong."

We all develop a hitch in our gitalongs of one sort or another in our later years. We might not limp, but we slow down. We can't walk as far as we used to. Maybe our hips hurt, or our knees, calves, shins, ankles, soles, heels, toes, whatevers. Maybe our stamina is not as long lasting as it was decades earlier. Maybe our mental capacity isn't as cooperative.

Whatever the reason, don't drop out; seek help. There are all types of assistive devices such as canes, walkers, wheelchairs, etc. I saw a man riding on his motorized wheelchair, not letting his hitch stop him. He was boogieing along, enjoying what the outdoors offers.

Too many people become reclusive as seniors, not wanting to display or even admit their various hitches. Many become depressed or withdrawn, embarrassed for others to see them as they've aged. Don't do that; be kind to yourself. What would you say to someone else you saw doing such a thing? Wouldn't you encourage him/her to move forward, hitch and all?

We must grab life with whatever means we have. Some of us have more capabilities than others. If you are not disabled, don't take that for granted. Be mindful of how fortunate you are, as not everyone is. If you are disabled, technology makes it easier for you to embrace life.

Take a walk whether it's with your own legs or your own wheels. Observe the bounty that nature puts forth. A wildflower growing at the edge of the road can be a thing of great beauty viewed with the right perspective.

We all have a finite time of life. We also have choices. Choose how you are going to live your remaining years, months, days, hours, minutes. If you decide to squander them on "poor me" behaviors, own the fact that you made that decision.

You are not committed to your choice in perpetuity. You can revise it at any time which, of course, is another choice. Utilize whatever is available to assist you. There is no shame in that. Wheels versus legs still access the same exquisite wildflower.

You Don't Get to Cherry Pick (March 19, 2018)

How many times have you looked at others and coveted something they have?

I wish I had such smart children. I wish I were thin like her. I wish I weren't burdened by a needy spouse like him. I wish I were rich like... Well, you get the idea.

Those types of thoughts begin to creep in, especially when we are feeling low or in a bad place. Our life sucks and everyone else's seems to be a fairy-tale with everything right and a happy ending.

Someone once told me about a friend of theirs. The friend was so attractive, had such a good personality, had... So, the relater of the story said he was so envious that he just had to stop being friends with that person. How sad for both of them.

Most likely the one who "had it all" was just putting on a good public face.

That's quite common. We want others to like and admire us, so we hide our bad apple spots. Some even fabricate tales to yield that story book presentation.

I've had so many instances in my life where someone I know or have just met or have read about seems to have it all. I'm always surprised when I learn the real truth, and that their facade wasn't at all what it looked like. A good example is the nasty split between long married and seemingly on top Hollywood couple Brad Pit and Angelina Jolie. Who knew that behind their shiny, solid oak veneer was actually dry-rot?

I remember when the adorable girl in grammar school who lived down the block and had the beautiful curls arranged just so and the expensive clothes I lusted for committed suicide. I remember in junior high school a girl who seemed so sweet, easy going, and well-liked having a nervous breakdown. I remember the popular, high school cheerleader whose parents turned out to be psychologically abusive and distant. I remember in college…, at work…, as a wife…, as a mother…, as a senior…, and on and on. It was the same at every stage of my life.

Take another gander, folks. All those people you're looking at and coveting have their problems, negatives, and bad times, too, just like you. You don't get to cherry-pick. You take their whole package or none. So, after carefully inspecting the entire life of the envied one, would you really trade yours for theirs?

I was discussing this concept with a friend not long ago, and she reminded me, "Be careful what you wish for." That's so easy to forget. When you long for another's life to replace your own, take a deeper look with a strong magnifying glass. Yours may start to seem a whole lot better than you thought.

Uber et al (March 4, 2018)

Ah, Uber and its brethren. They use technology to make life easier while simultaneously making it more complicated. Yes, I wanted to be "with it" just like my tech savvy son–to summon a car using my iPhone. So, I decided to brave the learning curve and set out to install the Uber app.

The first mistake I made in my confusion was to sign myself up as an Uber driver. I realized my error as soon as Uber congratulated me on becoming a team member and requested information about my car and driver's license.

Attempting to unenroll as an Uber driver is a lot harder than enrolling. Although I kept trying to tell the Uber God that I didn't want to be a driver but just a rider, he/she refused to listen to me and kept insisting I provide my car/DL info. Eventually, Uber got tired of my stalling and kicked me out as a potential driver. I was small potatoes, and they were having none of my foolishness.

I waited a few days to brave the Uber site again. This time, unbeknownst to me how it came about, I did manage to enroll as a rider. An Uber app appeared on the homepage screen of my iPhone. I became one of the cool, trendy types and was going to be chauffeured by Uber.

The first time I called for an Uber pickup, it worked! I was amazed how simple it was, and that I had done it. The ride was pleasant and the driver amiable. All was right with the world, and I was a functioning cog in the Uber machine.

Uber emailed me my receipt and requested input on how I liked the ride. They offered me a visual of five stars, each with a number under it from one to five in a horizontal row. I was supposed to click on these celestial bodies to rate my ride.

My driver had been great, and, of course, I wanted to give him the highest rating: five stars. So, I assumed I was supposed to click on all of the stars. I clicked the star above the number one first whereupon I was kicked off that page and a message appeared in its place sympathizing with me that I had not had a good Uber experience. Apparently, I was supposed to click only on the star over the number five, not on every star. Now, how was I supposed to know that?

Unforgiving Uber God refused to give me an option to revise my evaluation. Guilt took over; I had just given a black mark to the Uber driving record of a very nice guy.

What to do? I navigated the Uber website but couldn't find any way to connect with Uber. A half-hour later and still navigating, I stumbled upon a contact form to send Uber a message. I explained my error and begged UG to upgrade my evaluation to five stars. Later that day, I received an email that my wish had been granted.

I did not use Uber again for several months. By that time, I forgot about the quirky rating system. Again, in trying to rate my driver, I ended up giving him the lowest possible rating. No more guilt–every man for him/herself–I was sick of the whole thing and refused to play the half-hour navigation game again.

Cut to two years later. I had not used Uber in all that time and forgot the protocol. After arriving late and tired at my home airport, I summoned Uber to take me to my front door. The screen monitor notified me that the trip would cost $33.66.

The drive was pleasant and the driver sweet and chatty. Upon arriving home, I handed him two twenty dollar bills: $33.66 for the fare and the rest for his tip.

"Wow!" he exclaimed.

I couldn't understand what all the fuss was over a $6 tip. I mean it was about twenty percent of the bill—a fair tip, but hardly warranting a "wow." Maybe he wasn't used to any tip at all.

The next day I was checking my emails and found one from Uber. It was a receipt for $33.66 billed to my credit card. How could they do that when I had paid the fare to the driver? My son explained it all to me patiently–sort of.

"Well, Mom, you gave him a $40 tip. You'll just have to suck it up."

So, I have been sucking it up for a few weeks now. I'm getting weary of being among the trendy. The only good thing is that I probably made the guy's day. I am one of the positive war stories he can brag about over the coming years on the topic of his life as an Uber driver.

Hugs (February 18, 2018)

The subject of inappropriate touching has been in the news a lot lately. Many have experienced this during their lifetime, both women and men. It may have been as the hug giver, the hug receiver, or both.

I've had such experiences including some incidents years ago at my job which would today be considered sexual harassment. These acts are usually carried out by the perpetrator when no one else is around, so if reported by the victim, it becomes an uncorroborated "he said-she said" scenario.

From my youth until well into my adulthood, I was not a huggy type of person. Although I'm still not exceptionally huggy, as I've matured and been subjected to life, I'm more prone to offering a hug to relatives and good friends upon meeting or departing, or to someone who has been especially nice and giving in a situation.

I can think of three things that changed my hugging persuasion:

1. When I had children, they needed hugs, and I found that I loved embracing them.
2. I have some close friends who are very huggy, and I've grown to be comfortable with it.
3. When I became an actress as a senior, I discovered that the acting community as a whole is a pretty huggy/touchy bunch out of camaraderie.

Sometimes my hug has been well received and other times it has seemed to make the recipient uncomfortable. I think the response comes from how the hugee was raised, where they were raised (different parts of the country or world are not as huggy as others), his/her culture, etc.

I have had a few strange experiences when I've initiated a hug. I made the mistake of hugging a man out of friendship. He then expected us to hug every time we saw each other. He finally made it clear that he wanted our relationship to ramp up to the next level, which was not what I wanted, so I broke off the whole thing. It probably would have remained on the friendship footing I had preferred had I not initiated the initial hug out of good feelings.

Once, I invited a group of friends over for lunch. One I knew well, and the other two, a husband and wife, were his friends whom I had only met a few times. We had a lovely time, and when they were ready to depart, I gave each a hug. The husband and wife both seemed very uncomfortable with the gesture, and I was sorry I had done it.

I remember another uneasy situation. A program director had hired me to give a talk to a large group. Although our interaction prior to the event was purely a business relationship, she had been exceptionally nice and helpful to me. After the talk, we were chatting, and I thanked her. Out of excitement at how well things had gone, I moved forward to hug her whereupon she jerked back with an alarmed look on her face. I immediately backed off, but it felt very awkward.

Hugging or other types of touching can be interpreted incorrectly. If one gets a different idea from your initiation of a hug or other simple touch than you had intended, it is very hard to convey to that person that you were simply expressing your warm feelings in an embracing manner. Conversely, when people make themselves vulnerable by expressing affection for another whether physically or verbally, it is hurtful to them to learn that their overtures are unwanted. You take the chance of alienating that person and the discomfort whenever you encounter them again.

Don't stop hugging or enjoying hugs. Just learn to be prudent when engaging in them.

To get you into a hugging mood, check out the online video, "Free Hugs," which follows a man as he offers just that, free hugs, to passersby in public. Also, read the moving poem, "The Hug," by Tess Gallagher.

Free at Last! (February 5, 2018)

An oppressive lifestyle can be imposed from without or within. Sometimes, it is the people we live with or the situation we find ourselves in that causes the oppression. Maybe a spouse or significant other demoralizes us. It could be a parent or a child who is the culprit. We might feel ourselves excessively burdened by our job or daily activities. Humans are also quite accomplished at weighing themselves down. We might impose impossible-to-meet standards on ourselves or aim for perfection to the point where we always fall short.

If you are living in an ongoing state of oppression no matter how you got there, you must escape for your own well-being. That is easy to say but so hard to do. Our situation, no matter how burdensome, usually provides us with something that we desire or fear we cannot obtain elsewhere. It could be as basic as food and shelter. It might be the siren call of social position that binds us. Perhaps it is the fear of forfeiting something precious such as children, income, or even a pet that keeps us there.

It is scary to disengage from a situation that offers us things we crave or fear losing. Yes, walking away is chancy. "What ifs" pop into our mind, usually miring us in the status quo, often for years.

However, if you ever want to break free of those chains that hold you prisoner, you must take a risk. Decide if you want to escape, make your getaway plans, and do it.

Many years ago, I had a friend, Priscilla, who told me that shortly after she married her husband, she realized what a mistake she had made as he proved to be an abusive alcoholic. However, by that time, she was already pregnant and dependent upon him. So, she made her escape plans and spent the next several years carrying them out. Priscilla went to college part-time and got an education so she could find gainful employment. By the time she finally put her plan into effect and left her husband, she had two children. She had also found a good paying job and was able to support herself and her kids.

We've all heard about people leaving lucrative employment to start their own business or to take lesser paying work that they find much more fulfilling. I once had an attorney who handled a case for me. Years later, when I needed more legal work, I sought him out only to find that he had given up the practice of law and opened a ski shop. He told me he had never really enjoyed being a lawyer, and that he loved his new venture even though he made far less money.

Don't just wallow in an oppressive situation. Envision a goal of throwing off that yoke. Make your jailbreak plans and carry them out, even if it takes years.

Why Does He/She Treat Me So Badly? (January 21, 2018)

Have you always been confused as to why your spouse or significant other turns into a snarling dog and treats you with such disdain? Although in this discussion I'll talk about partner connections, this type of interaction can occur in other close relationships such as with a parent, child, sibling, boss, mentor, etc. I'll use the generic masculine tone when referring to your partner, but it can equally apply to both sexes.

You do everything you can to get along, have a peaceful relationship, keep him happy. You try to shape yourself to his demands and requirements. It may work for a while when he's in a good place psychologically, or externally driven factors such as a job, school, finances, and such are going right for him. However, the fall always comes. Nothing you do satisfies him. You are cast as the bad guy, especially when he needs someone to blame when his life sucks once again.

This scenario may involve your being emotionally abused including being insulted, dismissed, or ostracized. You might be given the silent treatment (for hours or even days), a particularly cunning form of cruelty. Or, you might even be physically abused. It's like living on a roller coaster. He can be loving and caring or hateful and rejecting, and you never know which version of him is going to show up.

You soon learn to watch for it, always a bit tense even in the best of times. You wait for him to sock-it-to-ya because you know instinctively that it's coming sooner or later.

This is typical of the "Battered Woman Syndrome (BWS)," so named because of its frequency in incidents of domestic violence. As I said earlier, men can be the victims of it, too. Examples of BWS fall on a continuum because each situation is different, some more extreme and some less. You can still be a victim even if no physical violence is involved. Emotional battering can be just as painful; it may be so subtle you can't even verbalize it, but you feel bad, strange, off-kilter—something doesn't sit right. It might be a small remark said in public or private that is demeaning but disguised so that the perpetrator can claim,

"What are you talking about; you're crazy?" if you try to call him on it. Behavior such as this is wily, conniving, deliberate, or passive/aggressive: amiability which conceals antagonism.

You start to feel worthless, baffled why everything you do seems to be wrong. You may doubt your own sanity. It doesn't dawn on you that your abuser might not be correct in his assessment of the situation. You buy into whatever he sells, never questioning.

So, why does your loved one behave like that? One contributing reason might be poor self-image—not yours, his. If your partner doesn't think much of himself, then he probably feels that anyone who cares for him, loves him or respects him must not be much either.

How can anyone love me, I'm such a loser. They must be horrible, undesirable, a loser themselves. So, not only am I despicable, but I'm with this loser.

Thoughts such as these on the part of the victimizer are usually subconscious—ingrained from childhood. This scenario is often played out with partner after partner.

Even if you understand why your mate behaves as he does, that doesn't alter your interaction. He's honed this personality for decades, and he doesn't plan on changing. Not only that, but he has no problem with how he is; only you have a problem.

So, what do you do? As I've encouraged many times in past blogs, you must survive. Whether his technique is the subtle type or the go-for-the-jugular, take-no-prisoners model, you must negate his power to control you.

When you get the feeling that you've been put down by him, trust your gut! Keep in mind that you are not on this earth so he can play out these types of conscious or subconscious feelings. Refuse to accept that role! Don't engage. Leave the staging area. Pursue activities apart from him. In extreme cases, you may have to extricate yourself from the relationship entirely to get healthy.

Take charge of your life and your happiness. Don't be willing to put it into the hands of another, even someone as close as a spouse or significant other.

We All Have "Something" (January 7, 2018)

I saw an all gender bathroom sign at an airport terminal recently. I have no idea who was enlightened enough to create a bathroom for everyone no matter their persuasion. However, that person simply posted the sign, and the thousands of humans passing by in that busy location didn't seem to suffer any harm from it.

All of us have something about ourselves or our lives that is viewed as less than ideal in our current culture, or we have a friend or relative who does. We think that our something merits special consideration, tender handling, understanding, tolerance.

Maybe you or they are handicapped in some fashion. Maybe you or they respond slower than others, are of a particular physical build, intellectual level, sexual orientation, hue on the color spectrum, or whatever which is not so highly prized by our society just now.

So what do we do with you or them? Well, everyone hopes that others will be kind and forgiving of their particular affliction or situation. However, let's take a good look at ourselves.

Are we as kind and forgiving of others' oddities, needs, or differences as we hope they will be of ours?

Why does a group of boys attack another boy who is homosexual? Why does a person insist his religion is the only way to believe and then kills non-believers to that end? Why does someone with so much money go out of his/her way to disadvantage others merely to make more?

Our country and much of the world is divided by prejudice against race, sex, gender identity, religion, politics, and all manner of things. However, I'm sure you have heard the aphorism: *let he who is without sin cast the first stone*. Are you so perfect that you can judge others and find them wanting?

Remember to treat everyone with love, care, consideration, and compassion no matter how different they seem to be. We all share humanness; we are far more alike than different. There's another old saying that has been termed "The Golden Rule": *Do onto others as you would have them do onto you.*

Why do so many forget that? It's often those screaming the loudest to denigrate another who are hiding the most in their own lives.

BLOG POSTS FROM 2017

The Time We Have Left (December 24, 2017)
I was having an email discussion with my friend, a cancer sur-

vivor, about an article we both read listing predictions for our future world. One involved longevity.

According to the article, our current average life span increases three months per year. Within the past four years, life expectancy has increased from 79 to 80 years. By 2036, it will increase by over one year per year. Therefore, many more people will live to be over 100.

We had this email back-and-forth:

Her: "I went to see my new primary care doctor, a geriatrician, and got quite a shock. I asked her at what age I can stop getting colonoscopies. She said that the average for female death is 84, so there is no point in trying to prevent diseases such as colon cancer that take time to develop, unless I plan to live a lot longer than that. It's not as though there is any of that that I didn't already know, but it hit me like a punch in the stomach. I feel the same way I would feel if I were 30 and got the news that I had a life expectancy of 9 years. I now evaluate everything I do to make sure I'm not wasting any time."

Me: "As for your punch in the stomach, don't assume that you only have a life expectancy of 9 more years. That email said that longevity is predicted to increase. Therefore, assume you're going to live to 100, which means you have 25 more years. So, get that colonoscopy and go ahead and waste some time:-)"

Her: "The average for women now is 84, 82 for men. I'm pretty healthy so far as I know, and my parents both lived longer than 84. Still, I am confronting a short life."

Me: "We are all confronting a short life. Stop focusing on that and focus on enjoying it. Try the AA mantra: one day at a time."

Her: "…my short life isn't because of cancer, it's because of my age. I do focus on enjoying life—I certainly don't want to piss away whatever time I have left."

If you are in satisfactory health, I'm not sure which is more destructive to your enjoyment of life, excessive worry that you might get or have a recurrence of a serious disease such as cancer or apprehension over statistics predicting at what age you might die. Dwelling on such considerations spoils embracing the time you do have left.

Among the more inspiring people I have known was Rose Freedman, a classmate in a community Spanish class I attended many years ago. She was the last living survivor of the terrible fire in 1911 at the Triangle Shirtwaist Factory in New York City where 146 young, immigrant garment workers died. That tragedy led to significant changes in labor laws.

Rose was full of life, dynamic and always well-dressed with her hair nicely coifed. She consistently arrived at class with her homework completed, spending the opening moments before the teacher arrived socializing with everyone. She was also an artist and an avid, Lakers basketball fan.

One day, the teacher announced, "Rosa (we used the Spanish version of our names during class) has invited everyone to go to the bakery down the street after class for cake and coffee to celebrate her 100th birthday." I was blown away! Given her exuberance and youthfulness, I always thought Rose was in her eighties.

I continued going to that class for many years with Rose until she was hospitalized and died a few months later in 2001 at the age of 107. Yes, good genes and healthy living had a lot to do with Rose's longevity. However, a positive attitude and a love of life contributed significantly.

Let Rose serve as our role model. It's our choice how to embrace our final years. If we live our lives in agitated worry about our waning days, can we really enjoy that precious time to its fullest? Yes, we want to be productive—leave a legacy. However, the pressure to do so caused by fear we might die sooner rather than later spoils our journey.

In your final years, be productive for the joy of it, not in a race against some elusive calculation about the amount of time you have left.

Let It Go (December 9, 2017)

We all get upset, pissed off, angry, enraged, and worse at circumstances, the behavior of others, life... Yes, we need to vent; it releases tension. But, be careful who you choose as your ventee. Is he/she the right choice–the one who done ya wrong?

Are you dumping your situation on whomever you stumble upon? Are you taking any and every opportunity to steer the conversation around to your hurt or bad luck? That gets very old very fast, and others don't want to constantly be at the receiving end of such conduct. After all, they have their own issues for which they'd like to vent, and it's so easy for your interaction to devolve into a mutual ventfest.

Whatever it is that is bumming you out, there comes a point where you just have to let it go and get on with your life. Easy to say; hard to do, but, what is the alternative?

You can continue to stew for days, weeks, months, even years. While you're doing so, what else is happening? Have opportunities passed you by because you were too angry and distracted to grab them? Have you missed out on jobs, relationships, etc. because others picked up on your rage and backed off? Who is the loser with your attitude? The way I see it, it's you!

I'm still carrying around pain as the result of being hurt or let down by others whom I trusted. I'm probably pretty typical of most people. Very few get through this life without those types of experiences. Yes, I'm still a work in progress, but I try. I think about it and work at moving on. Sometimes I do a better job than at other times.

Letting it go doesn't have to be done all at once. It can be done in stages—baby steps. I have been estranged from a family member for several years. I thought a lot about letting it go, mainly to heal myself. Recently, I sent her a birthday card. It was very difficult to do and took a lot of mental back-and-forth while buying the card, addressing it, putting on the stamp, and releasing it from my fingertips into the mailbox. I lived with that small act for a while until I was able to digest it. The next step I took was some very light, superficial email correspondence. I'm currently in the process of living with that and trying to digest it. The next step may be a telephone call.

Keep working at letting it go even if you're not always successful. View yourself as a wounded child, and take care of yourself with tenderness, support, and encouragement as you would any troubled youngster. Help that child heal. Strive to make yourself the winner, not the loser.

Remembering (November 25, 2017)
We all have our memories, and we spend significant amounts

of our awake and our asleep time pondering them. One of the most compelling things we remember are the significant people who have impacted our lives.

This month marks the one-year anniversary of the death of one of my dearest friends. She was such a major part of my life for decades, and so many things in my home remind me of her.

There is the fleece shirt I put on each winter morning to break the chill when I get out of bed that Sue bought me for my birthday years ago after seeing me finger it on the store rack while we were shopping.

There are the 1600 threads-per-inch sheets I sleep on nightly which I, along with many of her friends and relatives, ordered through her secret source with the amazing discount.

There are those small decorative, bolster pillows that sit atop the regular pillows on my bed. We each got one that day Sue took me to visit the Wolf Rescue Compound, a two-hour ride from the city where we lived because I'd chosen it as my birthday gift excursion. We had been giving each other events for birthday presents in those final years, a way to spend more meaningful time together as the annual exchange of yet another sweater, scarf, or pair of earrings had become old and tiresome. The compound owner had made the little pillows which she presented to each person who braved the trek to her isolated location and contributed a donation upon entering. Sue gave me hers so I'd have a matching pair for my bed.

There is the...

Last week, I saw Sue's children for the first time since her death. Her daughter held me and cried giant tears, the sight of me bringing back memories of her mother yet again. I cried my own internal tears, as external ones don't happen for me. We all have our own way of grieving and responding to pain; mine is the dry, lump-in-your-throat type. Neither are right or wrong; they just are.

When someone has been significant to you, that never ends, it merely changes. Everyone has had a Sue in their life, and they live on in the memories of their friends and family members.

Silence and Stillness (October 28, 2017)

A friend recently mentioned that she had attended a retreat on the topic of silence and stillness. What a concept!

All my life I have had trouble with being silent and being still. My interpretation of silence on the part of others in my presence meant that they were unhappy or bored with me. So, to ease my discomfort, I would fill the silence with chatter. Of course, that meant animation—the opposite of stillness—even if just body language. It was an exhausting enterprise, but I had no control over it; I did it without thinking—a compulsion.

I remember the turning point. I was driving with my then boyfriend when I noticed that he had become very quiet. I thought he was angry at me because that's how my ex-husband used to behave—the silent treatment, a cruel form of punishment. I went through a mental back-and-forth with myself, vowing not to be the first to speak.

Who does he think he is? He's not going to get away with pulling that crap on me. I'm not going to have that in my life again. Yadda, yadda, yadda.

I was nervous, anxious, and worked myself into a defensive state. After a little while, my boyfriend made some inane remark such as, "look at that tree over there." I was amazed.

What I thought was going to grow into a big argument was just him being quiet. I had never realized that anyone could be quiet deliberately with no other motive.

It is very difficult to change a behavior pattern that took years to perfect. Although I'm still struggling with it, I've slowly gotten better with being quiet. My inclination is still to jump into those silent spaces, but now I can stop myself. Sometimes, it requires a mental dialogue (I do a lot of those) that my role doesn't have to be the entertainment committee—that it's okay for me to just stay muted.

These days, I seem to crave quiet and calm more and more. I cherish my down days where I can pad around my house alone with no appointments, deadlines, or obligations. The space to spend my time reading, writing, thinking, and whatever else strikes me has become precious. I surprise myself with this new outlook; it's so different from my former self. There is a peacefulness I didn't have when I was younger.

Try adding periods of silence and stillness to your life. Schedule time for it if it doesn't come naturally. Embrace it instead of fighting it. It is cleansing, calming, and healing.

Taking Care of the Caretaker (October 12, 2017)

Some of us go willingly into the role of caretaker, and some of us are thrust into it without being consulted. Examples of voluntary caretaker roles are: parent, teacher, nurse, and even pet owner. (Yes, owners of sick pets have been found to have more than normal stress, anxiety, and depression.)

Some people deliberately choose caretaking involvements and thrive on them. But, what about when the role of consuming, full-time or almost full-time caretaker ensnares us when we hadn't planned on it, hadn't desired it, and it does not fit our personality type?

A typical scenario might be when an ailing spouse requires ongoing, long-term care. There may be no one else available to step into the caretaker role other than the remaining, healthy spouse. Other examples might be when children have to care for an aging parent or when parents have to care for a child who has become permanently disabled. We're not talking here about just bringing them lunch in bed. We're talking about hands-on care of their bodily needs and functions, entertaining them, transporting them, and maybe even supporting them financially.

You might be a caretaker from afar. Maybe you are responsible for someone in a placement of some sort or who resides a long distance from you. Perhaps you're the go-to-person for any problems, crises, concerns, questions, or decisions. Although your life is not necessarily hampered on a continual basis, that responsibility is always capable of demanding instant attention, superseding anything else you had planned. You live with an underlying tension, never knowing when your remote caretaker duties will kick in.

You may feel overwhelmed and no longer able to cope with that role no matter how much you are concerned about your charge? You might find yourself becoming resentful, angry, bitter, impatient, irritable, and stressed out. This can lead to negative behaviors toward your dependent such as yelling, ignoring, pushing, or worse. After that, you may feel guilty as he/she did not choose to require caretaking and is helpless to help you. Cyclical emotions such as these can spiral you into depression which renders you less capable of being an effective caretaker.

To the outside world, sympathy and attention usually go to the sickly or helpless one. People rarely have much left for the caretakers or even think of them as needing any. Yet caretakers burn out. Caretakers may become sick themselves simply from the job of caretaking.

So what can you do to break this cycle and stay relevant and capable in your role as a caretaker? How can you take care of yourself, not only for you but for your charge? Both you and they need you to remain strong emotionally and physically.

You can seek respite from time to time. Find outside activities that bring you pleasure and enjoyment. Take breaks from the caretaking business just as anyone with a job has weekends or other days off as well as periodic, longer vacations. In short, refresh yourself on a regular basis.

To do this, you need someone or several someones to step in as a substitute caretaker while you're gone. Start seeking suitable candidates. These might be your children; other family members; friends; neighbors; members of your church, temple, or mosque; hired help; volunteers from an organization; home-health aides referred by an insurance plan or a governmental agency, etc. You must do this for yourself, even if you feel that no one else can take care of your ward as well as you can.

By taking better care of yourself, you are indirectly taking better care of the one who is dependent on you. You return to duty refreshed, in a better mental state, and with a better outlook knowing that your next break will come soon.

Boredom (September 27, 2017)

We come into this world yawning with boredom and go downhill from there. Recently, in my philosophy class, we were discussing whether we would want to live an extra hundred years. One class member commented that he would not want to do so because by that time, he probably would have done or learned everything interesting, and life would be just too boring.

We all laughed while nodding in agreement. Yes, we scurry from boredom the moment we encounter it. Humans seem to need constant engagement, constant entertainment, constant stimulation.

We don't just sit around and do nothing. When we are not actively involved in a goal-oriented pursuit, we will grab a book or magazine, turn on the television, check our email, surf the web, go shopping, and on and on. We flee boredom like it's a disease. The idea of nothing new to learn, nothing new to experience, only eternal boredom is horrifying.

I am always weighing the amount of stress I put myself under against the boredom that I can't tolerate. I'm trying hard not to cram too much into my life, but it's an ongoing challenge. Every time I hear about something that sounds exciting, I want to get involved. Like usual, I'm involved in too much stuff. It's so difficult to pick and choose because it's all interesting. Everyone lives with the dichotomy of that struggle between boredom and stress.

A few years ago, a friend visited me with her daughter and two young grandchildren. We chatted for a short time whereupon the oldest child announced, "I'm bored." My friend's daughter quickly wrapped up our conversation, telling the child, "Okay, okay, we're going." I'm not passing judgment one way or another on her parenting skills. However, the child could have been encouraged to walk around my house observing all the interesting things I have displayed on shelves and walls.

So, how do we grownups combat boredom? We can whine to anyone who will listen, pandering to be entertained. Or, we can adopt the maxim about using stones in our path to build a house. Yes, we can walk around wherever we happen to be, observing all the interesting things there. We might actually learn a thing or two or ten or at least have a pleasant experience. We can also accept the stress and learn to flourish under it, remembering that we can back away whenever we desire.

Man in a Bucket (September 12, 2017)

Each of us lives in a bucket–many buckets to be exact: our homes, our schools, our jobs, our extended hood, etc. Buckets are the catchment areas in which we roam, but they are for the most part relatively circumscribed. Some buckets are very small like that of a tree trimmer high up in an extended mechanical arm, and some cover miles. Our various buckets bump up against each other, and we move from one to the next.

It is our responsibility to participate in keeping our buckets pleasant, tidy, positive, and all other adjectives we can think of to describe a comfortable life. We do so not only for ourselves but for others who might share them with us.

I remember standing at a bus stop once with a man who was also awaiting the bus. He was eating some sort of fast food and dropped the wrappers as he finished each item. I watched him as he opened his fist and, with as little effort as possible, let the napkin, paper cup, or container float to the ground. In a short time, there was a small circle of trash surrounding him, but he was oblivious to it.

What if we all did that rather than throwing our discards into the nearest trash can? We would soon be maneuvering our way through our bucket by scaling a garbage heap. It is an unpleasant and unnecessary way to live.

How about the emotional trash we discard in our buckets? Are we going to spend all of our time posturing and fighting with everyone else? What if we all did that? Our buckets would soon be filled with anxiety, nervousness, upset, and negative feelings, also an unpleasant and unnecessary way to live.

Remember to do your part to care for your particular buckets, and encourage those close to you to do the same. Buckets can be a comfortable, joyful cocoon, or they can be a stressful, distressing jail.

Rest and Regenerate (August 29, 2017)

Rest is mandatory for all animals to renew their energy and vitality including those living helicopters: hummingbirds. I spotted one little guy hovering near a bush outside my window. Then, much to my surprise, he landed on a branch. I had never seen a hummingbird before that wasn't humming. I stopped what I was doing and just hung out with him. Mr. H. stayed there for about ten minutes, resting, regenerating, and allowing his heart rate to slow down before continuing his frenetic activities. Such a smart bird.

Hummingbirds' wings flutter 80 times per second and their hearts can beat as much as 1,263 times per minute or as little as 50 times per minute when conserving energy. Compare that to the human heart which beats as low as 60 and as high as 200 times per minute depending on age and activity level.

Do you remember to rest and regenerate? We must learn to pace ourselves—land on a branch—and allow plenty of downtime in order to be able to function well when we are active. Rest and especially sleep have an unexplained yet proven impact on our health and productivity. A very rare hereditary disease called fatal familial insomnia manifests itself in midlife to its victims and eventually renders them unable to sleep. At that stage, death comes within months. We cannot live without sleep.

Have you noticed that when you are not rested, your responses become dull and sloppy? We make many more errors and bad decisions when not rested. It's tempting to overdo. There are so many interesting and compelling projects and activities. Sometimes, it seems there is never enough time to do everything we want to do. However, over-scheduling and cramming in too much becomes counterproductive.

Remember to do your resting in a location conducive to that end. Choosing a roomful of people, noise, and stimulation does not yield good quality relaxation to most. If out and about, try to find a quiet, isolated place. If one is not available, you might decamp to your car. No car? Try a stall in the bathroom. It's a one-holer, people are banging on the door, and you've run out of options? Then find any seat and use the earplugs and eye mask you always carry with you in your purse, pocket, back pack, wherever. (You do carry them, right, along with a granola bar for quick energy when needed?) If all else fails, take a tip from a gal I saw catching some Z's on a commuter train instead of grabbing her cell phone to read her emails, navigate the Net, or play mindless computer games. Make it work for you!

Remember to schedule plenty of rest time into your life. It takes discipline but is an art that you must master. Then, the things that you do participate in will be so much more fruitful and rewarding.

Playing Well with Others (August 17, 2017)

Are you a person who has trouble playing well with others? Or, perhaps you know someone like that. Getting along with other humans is a talent gained from part nature and part nurture.

It almost doesn't matter what you say or convey to others. If done in the right way, just about anything is acceptable. For example, if someone is wearing clothing that you think looks terrible, you can say, "You look awful in that dress," or you can say, "I think red looks so much better on you than blue." If someone is doing something you don't think is correct, you can say, "Don't do that!" or you can say, "I don't think they want us doing that."

If you're not a natural at warm/cozy techniques of com-munication and are tired of people drawing away from you or completely ostracizing you, consider practicing some basic requirements. Here's a list of "musts" that I came up with. Per-haps you can add a few of your own.

1.   It's not all about you. Don't spend the interaction talk-

ing only about your stuff or sucking the focus onto yourself whenever possible.

2. Show interest in the others present. Everyone wants a chance to be the center of attention for a while. Aid in that goal by asking questions of them, and really listen to their answers. You show that you're listening by maintaining consistent eye contact and asking meaningful, follow-up questions.

3. Check your attitude. Don't come across as irritated, impatient, hostile, and pissy. People don't like that and will begin to avoid you.

4. Don't be the resident expert-in-everything even if you are. It gets old very fast. As my father used to say, "Nobody likes a smart ass."

5. Be gracious. Say things like "thank you" or "that was really interesting" or "nice to see you again." People love compliments and acknowledgement.

6. Be aware of the tone and volume of your voice. Dial both down a notch or ten. Practice exchanging verbal coldness for warmth. Record yourself and listen to how you come across when you talk.

7. Body language speaks volumes. Chill out and relax.

8. Facial expressions are huge. Everyone is always reading people by the look on their face. Does yours come across as sourpuss, angry, negative, critical, bored, or disinterested? If so, practice in front of a mirror making facial expressions which are positive, accepting, warm, upbeat, supportive, and interested. Experience how your face muscles feel with those positive contours, and repeat them in public.

If you can't figure out how to put into practice some of the aforementioned suggestions, study others who seem to do so effortlessly. Then, wiggle into your actor robes and perform, using them as role models. It may seem strange at first, but you'll get used to it. Remember, the content is far less important than the delivery.

Lighten Your Load (August 1, 2017)
We all carry heavy, emotional loads around with us. Some call it "baggage." Whatever you call it, it exhausts you and depletes your energy. This angst you create for yourself is manifested in worrying, ruminating, stressing, fixating, or obsessing over what has happened or what might happen.

The current, trendy advice is: live in the now. It sounds wonderful, but it's so hard to do. We all suffer from mind drift. So, how do you turn off your thoughts from remembering your upsetting, negative experiences? How do you control your reflections from worrying about life's possible, future land mines?

Like acquiring any new skill, it takes practice—constant practice. It also takes awareness of when your mind is drifting to those types of deliberations. So, it's up to you to work at lightening your own load. And, it will only be successful if you want it badly enough. Here's an idea to get you started:

Develop the habit of checking in with your mind on a regular basis to see if and where it has drifted. When that drift is to a negative place, stay vigilant and replace those thoughts with something positive or at least neutral. Use your environment as an aid.

In my new home, I have a variety of animal life that

passes by. I've made it a point of stopping whatever I'm doing when I hear or spot a candidate from my window. I watch the free performance nature provides which puts my mind in a positive place.

That exercise can be done with all types of external stimuli found everywhere. For example, have you ever really looked at a flower growing outside? Don't just glance at it; approach it and stare deeply at its structure. Notice each petal; notice the stamen and pistil in the center. Assess the color as it varies in shade from one part of the flower to another. Smell it. Does it have a strong scent, a mild scent, no scent? While you are doing this, your mind is focused totally on the flower.

It seems like a constant struggle to take control of our thought patterns. However, like learning any new skill, it becomes a bit easier each time you are successful. The aggregate of many successful experiences makes you more proficient at the task. Keep at it, and see if the outcome leads to more contentment in your life. If not, you can always go back to wallowing in the turmoil your mind creates.

Help: a Noun and a Verb (July 16, 2017)

I had just exited the airport after flying in from out of town and was waiting for the metro to take me home. When it arrived and the doors opened, I realized I had hit it at rush hour. The car was crammed with humanity—standing room only. That was fine with me; I liked the idea of remaining upright as I had been sitting on an airplane for two hours.

I positioned myself between a post and the back of a seat, holding on to the former. At the next stop, a boy of about nine years of age walked toward me gesturing to a seat. A woman, obviously his mother, was standing nearby and nodding at me. They had been occupying a place designated for the handicapped, pregnant women, and the elderly. To my consternation, I fell into the last category. Even so, I am in good physical condition and was quite capable of standing. However, the young boy looked so eager charged with his important mission that I simply couldn't tell him I had no need of the proffered prime location. So I thanked him very much, walked over, and took my seat for the elderly. The boy was beaming and looked at his mother who gave the requisite approval.

Sometimes, even if we don't need assistance, it is a kind gesture toward the giver to accept an offer of help. People feel good when they assist others, and we can get some good feelings for ourselves by being gracious toward their sacrifice in our behalf—a definite win-win situation.

I think the same applies if we really do need help. What's the matter with that? Some find it so difficult to request and/or accept assistance. They feel it demeans them or indicates they are lacking in some way. They might feel a burden that they must reciprocate. No, you don't need to give like-for-like. Sometimes, there is no way to repay a good deed done for you. The only payback is to perform a kindness for another.

Offer help generously, and don't be ashamed to accept it either. We all need help from time to time no matter our age or physical condition. Participate willingly on either side of this caring, human interaction and reap the emotional rewards that it bestows.

Feeling Invisible (July 2, 2017)

Have you ever been in a situation where you're surrounded by people much younger than yourself? Have you ever felt invisible as they talk past you? A similar experience might occur even when the others are closer to your age, but they all know each other or attend the same class/club/church/temple/mosque/whatever, and you're the odd man out. This might happen when you're seated at a table while attending an event, marking time in a waiting room, or at any other venue where you find yourself surrounded by strangers who are with others in a common grouping.

In situations like that, it's often hard to strike up a conversation. People near you seem only interested in talking to those of the same age, pursuit, social history... You might try to steer the conversation around to something universal such as the current political situation, a recent news item, whatever. However, the conversation segues back to their niche interests.

The others might be polite to you if you do manage to interject something, but they quickly turn back to their peers. In the case of those much younger, you notice the chatter centers around subjects that don't interest you: a certain type of music, jobs, children's play dates, someone you don't know, or things that you've outgrown.

You want to shout out your credentials: I'm bright; I'm educated; I'm well-traveled; I'm interesting. But, of course, you don't; that's socially unacceptable. So, you sit there in silence feeling awkward and rejected.

I've heard some seniors say that they don't like being around large groups their own age. They prefer to be with younger people as it makes them feel young. I've never understood that. I can't imagine what they even talk about.

Yes, there are some situations where the meeting centers around a specific topic common to all present, and age differences don't matter. There also might be specific individuals who easily bridge the age gap. But, those are the exception, not the norm. I find it much more comfortable to be with others in my same age group. We have a commonality of experiences and are no longer focused on the things done by age specific younger generations such as child rearing and careers.

When you find yourself in situations like these, it's time to look around the room for the senior folks. If you can't find any or are stuck at a table with those half your age, you might whip out that book you always carry with you. You forgot to take the book? Your cell phone can entertain you for a while. Or, you might simply relax and enjoy people watching. That's always a fun sport. And, when you hear such talk as diaper rash, pediatricians, and the like, you can rejoice that you're in the "been there, done that" age group.

Mackinac (June 18, 2017)

Clop, clop, clop—the sound of the horses' hooves as they pulled the wagon taxi carrying me around Mackinac Island, Michigan last week. It was the time of the Lilac Festival during which all of the lilac bushes covering the island in their various colors and hues perform for the tourists. It seemed that every hotel, restaurant, park, private home and anywhere else something could be planted had its own lilac bushes for passersby to admire, sniff, and use as a backdrop to pose for photos.

The island is supported by tourism. However, despite the thousands who descend each year, it has been kept pristine and is a little step back in history. No cars are allowed. All transportation is accomplished by horse drawn carriages and drays, bicycles, and good old-fashioned walking. Humans with pooper scoopers as well as machines pulled by draft horses, Belgians and Percherons mostly, ply the roads gathering the equine droppings. They are then composted and spread throughout the island to assist in the growth of those magnificent lilacs as well as other flora.

Here's another fact that grabbed my interest. The three-mile-long body of water to the closest mainland freezes shortly after Christmas forming what the locals call the "ice bridge." The full-time residents have created a folk remedy of sorts to delineate the path as they traverse it atop their snowmobiles. People simply save their Christmas trees which are then set up on the ice to mark the route.

Yes, the five-hundred full-time islanders certainly do enjoy modern lifestyles that technology has brought to all of us. However, they seem to have found some simple solutions to their unique challenges. My little peek through their keyhole tells me that they have a less stressful, less emotionally demanding cadence to their lives than we in the big cities experience.

My auditory sense relaxed in the replacement of engine noise with the resonance of the horses' steps as they went about their duties. I like that their emissions help the life cycle unlike that of automobiles that only contribute their noxious gases to the destruction of our planet. Is progress really all it's touted to be? Can we learn from Mackinac Island residents?

Might a return to simpler times and simpler ways be the answer to our angst?

Generational Differences (June 5, 2017)

It is often so hard for distant generations to understand and accept each other and to even communicate. Differences are greater as the years between generations increase. Behavioral and linguistic disparities between parents and children are hard enough, but it becomes more extreme between age spans separating grandparents and grandchildren or great grandchildren. This, of course, can be extrapolated to anyone, not just family members. However, if we are going to live together and benefit from each other, we must adapt and cope, as hard and confusing as it may be.

A few weeks ago, I had a young workman approximately age twenty fixing some damage to my wall. He arrived with tools in his hands which were attached to fully tattooed arms. This contrasted sharply with my tattooless ones. In his earlobes were hole stretch earrings (also called gauges as Google informed me) which expanded those lobe holes to about a three quarter inch diameter. My own lobe holes are pinhead width, my norm for voluntary body mutilations.

Check the Internet for a how-to primer on ear lobe stretching for those so inclined. As you will learn, it's not an easy thing to become a practitioner. If you are still determined to stretch your lobes, check out Amazon.com's offers of do-it-yourself ear stretching kits.

Despite our stylistic differences, the young workman was a sweetheart. He set to his task with diligence. About an hour later, YW appeared at my office door and announced that he was finished.

"I'm sorry it took me so long," he said. "I had a brain fart and cut the wood too short, so I had to do it again."

"What?"

"I had a brain fart and cut the wood too short. The reason I didn't finish earlier is because I had to do it over."

Yes, I had heard him correctly. *A brain fart.*

I swallowed and just responded, "Oh."

He had used that compound noun twice in his explanation with no sign of jest, sarcasm, or a goal to shock. It was simply part of his natural speech, and he never even thought that it might be offensive to someone else.

I was not exactly offended—more surprised and amazed. In my lifetime, I've experienced confusion, distraction, misunderstanding, mistakes, but never a brain fart. Or, maybe I have but just didn't know it. "A word is a word is a word," as I've heard it said.

We should be grateful if the younger generation beings in our lives are loving, giving, goal oriented, and possess other traits we value. Mild rebellions such as tattoos, shaved heads, trendy words and phrases, bodily piercings of various types, or rainbow colored hair are tolerable and non-destructive—so much better than drug experimentation, criminal acts and the like which some use to rebel. So, get in sync with the young people in your life; go ahead and stretch your earlobes.

Don't Be a Crappee (May 21, 2017)

While on a trip to Scotland last month, I was taking a tour of

Edinburgh, the capital. As the guide was waxing on about all the attractions, I noticed an interesting duo: a statue of Dr. David Livingstone, the nineteenth century Scottish medical missionary and African explorer of "Dr. Livingstone, I presume?" fame, topped by an uninvited seagull. The statue graces a park in the center of the city. The foul fowl had assumed the role of crappor with poor Livingstone as the crappee. I wonder how the renowned doctor would have felt about that scenario if he were still alive.

How can we avoid being the crappee? I've written about this subject in previous blog posts, but it bears revisiting as it's so important to our emotional well-being. The answer is: it's not always easy with the various roles we play in our lives. We may be a spouse, a child, a parent, a sibling, an employee, a student, etc., or a combination of these at the same time. Many of our roles are hierarchal in nature, and it's particularly hard to avoid being dumped on by someone who has power or authority over you. So, what can you do?

There are several tactics you can employ when another is castigating you. You can choose to verbally stand up for yourself and suffer the possible consequences. Be aware that they can be serious such as being fired from a job; losing a spouse or significant other; becoming estranged from a parent or child; or being expelled from a school, club, or organization. You must decide if such a potential outcome is worth it.

You can mentally turn off your receptors, choosing not to receive what the crappor is sending. To avoid extreme results, tune out but behave as though you are attendant. It's a hard art to master but with some practice, you can become adept.

You might try deflection. Interject something into the diatribe to turn your adversary's attention in another direction. Example: "Oh, (insert crappor's name), I heard that the (insert something significant to crappor) just got (insert negative outcome)." That should send him/her in another direction mentally or physically, long enough for you to regroup and escape, at least for the moment.

You can physically remove yourself from the field of battle. Create an emergency that requires you to exit immediately. It can be something like a just-remembered appointment, a bathroom call, a pot on the stove ready to boil over, whatever. You might even think of some excuses in advance to use when the situation requires it.

Don't be a statue with bird droppings dripping down your face. Plan and execute tactical moves to protect yourself from the onslaught of others.

The Perils of Communication (May 8, 2017)

Being an effective communicator requires talent. Engaging others with our message and receiving theirs is fraught with danger: misunderstandings, mixed signals, confusion, and all sorts of other roadblocks from differences in age, sex, culture, language, education, and racial/ethnic group. However, communicate we must if we're going to interact with other humans and depend on each other to get along. So, how do we do it effectively?

That is a massive task but with practice, we can all master it. First, let's discuss what communication is. For our purposes, it will be defined as a human exchange of information using agreed upon actions, language, or symbols.

Communication methods utilize our five major senses. They can be written or pictorial; verbal using words and other sounds; or behavioral such as body language, facial expressions, or a handshake. Babies make their needs known by communicating with cries, grunts, and smiles. We become more sophisticated in our communication methods as we age.

There are many subtleties to communication. It can be controlling, manipulative, friendly, warm, cold, straight forward, duplicitous, honest, conniving, and on and on. Different styles and personalities dictate the tone of the communication.

Remember, communication is not all about you. It is not just a one-sided "sending" of information significant to the sender. It also involves "receiving" of information significant to the other person in the interaction. Finally, a switching of roles occurs with the original sender becoming the receiver and the original receiver becoming the sender. This rapid-fire reversal takes place continuously throughout the exchange.

Not only must the parties involved be able to switch from send mode to receive mode quickly, they must also be able to interpret meaning. We practice this as children and hopefully perfect it by adulthood. However, not everyone masters the lessons so well. If you fall into that category, watch how effective communicators do it and try out their techniques. They may feel strange at first, but it will get easier with repetition.

Effective communication requires an awareness of goals— what the parties want from the interchange. Do you strive to win favor; do you want an extension of good will; do you simply want to experience the good feelings you get from talking to a friend? Be careful that your approach matches what you hope to gain. If not, then you are wasting your time and effort.

An acquaintance and I recently discussed how valuable laughter is in communication. Including humor and creating an opportunity for laughter usually yields much more than aggression does. There's an old proverb to the point: "You can catch more flies with honey than with vinegar."

When attempting to communicate, lighten up and make the exchange pleasant and even fun, no matter the subject matter. It can be done and is often significantly more effective. Just give it a try.

Wrangling Seniors (April 19, 2017)

A dear friend and her husband from out of state visited me last weekend. I have known them for over forty-five years and hadn't seen them for quite a while. We were young and healthy when we met, and we have aged together over the decades.

They are older than I am and have become quite frail. Still, they managed to board a plane with the help of airport wheelchair attendants and arrive at my place by taxi with the aid of the driver. A good tip helped, I guess.

I opened my door to two seniors, both upright with the assistance of their respective walkers. Although a senior myself, I am in good physical condition, and I was pained by their deterioration since I had last seen them. Nevertheless, I was excited by their visit and anxious to show them around my new 'hood.

It quickly became evident that for each excursion, I would be the pack animal, collapsing and loading two walkers into my car trunk and unloading them upon arrival at our destination not to mention securing seat belts and the like. Ditto on the return ride. All progress was excruciatingly slow. All plans had to be made with time buffers to allow for the lengthy preparation both before and after the event.

I also fell into the role of fetch person as their ability to stand up and make their way to get the sugar, a Kleenex, a shawl for warmth, or just about anything was so much more quickly accomplished by swift me. It reminded me of what my son and daughter-in-law go through with their young children (my adorable grandchildren): strollers, snacks, bathroom breaks, and all events planned around rest time.

At the end of each day, I was exhausted, impatient, and irritable. It's tiring being a wrangler whether your charges are horses or seniors. I tried hard to keep in perspective what I was getting out of the experience. It was such a gift that my dear friends who had been there to nurture and care for me through the years had made the extreme effort to visit me. It was a privilege to help them experience a trip away from their now confined quarters in an assisted living home. It was a way to pay them back for the love they had always shown me.

Modify your viewpoint toward the elders in your life. Yes, they have become childlike in their needs and even in their behavior. Have patience; be loving, kind, and giving. Don't forget what they did for you in earlier years which probably caused them to become exhausted, impatient, and irritable.

Nature's Floor Show (April 4, 2017)

I was doing my morning back exercises when I glanced through my window and spied a feathered guy hanging out on a nearby tree branch. What could be more inspiring? I am regaled lately with a variety of birds hovering, preaching, pecking, warbling, chirping, soaring, and all of the other things birds do. I have never been a "birder," but I am rejoicing in their exaltation. They tell me that spring is here, and that I too can exalt in it.

Do you look out the window of your house, car, office, or any other structure in which you find yourself with glass interruptions in its solidity? I don't mean a glance while you're doing much more important business. I mean really look!

There's so much to see. From my window, I enjoyed a glorious flowering tree. Yes, the plants, bushes and trees dress up in springtime for our pleasure. Nature offers us a free floor show. Don't forget to attend.

We all have interesting things to observe around us wherever we live. Here are some we might spy looking out of windows: hills or mountains, children playing, passersby strolling, dogs running, cars of all shapes and colors, and so much more.

Let the visual panoply engulf you. Feel yourself drawn into the details of a leaf, a bird searching the grass for food, a ball bouncing away from its thrower. These sights and sounds are cleansing. Be mindful; notice as you are being swept into the experience; allow it to overtake you. Don't worry, you can always go back to that important business you left, refreshed and invigorated. And, this psychic infusion doesn't require dipping into your wallet.

Secrets (March 19, 2017)

Keeping secrets is something we all do for various reasons. It usually starts with fretting about negative blowback we might experience if others knew the truth. This can be worry about being judged and found wanting, concern about being pitied, fear of reprisals, and on and on. The reality is that whatever our oh-so-important secret, others usually spend only moments on our situation and then revert back to focusing on their own lives.

There's a saying: "A secret is something you tell one person at a time." Most of us have a need to unburden by sharing our secret with someone whom we think we can trust with it. Although we swear our trusted agents to secrecy, we ruminate that they might deliberately or by accident tell another. Sometimes, we instruct our agent not to share our secret only with select persons.

That puts an additional burden on our designee not only to live his/her own life with all its attendant stresses and yes, even secrets, but to remember not to share our secret and with whom not to share it. That's called "dumping," people.

It's not easy being the dumpee. The one placed in that role now has a new stressor: keeping your secret. It's hard enough keeping their own, but now they have the worry of yours they might accidentally spill, potentially incurring your wrath and/or damaging the relationship. Sometimes, the dumpee may deliberately spill your secret for their own gain—remember Linda Tripp? Google her if you don't.

Secrets range from tiny ones to great big ones. The degree of weight of the secret is usually decided by the owner. However, it's often not given the same level of importance by those learning it.

The keeping and managing of secrets is a wearisome process. We must remember who we told and didn't tell, why it was so important to keep the secret, what to do if others learn about it, and what we must do if we want to divulge it to the world and finally get on with our lives.

Will we ever reach the time where the matter kept secret loses it power over us? How about now? In my memoir, I shared my secret of feeling self-conscious and inadequate in my younger years and of having crippling stage-fright for so much of my life. When I had the nerve to tell the world, those bonds lost their power over me. Revealing our secrets can be so liberating.

Strutting Your Stuff (March 6, 2017)

My visitor knew how to strut his stuff. A wild tom turkey appeared on my patio a few days ago, staying about fifteen minutes as he fluffed out his feathers, fanned his tail, and walked from one end to the other and back again, periodically stopping to turn around slowly so he could be seen from all sides by potential, admiring onlookers. I grabbed my camera to memorialize his display. How could any female resist him? I know I couldn't.

Another euphemism for strutting your stuff is "tooting your own horn." Some humans are good at it just like feathered Tom. Successful practitioners know how to display their talents and attributes. Others are too shy or embarrassed while wishing they could and envying those able to do so with such seeming ease. Some withdraw from even considering such behavior, finding it too prideful and self-indulgent. However, let's consider if occasional strutting or tooting can aid in our fulfillment.

We all need attention; we all want to attract others. That is neither positive nor negative; it is simply a human trait. With over seven billion of us on this earth and counting, the competition is fierce. So, how do we get some of that elusive, oh-so-valuable acclaim? We must do something to make others notice us in some way.

Yes, many overdo it—again like Tom. It gets old when someone seems to be constantly bragging or promoting him/herself. Not everyone has mastered the art of subtlety or sophistication in seeking attention. We really don't need to puff up our bearing and prance around in the best finery we can afford, folks. But, we can do other things to bring accolades and favor to ourselves. We can aim to excel in areas where we seem to have talent. Even introverted people can find quieter, less conspicuous ways to shine.

Think of something you can do well. Seek out opportunities to display or utilize that ability where others will notice. Allow yourself to experience the rewards of a compliment, praise, or kudos.

Attention from others is nourishing. Remember to be generous and not hog it all if you're the aggressive type. If you're the timid type, remember that you deserve notice, too. And, let's remember to practice tolerance toward those who seem so needy of approval. We are all on that scale somewhere.

Kick Up Your Heels (February 20, 2017)

We've all heard the expression, "kick up your heels." What exactly does it mean? A Google search yielded these explanations: doing things that you enjoy or having a good time by discarding your inhibitions.

I visited a stable not long ago and hung out with some of the horses. One was led into the ring and immediately hunkered down, rolled over, and kicked up his heels for the sheer joy of it, all the while wiggling around and changing himself from white to tan to the consternation of his groomers of which I was to be one. We would have to spend extra time at our upcoming task to transform him back to the white of his birth. No matter, we human onlookers became childlike along with our stallion, basking in his exuberance.

When was the last time you kicked up your heels? It doesn't have to be done by rolling around in the dirt with your legs in the air. It might be singing loudly with the radio as you drive to work, enthusiastic dancing, laughing uncontrollably with friends, swinging on a swing in a playground, or any of scores of activities done without inhibitions.

Too many of us are constrained by social niceties, conventions, or other governors on our behavior. I've seen people deliberately stifle laughs or even walk out of the room to avoid looking foolish by kicking up their heels. Members of some cultures cover their mouths with their hands to avoid emitting too much laughter.

Young children kick up their heels naturally until they become old enough to learn that it's unacceptable, not polite, not ladylike, and all the rest. Why does society teach them that?

Why does the collective body insist on sublimating the good feelings that can come from kicking up one's heels and redirect us to socially acceptable venues to do so such as sports stadiums where kicking up one's heels is only to be done in a group setting by screaming at the athletic teams, sometimes while wearing ridiculous garb and/or face paint?

Give yourself permission to kick up your heels on a regular basis wherever you are. Experience the heeling that comes from it.

Your Remains (February 4, 2017)

It's a morbid and depressing subject, but somebody's got to tackle it. What's going to happen to your body after you're done with it? The majority of people or their family members spend a lot of money on fancy caskets, cemetery plots, and funeral services to bury the deceased in the ground. If you've served your country in the military, your coffin may come draped with an American flag, and you can even arrange to have an honor guard at your funeral.

You can have a closed casket service, or people can view you lying in your expensive box, made up to look better than you ever looked when you were alive. Now, you can even buy your coffin in advance and store it in your closet or garage, or use it as a backup bed when guests arrive unexpectedly (that will get rid of them quick.)

You can be cremated and your ashes dealt with however: buried; entombed in a crypt; set in a niche of a columbarium (a room at a cemetery for urns containing cremation ashes); given to someone to take home and save in a decorative container on the fireplace mantel, a china cabinet, an unused back closet, or any other location of your choice; or scattered in your favorite place such as a hiking trail, beach, mountain top, or even flushed down the toilet of a favorite restaurant as someone I know did to fulfill a request.

You can opt for a sky burial, but your body will have to be shipped to Tibet, Mongolia, or parts nearby. Then, you will be placed on a mountaintop to decompose while exposed to the weather or to be eaten by scavenging animals, especially carrion birds such as vultures. Hey, vultures gotta live, too, ya know. And, they will excrete you as they fly, scattering you to add to the cycle of life.

On the other hand, there are other options. Here are a few particularly interesting ones:

Donate your body for medical research. Call the medical university nearest to your residence, and they will arrange to have your remains picked up when the magic notification is received. It requires some advance paperwork by you, but think of how you'll be contributing to medical science to help humans of the future, maybe even those carrying your own genes. And, it is free. My parents first foisted that idea upon me when they announced it as their choice. I was upset, refused to talk about it, and avoided the discussion for years. Now, I like the idea and am thinking about doing the same.

The Neptune Society has been around since 1973. It, also, requires advance planning but is not a freebie. For a fee, you will be cremated, and they will scatter your ashes at sea.

Here's another very compelling idea I just learned about. It's a true ashes-to-ashes, dust-to-dust cycle that makes me feel good. Bios Urn places your ashes into a biodegradable urn designed to convert you into a tree after life. The urn contains a seed which will grow to be a tree aided by the essence of you. Although I haven't researched it, I think it can be planted in the location of your choice. I'm not sure about the type of tree you get. If I opt for this path, I'd like mine to be a Redwood; why not go out with a bang? There are also biodegradable coffins.

If you do choose one of the above, you or your family can pay or donate money and have a plaque installed in some special place such as a mortuary, university, or park where your loved ones can visit and remember you. Or, they could just remember you on their own. Be kind and generous to them when you're alive so they will want to do so when you're not.

Speaking Out (January 22, 2017)
There are many ways to speak out and be heard. One is in a group situation. On January 21, 2017, the Women's March took place across the United States and around the world. Ground Zero was Washington DC where an estimated 500,000 people marched to show their support of different issues they felt might be threatened by the new Trump Administration. They included women's rights, the environment, racial equality, sexual orientation, economic justice, immigration, science, and more.

I marched with my family at the rally in Oakland, CA which drew tens of thousands. I devoted this blog to photos I took of signs held by random marchers, some plain, some colorful, some simple, some creative, some angry, some staid, some crude, some philosophical, all speaking out and expressing a point of view. Here is the link to see those photos: https://leegalegruen.wordpress.com/2017/01.

My New Get-me-from-here-to-there (January 8, 2017)

Yes, I bought another one recently because my sixteen-year-old one conked out. You call it a car or automobile. I call it a get-me-from-here-to-there. That's its purpose. A bit of comfort is nice: protection from the sun and wind, controlled climate, a smooth ride. In case you weren't aware, the year, brand, color, and horsepower don't add to that.

Here's a not-so-secret secret. I bought a used one even though I could afford a new one. The reason: I didn't like the styling or increased size of the new, "small" SUVs which is what I wanted. I test drove almost every brand out there but wasn't satisfied with anything available. So, I researched and found the most recent year I could that had the features which matched my needs.

Our vehicle of choice has become a status symbol with full bragging rights. *My get-me-from-here-to-there is better than your get-me-from-here-to-there;* ergo, I'm richer, more successful, more desirable, more popular, more lovable, and more (add the descriptor of your choice).

We humans have lots of similar examples in life. Let's name a few: job, house, furniture, clothing, vacation, spouse, pet, and even our innocent children. Now, come on, folks; you're still the same freckle faced, too plump, too skinny, too tall, too short, too (add the descriptor of your choice) human that you always were.

Wrapped in an overly expensive (add the material possession, position, relationship, whatever of your choice) doesn't make you any different. It also doesn't make you better than anyone else. That comes from the inside. So, cut the crap and stop trying to buy your way into acceptability. It won't work. For that, you must become a mensch. (Google it for a translation if you must.)

Be kind, donate to a good cause those dollars you waste on the toy du jour, mentor someone, or give your time and energy to something worthy that isn't your own aggrandizement. Those are the sorts of things that will gain you admiration. Throwing money around on status symbols only makes people snicker behind your back mumbling words like: pathetic.

BLOG POSTS FROM 2016

Words That Diminish (December 29, 2016)

"Sticks and stones may break my bones, but words will never hurt me." We learned that rhyme as children. We tried so hard to remember it when we ran home crying after someone called us a name. Words are powerful. They can enhance or diminish. Wars have been fought over words.

A friend, a retired pathologist and now a widow, recently lamented how demeaned she feels when someone refers to her as granny or honey. A few have done so even knowing she is a medical doctor, an amazing accomplishment especially considering she became one so many decades ago when very few women did.

Denigrating or childlike terms are often applied to elderly women, terms much less frequently used toward men. My friend mentioned that she is often targeted by high pressure salesmen whom she feels see her as an easy mark due to her age and being without a man to protect her. She had an assertive husband most of her adult life and now finds it difficult to stand up for herself.

Many women hide behind a husband or partner to deal with a hostile world. Even though some may consider themselves assertive, often they are better at it when they know they have a man to back them up. It's like the child who dares to stand up to the neighborhood bully, but when it becomes too overwhelming, he runs and hides behind mommy's skirt.

Somehow, men seem better at setting boundaries than women. Why is that? Is it inherent or simply taught to us as young children? Why can't the bulk of women and even a lot of men be assertive and stand up for themselves? What is the secret and how can we tap into it? I'll venture a guess.

Stop being invisible, people! It's time to get tough. Imagine how you would like to be treated by everyone with whom you come in contact, and then refuse to accept anything less. The term "dissed" has become popular in recent times. It means disrespected, and people kill over being dissed.

Your first clue that you've fallen into that vortex again is when that wonky feeling overtakes your body after someone has spoken to you in a manner that minimizes you whether done subtly or overtly. Everything becomes surreal, and you have a vague sensation that it has something to do with what that person just said to you.

Halt everything you're doing. Take a moment or two or ten to identify what is bothering you rather than waiting hours or even days to figure it out. If you must, ask the other person to be quiet while you think. Once you've identified it—*he just called me* (fill in the blank), *and I don't like that*—you are ready to start. Don't let it pass; let it energize you to action.

There are tools we can use at any age when we feel verbally discounted by another. Confrontation is one that yields rewarding results. If someone addresses you in a way you consider disparaging, call them out. Here are several suggested approaches using the irritating salesman as an example. Of course, it can be extrapolated to other scenarios.

Approach #1: Interrupt all interaction and transactions by saying "excuse me" repeatedly until your opponent stops talking. Then, pause, look him or her in the eye, and say something like: "What was that you called me—(fill in the derogatory term he/she used)? I'd prefer that you address me as (fill in the blank) rather than (fill in the aforementioned derogatory term)." Continue the interaction if that suits you.

Approach #2: Do the same initial behavior as in Approach #1, and then say something like: "I don't like being referred to in disrespectful terms like (fill in the derogatory term he/she used), so I'm going to leave now." Stay calm; do not get into a cat fight; and follow through. Walk out! You were born with feet. This is one of the best times to use them.

Approach #3: Do the same initial behavior as in Approach #1, and then request another salesman, server, bank teller, whatever. Your errant foe will apologize, posture, get angry, and use other types of behavior to convince you to change your mind. Don't settle. When he/she pauses for a breath, repeat your request. Keep doing it at each pause, like the proverbial broken record. If that isn't working, ask to see the manager. If nothing works, don't say another word. Walk out! (Remember, you have feet. And, by the way, feet can be used in all sorts of situations without requiring the mouth to set the stage.)

If you're not used to assertive approaches like these and have a more reserved demeanor, it will be hard at first. Keep practicing; it will become easier. You can still be true to your usual nature as none of these approaches has to be done in an angry, defiant, high-pitched manner. Don't sacrifice your dignity to gain your dignity. Retain your decorum, but be firm and insistent. If you must walk out, you may cost yourself some time and the product or service you came for. However, it will be worth it for the good feelings you'll reap after taking charge of how you allow yourself to be treated. And, you will have done a good deed. You will have taught your adversary a lesson on how not to address older people. I bet he/she will never do that again.

Insist on being dealt with respectfully. That's what the big boys do.

Trumpet Yourself (December 16, 2016)

The transitive verb "to trumpet" means to talk about your own or someone else's accomplishments in an enthusiastic manner.

Yes, it's always been considered acceptable to trumpet someone else's achievements. But, what about when you do so for your own achievements?

I've always found it hard to tell people about my accomplishments. It makes me feel like I'm bragging, and that's an uncomfortable position for me. After I wrote a book, I learned that I would have to market it. That meant going against my grain and inserting it into the conversation whenever I had a chance.

I'm still timid about it. I do it in an almost apologetic manner. However, when you must promote and market, you simply can't wait and hope for someone else to trumpet it for you. You must blow your own trumpet.

I was a participant at a recent book sale and signing which was part of a large event offering numerous items for sale. As attendees made their way to my book club's long table and over to me, I would have to quickly start my spiel about my book, giving my brief elevator speech to grab their attention. I was competing not only with the other authors at my table but also with the scores of other tables in the hall, each with hawkers of the wares they and their fellow group members had made: jewelry, ceramics, wooden objects, sewing items, bakery goods, and lots more. All this tumult was noisy, confusing, and distracting. I felt like a circus barker having to yell louder, be flashier, or spin a more interesting and compelling yarn than my competitors.

Participation in fierce competition can be exhausting and off-putting. How does one function in a situation like that, especially when it is against your nature? You can start by accepting that it is okay to trumpet yourself from time to time. Of course, it would be nice if you can avoid becoming obnoxious about it. View it as a challenge to learn a new skill. See it as a growth experience to broaden yourself. Do it sparingly to avoid wearing out your audience.

As grownups, we sometimes must be involved in disquieting situations which are against our normal inclination. Changing your mental attitude can help you get through it.

The Death of a Friend (December 4, 2016)

I lost Sue, one of my closest friends, a few days ago. She just couldn't fight the complications her body imposed on her from the recent onslaught of leukemia and subsequent chemotherapy. I was told she died peacefully in her daughter's arms. I hope she was aware enough in her morphine haze to realize that she was lovingly cradled through her passage.

I'm walking around in a fog—can't quite grasp it all. It doesn't make any sense that I can't just pick up the phone, call Sue, and hear her on the other end: "Oh, hi Trixie," a nickname she anointed me with on our trip to Europe together thirty-five years ago shortly after we became friends. How can I now be speaking about her in the past tense? I don't like it; I refuse to do it! Will my pathetic rebellion bring her back?

So many thoughts, memories. I look at things in my house and remember a comment she made, an item she gave me, something I purchased when I was with her. A few weeks ago, I finally threw out the package of all-natural pineapple popsicles wasting space in my freezer that she bought after making the four-hundred mile trip to visit me in my new home just two and a half months ago. She loved them; I hated them. I wish I had kept them.

During that visit, Sue treated Cousin Judy, me, and herself to manicures following our lunch at a local restaurant. We dominated the shop, talking, laughing, just hanging out as the staff worked on us. A few weeks later, I told her I wanted to do that again; I feel cheated out of our second act.

I'm thinking of revisiting skiing after a hiatus of a few years. Sue started me on that addiction.

"Let's go skiing," she suggested one day early in our friendship.

"Oh, not me. I don't know how to ski. I'm not that athletic. I don't have any skis or ski clothes."

She ignored my protestations and brought me into her bedroom. Drawers were opened and an assortment of ski clothes, nothing matching, was thrown onto the bed. My first days on the bunny hill announced to the world that I was a newbie and had had to beg my ensemble. I learned, became hooked, bought myself the equipment and attire, and we skied together for years.

I don't understand death. How can one so vital be here one moment and not the next, leaving only an empty shell that looks like her but can't say, "Oh, hi Trixie"?

You Win Some; You Lose Some (November 20, 2016)
We've just come through a grueling, national election. I won't even attempt to grapple with people's feelings if their chosen side didn't win. Some are taking it in stride while others are out demonstrating. They are angry, down, refusing to accept it, and unable to move on. That can be extrapolated to everyday life.

How do you handle it when things don't go right? If you're like me, it bums you out. You try to reason with yourself, but somehow the rest of the day just sucks. I experienced two events within the past year, both involving my car that are illustrations:

My Example 1:

The first time I ventured into "the city" near my new home in the suburbs, I got involved in rush hour traffic and was forced onto a toll bridge not even knowing it was a bridge. Where I had lived all my life before my recent move, we didn't have toll roads or highway length bridges.

I didn't know where I was or how to get off. I cruised along in the outer lane, ignoring the booths several lanes to the left with all the cars lined up which I noticed out of the corner of my eye. After all, my lane was doing fine. Three miles later, I was able to turn around and return without incident.

That night, my son explained to me what had happened. I was on a bridge driving solo in the carpool lane and hadn't paid the toll. I could expect a ticket in the mail. Bummer!

"I'll go to court and fight it."

"Yeah, sure, Mom."

We did a little role playing:

Me: "Your honor, I'm new to this area, and I didn't know I was on a bridge, and that I was supposed to pay."

My son as the judge: "Ignorance of the law is no excuse, madam."

Me: "Have some mercy, your honor. I'm just a sweet, little old lady." (I become sweet and old in situations like this.)

My son as the judge: "Just pay the fine and learn a lesson. NEXT."

My Example 2:

Earlier this year, I hit, or should I say tapped, the car, or should I say pickup truck, in front of me while coming to a stop at a red light. Who knows how or why I did it? All I know is that I felt a thud and looked up to see myself flush with the vehicle ahead.

The driver and his passenger both got out and walked toward me. I got out to meet them. I knew it was going to go badly when the driver wagged his finger at me as though I were a wayward child.

My car had just two small chipped areas in the paint on the front bumper about three feet apart. His back bumper was twisted upward in the middle with my paint transfer far to each side of that area. He, of course, insisted the damage had not been there before, and that my car bumper must have forced each side of his bumper to move toward the center. Did I mention that my bumper is plastic and his is metal?

The driver appeared to be approximately late-fifties and in decent shape. His well-built, muscular passenger appeared to be in his twenties. Their pickup truck had one of those toolboxes stretching across the front of the truck bed. I concluded that they performed labor of some sort and were in good physical condition. I was not hurt, and they were talking and walking around with gusto which suggested to me that they, too, were not hurt. Silly me!

Jumping forward, my insurance company bought their stories that their vehicle bumper damage was caused by my car, and that both the driver and passenger were injured. Over my protestations, they paid the two men a total of $11,000 for their injuries and paid for the damaged bumper on their truck.

It was cheaper to pay the nuisance value of the claim than to fight it in court. That is how insurance companies function. The fallout to me is that I lost my good driver discount.

Ah, yes, you win some and you lose some. The above are just two small examples of the latter. When things like that happen, the only salvation is to focus on the former. Thankfully, we do win some. Let's be grateful for that. They could all be losers, you know.

I Am Not an Aquarian! (November 4, 2016)

I was on my way from my car to a store last week when I noticed a woman walking next to me in the parking lot. She pointed to my shoes and said, "Oh, you have those new arch support tennis shoes. I saw them on television."

"Oh no, these are quite old. They're nothing special."

"Yeah, those are the ones. They've got arches built into them."

I went on to explain, "Well, I wear orthotics, so I don't depend on arches in the shoes even if there are any."

"Yeah, they have great arch supports, and they have those little springs in them," she insisted.

"No, I don't think they have any springs in them."

That's when she torpedoed me with, "Geez, you must be an Aquarian. You argue about everything."

I could feel my temper rising. I wanted her to know that I am not an Aquarian. I wanted to argue about the fact that I do not argue about everything.

The whole thing suddenly became silly. Was I going to get into a cat fight over my old tennis shoes? This was a total stranger who obviously had her own agenda. I did not start talking to her; she started talking to me. She was convinced that she was right about her assessment of my shoes, and nothing was going to change her mind. She also knew she was right about my being an argumentative type, apparently like those born between January 20 and February 18, who, she was certain, argue about everything. She failed to see her own role in our escalating discussion. I'm guessing that this was not a new situation for her.

I know very little about the Signs of the Zodiac including my own which happens to be Capricorn if anyone is interested. I don't believe that what month, day, time, or moon phase during which you were born has anything to do with your personality. I also don't believe that all those of the Aquarian persuasion argue about everything. I'm sure there are nice, pleasant Aquarians and not so nice ones as there are for every other Zodiac sign.

The point here is: What do you do when you find yourself in a situation where a stranger manages to insult you within five minutes of meeting them? There is not an easy answer. You feel your face flush, and you want to defend yourself.

Try to step back and realize how ridiculous the whole thing is. You're not going to dissuade your attacker from their conviction. Why waste your time and energy trying to do so? The best course of action is to concede the point graciously and get away ASAP. You know you're right, and it doesn't matter whether they know it or not, especially if you're an Aquarian.

Respecting the Priorities of Others (October 20, 2016)

We all have our priorities. Why can't lampshades be some-one's? I met that someone recently when I was shopping for the item in question.

I was wandering through a local shopping mall and strolled into a store that sold lamps and lampshades exclusive-ly. The threshold tripped the bell in back whereupon a man I presumed to be the store owner emerged and asked the stan-dard shopkeeper question: May I help you? I explained that I was looking for shades for a few table lamps. That was his cue.

The proprietor proceeded to educate me about lamp-shades and their importance in my life, a subject about which I had given very little thought. He made it clear that he was an expert in the field and, according to him, choosing the prop-er lampshade "is the most important decision you'll have to make." I never knew that, and I pondered over it for the ap-propriate period of time to satisfy him.

Together, we surveyed the store's offerings as my host ex-plained each shade's details to me. One had to consider pro-portion, material, light emitted or blocked, price, color, and more. However, I had made a grave error. I had not brought my shadeless lamps with me for a proper fitting. I was embar-rassed by my error and begged forgiveness. He succumbed, but only after I agreed to bring said objects the next time I came looking for their toppings.

After my guide told me he had been in the lampshade business for over thirty years, I understood his perspective. We all think that what we are doing is the most important, urgent, relevant pursuit there is. Although someone else's passion may be totally different than ours and even something that seems silly to us, can't we consider the point of view of others? After all, it may be something they have spent decades pursuing and perfecting, and who are we to decide that it has little or no relevance?

I've always treated lampshades as simply decorative filters for the lights I need in my home. However, to this man they were his field of expertise just as doctors, lawyers, and others have theirs, and it was refreshing to see him taking pride in his work. Lampshades were the vehicle to put food on his table and provide shelter from the elements. What's wrong with that?

Perhaps we can respect differences of opinion, priority, or emphasis even though we don't adopt them as our own? Although my focus in life is not lampshades, or least it didn't used to be, who's to say that what I deem most important needs to be so for others? Let's accept, appreciate, and acknowledge that something like lampshades may be compelling and significant in the life of another? It makes bumping up against each other in a crowded society just a bit easier.

Don't Squander Your Complaint Quota (October 4, 2016)
Complaining—ah, we all love to do it. Some do it very little and others more so. Then, there are those who have honed it to an art form. They seem to complain frequently and obsessively. This constant default position can render their targets weary, ditsy, spaced out, and generally down.

It's hard to confront the expert complainers about their behavior because their logical comeback is, "Well, you complain, too." How do you get it across that it is a matter of degree, and who sets the rules on where the line has been crossed? That's a tough one. Who am I to say that my amount of complaining is correct but yours is not?

To solve this conundrum, I've developed a philosophy that works for me; feel free to use it. It goes like this: We are all born with a given amount of complaints available to us, sort of like a woman is born with a given amount of eggs that she ovulates monthly until they are used up. Some people spread out their allotment of complaints over their lifetime, while others use them up long before the inevitable final bell.

Once you deplete your allotment of complaints, you cannot complain anymore. If you try to do so, those of us on the receiving end are justified in simply walking away, hanging up the phone, or otherwise ignoring you. You may get mad, posture, yell and scream, profess you don't understand, and all other manner of push back, but that's it—no more complaints from you.

So folks, and especially the serial complainers, guard, hoard, and care for your allotment of complaints. It is not infinite.

Drama Kings and Queens (September 23, 2016)

Do you have someone in your life who is a drama king or queen? Are you one? You know the type. They always seem to have a crisis, event, happening, whatever that is the most urgent, horrible, fantastic, important, (add your own adjective) thing in the world. If their current focus is on solving their problem du jour, preferably with your help, angst, time and attention, once it is over, a new one usually pops up. What's going on?

Everyone wants attention; it is normal. We take steps to achieve it such as talking about interesting things or trying to excel at something. However, many people with drama king/queen traits hunger for attention and never seem to get enough to satisfy them. To that end, they have figured out how well it works to be hyper-vigilant about a multitude of matters. The logical segue, of course, is to make a big deal about the goings-on in their life to anyone who will listen and jump into the fray. They are drawn to those who will play the game. Their approach can be to an individual or group and often starts with openings such as: "I really need your advice on this," or "Let me tell you what happened to me today (yesterday, last night, week, year, century)."

Are you tired of being sucked into this type of interaction? If so, how do you protect yourself from the ravages of being on the receiving end of someone else's hyped-up drama? It's hard, especially if that someone is significant in your life such as a spouse, child, parent, co-worker, boss, etc. However, playing the co-dependent doesn't help them or you.

Here is one approach: when the next performance starts and becomes too much to bear, make an excuse to get out of their presence. Feel free to use the following phrases and add to them:

1. "Excuse me, but I have to go to the bathroom." (Positioning yourself as having weak bladder and/or bowel control is a convenient deflector.)

2. "Oh, I have to rush off now to get to my appointment with my doctor (dentist, therapist, dog groomer, astrologer, guru, your service professional of choice)."

Remember, it's only fun being a drama king/queen if you have an audience.

Learning the Ropes (September 8, 2016)

This is a continuation of my three previous blogs about moving from my house of forty-five years:

In my new life, I am striving to drive an automobile less often. Having previously lived in Los Angeles, California since childhood, I drove my car everywhere. Yes, there is public transportation available there, but because of that city's greater distances and its being a commuter way of life, the majority of people drive. I'm sick of driving, of fighting rush hour traffic, and of the stress of trying not to kill myself or others as I speed along, a lone traveler leaving a carbon footprint that is shared with so many rather than a gentler impact on our stressed planet. So, yes, I'm learning to use public transportation.

I braved the local subway yesterday for the first time armed with my senior pass. Even applying for it was one of many in a very long list of new learning curves. I entered the train, positioned myself directly in front of the map on the wall, and compared it with the plans I had sketched out before beginning the undertaking. As we stopped at each station, I peeked out of the open door and read the sign to be sure I was where I thought I was. No one else was doing so. They all seemed comfortable with where they were located in space.

What a strange experience sharing a car with multitudes, most engrossed with their IT devices. I saw young professional types dressed in power suits presumably on their way to important business activities. I saw backpack wearers, some with predictable bicycles which they leaned against a railing installed for such gear. I saw mothers with their children, two-somes or threesomes engaged in chitchat, and homeless or al-most homeless souls.

Mass public transportation seems to have its own proto-col and mores, just like most activities. I was fascinated by a woman who entered the car wearing a spaghetti strap, cami-sole shirt. She seated herself, opened her purse, pulled out a small jar, and balanced it on her knee. Then, using a fingertip, she scooped out a dab of the glop it contained and applied it to one armpit, switched hands, and did the same to the oth-er one. All this was accomplished without missing a beat of her ongoing cellphone conversation. And to think I've always been timid about putting on lipstick with strangers nearby.

Once I realized that it was acceptable to groom oneself on public transportation, I took out the only thing I had to compete with her: a nail file. For the rest of the trip, I gave myself a manicure sans nail polish. It's amazing what you can accomplish when you don't have to obey the hands-free rule of the motorist. Next time I ride the metro, I might just arrive in my pajamas tugging my daytime garb along in a rolling suitcase. I'm sure it won't faze the other passengers as I change my clothes since most of them have their heads buried in their cell phones anyway.

Settling In (August 24, 2016)

This is a continuation of my two previous blogs about moving from my house of forty-five years:

I arrived at my new, empty condo and settled down for the

night on a mat on the floor which I'd brought tied to the top of my car. To put a positive spin on a bleak experience, I chose to view it as camping out complete with dinner by flashlight.

The moving van arrived with my furniture the next day. Aside from some minor damage to a few articles, most of my belongings were intact.

It's strange to accept that this is my new home and not just a vacation rental—temporary digs until returning to my real life. It's strange to realize that there are new people living in my old house now. They are cooking in my kitchen, showering in my bathroom, storing their possessions in my closets, and generally displacing me. Will my old house remember me and all the years I spent painting her, repairing her, gentling her as she broke down? We aged together, my old house and I, our parts wearing out and needing fixing.

My condo is becoming a home. It's an adjustment, but I'm slowly personalizing it. I've installed my own furniture, tchotchkes, and even some beloved plants which accompanied me in my car, gently covered to shade them from the harsh sun. Pictures and other touches brought from my former life to make me feel comfortable are coming out of boxes. Oh, the boxes—daunting as they stare at me, tease me. They are slowly disappearing as I tackle them, sift through their contents I so carefully packed, rediscover my possessions, and make decisions where to situate them.

I'm arranging, rearranging, and learning how things work. There are so many decisions to make—big ones, small ones, and all sizes in between. *Where's the light switch? Okay, I found it. Now, how do I turn it on?* In my new abode, the refrigerator opens on the opposite side from my old one. My kitchen sink is a double like before, but the garbage disposal is on the right, not on the left—grrrr. I concentrate hard on everything; nothing comes automatically—tiring, very tiring. I need a vacation from decision making.

There are lots of problems to solve: the toilet that leaks when flushed and the air conditioning that doesn't properly condition the air to name a few. Yes, my home warranty covers them. But, it still means I have to figure out who to call, be there for an appointment, and live with the problem until the problem solver arrives. I remind myself that they are only bumps in the road—first world problems as I've blogged about before.

My son mentioned how strange it felt to call my old telephone number, the only landline he ever knew for me, to find a mechanical voice referral to another number. I've spent hours on that new phone calling all the enterprises that define my life: credit card companies, insurance companies, utilities, my HMO, and on and on, to inform them of this major, traumatic change in my life and to give them my new address. Oddly, they were only interested in the latter.

I'm making almost daily trips to such establishments as Target; Bed, Bath and Beyond; hardware stores; and others of that ilk to purchase anew the things I left behind and, of course, now need.

On the flip side, I love my new condo; it's everything I wanted. Deer and wild turkeys stroll through my backyard from time to time, and I watch them from my office window. I can't get enough of that.

My son came over with his tools to help me set up a few things. This is the first time I have lived close to him since he left for college twenty-five years ago. He's coming over again next weekend to do more and just generally hang out. He'll bring over my daughter-in-law and grandchildren soon so everyone can see grandma's new pad.

My neighbor stopped over a few days ago to introduce herself and bring me a box of candy and a sweet note. Friends I made when I rented for a few months in this community last year to try it on for size have reached out to me and are eager to reconnect. It makes me feel welcome, like coming home again—back in a comfort zone.

I have downsized and aim for a slower, less stressful life. I love it here and don't regret my move. Yes, this was the right decision for me.

It's hard to admit when something has run its course. We hang on, hoping to return to a time of contentment, refusing to admit that it has passed and lives only in memory. Change is frightening, but we must forge on when life gets stale. It's calming and soothing when you know you've gotten it right.

Driving to My New Life (August 9, 2016)

This is a continuation of my previous blog about moving from my house of forty-five years:

The moving van left an hour ago carrying the majority of my possessions—so significant to me yet filling only a third of the huge transport. One last surreal glance back at the old house which sheltered me for almost half a century before I, too, leave.

I'm driving up the interstate next to tomato trucks, their trailers piled high with the red fruit. I pass them as I hurry on to my new life. A short time later, they pass me parked on the shoulder eating my lunch. They're like old friends, marking my progress.

Hung out for a while with an army convoy until they peeled off. Thank you guys for guarding me on this trip and in general.

Passed an industrial farm of thousands of cows crammed together with very little personal space. Makes me want to become a vegetarian.

Moseyed alongside hundreds of orange trees on the right and an equal number of almond trees on the left. Farmers had posted signs every few miles on the sides of abandoned trucks reminders such as: "No water, No jobs," as though their concern for their low-paid workers was their only reason for being. The desert landscape abuts the orchards—not an environment meant for thirsty, cultivated trees.

I spot in the rearview mirror my two-foot high dieffenbachia, leaves swaying gently with the motion of the road, waiting to be installed in its new home, too. Yes, I can buy a new one when I arrive, but I wanted something alive from my old life with me. It's comforting.

A friend gave me a toy rooster as a gift last year. Nearby motion causes it to crow three times making me want to strangle it. She insisted I place it next to my front door to warn me if intruders break in during the night. The rooster is ensconced in a box in the back of my car. Every time I go over a bump, it segues into crowing mode. That, too, is comforting—reminds me of home.

Snippets of the California aqueduct pass by, flowing liquid surrounded by an arid land. I come upon large mounds of dirt with giant, erector set machinery crawling over them, mining something undisclosed to passing drivers.

Around the next turn, a windmill farm appears upon a hill, three-leaf clover blades churning out renewable energy which flows through huge cables held up by giant electrical towers nearby—environmentally friendly power for a city. Diametrically opposed was an identical, long line of electrical towers a few cities back holding up their non-renewable energy powered cables—a contrast of changing times.

My anticipation is growing. I'm almost there. Excitement and apprehension.

Moving On (July 26, 2016)

The seventy-foot moving van arrived this morning (an aggregator, transporting the possessions of different people all going in the same direction.) I'm getting ready to move from my house of forty-five years into a condo in an active, senior retirement community almost four hundred miles away. It's a seismic change for me—scary and exciting all rolled into one. It's a good thing I didn't know how awful such an endeavor would be, or I don't think I would have started it.

I am a hoarder—not to be confused with a clutterer. My house is neat and clean. But, my closets, cupboards, cabinets, drawers, garage, and anywhere else you can stuff stuff are bursting with the things I've been saving for decades in case I might need them. You know what I mean; the minute you throw something away, it's not a week later that you'll be searching for it.

I've spent the last months sorting through it all, including the boxes of stuff my son dropped off when he graduated college almost twenty-five years ago. So, now I must decide what to keep, give away, donate, recycle, or throw away. It's been painful, exhausting, devastating, cleansing, liberating, and consuming.

These days, you can't just carelessly discard those important papers you've been accumulating. Now you must shred them as they contain sensitive information which can be retrieved from dumpsters and used to steal your identity. I attacked those papers with my little office shredder, but when that became cumbersome and didn't make a dent in the job, I hauled about four hundred pounds of documents to a local shredding event put on by the city.

I culled my collection of thousands of old photographs taken before the technique became digital. I threw away snapshots of beautiful rivers, mountains, deserts, canyons, and other assorted scenery I long ago forgot the locations of. I vow I will never take another picture of anything that doesn't have a human in it whom I know and like.

You can no longer throw paint, medications, household cleaners, electronic devices, and the like in the garbage. You must haul them to the toxic waste and electronic disposal sites. Each time I tried to throw such an item in the dumpster, my good citizen guilt pulled my arm back and made me put it in the trunk of my car for proper handling.

Of course, I elected to pack my own things; I'm no wimp. To that end, I trolled alleys visiting those same dumpsters seeking cardboard cartons to pack what remained. Loading up my car, I drove home with my daily harvest. Finding the boxes was easy. We have become an "order online" society, throwing away the wonderful containers used to deliver our purchases. Huge boxes grew in my garage to a total of twenty-nine, waiting patiently for the moving van to collect them along with the furniture I chose to keep.

I have become buff with all the physical labor I've been doing. It's more effective than working out at the gym and a lot cheaper. I will be sad to leave my home city since childhood and my friends of many years. Conversely, I'm eagerly anticipating my coming life and the new friends and experiences that await me. Is it time for you to move on? It's better to do it when you can rather than when you must.

Mercurial Personalities (July 8, 2016)

Some people swing rapidly from one emotional extreme to the other, just like the liquid metal mercury used in thermometers which shifts dramatically with the temperature. In the human form, it's not the temperature that sets them off, and you will never know what does. They can be fun, loving, upbeat one day or even one moment and without warning, switch to the polar opposite—angry, rejecting, a real downer.

Those that experience such swings to a pathological degree might be diagnosed as bi-polar or what used to be called manic-depressive. Their emotional lives are a constant roller coaster. There are psychiatric medications that help with their mood swings. Sometimes they work; sometimes they don't. I've often thought how difficult life must be for the bearer of such a personality.

But, what about the rest of us who must interact with someone like that? It might be a spouse or significant other, a relative, a co-worker, a teacher, or the cashier at the market. We are sucked in by how charming and exciting they can be in their up times and bitterly disappointed and hurt when we are attacked or shunned in their down times. We ruminate, wondering what we might have done to offend them, not realizing that the problem lies within them, not due to anything we did. We were simply the nearest human available to dump on. If it is someone we're close to and see regularly, we ride right along on their roller coaster albeit not of our choosing.

I have had such an experience with someone significant in my life. I grew to always be on the defensive when dealing with him, never knowing when I'd get it right over the head. Even when we seemed to be having a happy time, I was anxious, wondering when it would turn. Our interactions became more and more stressful, and I came to dread them. I once asked if he were bi-polar. He said his psychiatrist told him he wasn't. Well, if that's the case, in my opinion he's as close to being bi-polar that one can get without being bi-polar.

In looking back at my history of friends, I realize I've had several of a capricious nature to one degree or another. They can be fascinating, stimulating people, and that's the hook for me. However, I've learned that being victimized by interaction with a mercurial character is miserable, causing me nothing but tension and angst.

I frequently write in my blog that we must protect ourselves from victimization. Yes, we must take the strain out of being on the receiving end of a personality that switches with lightning speed, always catching us off-guard, always creating anxiety.

If the person is so significant in our lives that we choose not to cut them loose such as a parent or a child, what can we do? We can refuse to engage when they get into attack mode. We can leave the room. We can exit the location and take a walk or a drive. If this type of thing has happened to you when you're out together socially, always take your own car so you can make a quick get-away if necessary or be prepared to hail a taxi or ride sharing service. Protect yourself; Mr./Ms. Mercurial won't.

When Strangers Behave Offensively (June 24, 2016)

What happens when a stranger you encounter in public says something or behaves in a certain way toward you that you find uncomfortable or disagreeable? The stranger's behavior may be so sudden and unexpected that it catches you off guard. That, along with knowing that your reaction will be on display for everyone nearby to observe, can be disconcerting and cause you to fumble and stumble in your response. The whole matter becomes embarrassing with the stranger seeming to win the day.

I've had that type of scenario happen to me many times, and it always upsets me since I didn't invite or desire to be placed in that position. Recently, I found myself in yet another such situation and was proud of myself for handling it on the spot rather than mulling over it and coming up with a good response several hours later—way too late, beating myself up with "I-should-have-said" thoughts.

I was in a restaurant with a group of people I didn't know after we had all attended the same lecture. I sat down in a seat with no one on either side of me. Suddenly, a swaggering, blustery type of man entered, looked around the room, and announced in a loud voice for everyone to hear, "I think I'll sit right here next to this nice young lady" as he plunked himself in the empty chair directly to my right. His line was condescending and sexist, especially considering that he had no idea whether I am nice, and I am certainly not a young lady. Yes, given his age, he was probably old school. You know the type: women are just objects to be available for the enhancement of men. To be clear, men can be the victims of offensive behavior from strangers, too.

These situations are frequently foisted upon us without warning and with no time to prepare. I managed to blurt out, "Oh, I probably will be moving my seat soon as I want to sit near the speaker when she arrives." It was both the truth and a good, take-charge response.

Mr. Swagger, still playing to his audience, continued in his booming baritone, "Oh no, you sit right here next to me." Having a history of feeling intimidated when confronted by strong personality types, my normal reaction would have been to just laugh politely, try not to attract any more attention, and follow his orders to stay where I was not knowing what else to do.

Instead, picturing the entire meal with this controlling bore sitting next to me, I said, "I came to this lunch for one reason, and that is to be able to converse with the speaker. I will sit where I choose when the speaker arrives." Mr. S. never said another word to me as I guess I made him look foolish after his great pronouncements.

I was proud of taking care of myself and my needs and not letting someone else dictate how the occasion was going to progress for me. If a stranger, or anyone else for that matter, chooses to behave in a manner that sets up how things are going to go for you, you have a right to be just as obtuse and set them straight. This is difficult for more reserved types, especially if public display or rocking the boat are not your thing. However, you must take care of yourself folks. No one else will.

Pet Peeves (June 13, 2016)

We all have pet peeves, those things that irritate us as we go about the business of living. How do we weather them and decrease the stress they cause? Before we attack that question, I thought I'd list a few of my favorites:

1. Bar code stickers on fruit. Many require you to cut with a knife or jam your fingernail into the fruit in order to peel the damn thing off.

2. The driver in the left turn lane with a long line of cars behind him/her who creeps up just a few inches into the crosswalk when the signal turns green. He sits awaiting the oncoming traffic which never seems to end. When the light turns red, he finally moves fully into the intersection, which he should have done in the first place so that I might have been able to creep up and shadow his bumper, thereby enabling two people to turn left instead of just one.

3. Self-flushing toilets in public lavatories which wait until you put down the paper toilet seat cover and are about to enthrone yourself when it decides to flush and whip away the target just as you are descending.

I'm sure everyone has at least one to add to my list. Yes, each of these incidents and so many more take just a few seconds off of our projected lifespans. The only way to cope in a beneficial manner is to try to turn your pique into humor.

Some years ago, I used this approach with yet another pet peeve. I love dogs but really hate when one leaves its bountiful deposit on my grass and the jerk on the other end of the leash fails to pick it up and dispose of it elsewhere. So, I put up a sign which said, "If your dog poops on my lawn, please pick it up. If you can't bring yourself to do so, please leave me your address so I can bring it to your house and drop it on your lawn." I don't know that it cured the problem, but at least it gave everyone a laugh.

When pet peeves happen over and over again and you have no power to change them, turn them into something positive for yourself so that you're the winner. It certainly is better than the alternative.

You're Fine Just the Way You Are (May 29, 2016)

This is a continuation of the conversation in my last blog post.

Few admit to having a face lift or bags removed from under their eyes or (fill in the cosmetic procedure/surgery of your choice). The euphemism "I'm having work done" has replaced the embarrassing to admit, "I'm having plastic surgery." The euphemism "to look more refreshed" has replaced the truer "to look younger."

Many go to great lengths to keep their latest cosmetic surgery a secret. If it's so okay, why the privacy, shame, and avoidance of public discussion? Do the refreshees think that others don't know what's going on; if it isn't spoken, it doesn't exist? Do they think that others don't know the huge amount

236 | *Reinventing Yourself in Your Retirement Years*

of money they've expended to look youthful which could have been spent on something much more substantial like their retirement? Do they think that a face without wrinkles and bags really matches nicely with stooped bodies, age spots, sagging necks, and loose skin?

Shakespeare, that sly bard, said, "What's in a name?" Yes, if we can use a different terminology, we think it changes the stark reality of what's really going on: *I want to look younger because I've bought into the hype that it's more desirable than how I look now*—your true age, God forbid.

Marketing for elective cosmetic procedures and surgeries has played on our insecurities: *I'm ugly, undesirable, and unlovable the way I am. If I do* (again fill in the blank), *I will be beautiful, desirable, and loved.*

We all know on a visceral level this is not true. But, we're flocking to the purveyors of these myths "just in case."

Recently, a friend had cataract surgery. I emailed her to inquire how it went. We had the following back and forth emails:

Lee Gale: How are your eyes doing?

Friend: The great part is the richness of color and the clarity. I feel like Dorothy in Oz. The bad part is looking in the mirror and seeing all the lines and bags and spots so clearly. I aged 25 years in 24 hours.

LG: You are Dorothy. People are attracted to you because of your talents, your enthusiasm, and your zest for life. That was so 24 hours ago and has not changed just because you can see your physical self more clearly. You're fine the way you are. Don't start getting crazy notions into your head. I just saw a current picture of (famous 1950s movie star) who now has one of those grotesque, plastic surgery faces. OMG!

F: I am going to copy your words, enlarge them and hang them next to my mirror. THANKS a hundred mil.

The singer, Michael Jackson, was a sad character who, despite talent and success most people never achieve, was so insecure that he became a plastic surgery junkie and, in his own description of himself, ended up looking like a lizard. We can all name one famous person after another with a similar story. Most of us can name one not-so-famous person, too.

I call it the plastic surgery merry-go-round which is my euphemism for addiction to those types of procedures. I've heard of physicians who put out newsletters about the latest tweaks available for potential buyers of their wares. Others have parties so their clients can show off their most recent, surgically-induced look to each other and shop for what their next youth-enhancing move will be. Then, there are those addicts who are so self-critical that they have the same procedure repeatedly because the outcome from the previous one wasn't exactly what they had envisioned, or now that look is out and another is in—kind of like trendy clothing. Michael Jackson became a man with almost no nose at all.

So, what I want to know is where are the spouses, the significant others, the children, and the good friends to tell people that they are fine, lovable, and desirable just the way they are—that they don't have to spend thousands of dollars, put their health or life at risk and take the chance of looking grotesque just to get people to like and accept them?

Being at the Whim of Marketeers (May 13, 2016)
Marketeers spend a lot of time, energy, and money defining what is desirable and attractive—what we absolutely must have. They hawk it to the masses via advertising and the media. Then, they sell it to us.

I have been a victim of this all my life with my skills, my possessions, my appearance, and so on. My insecurity, carefully nurtured from childhood, has always convinced me that if I look a certain way, possess a particular talent, own a specific object, etc., it's not a big deal—anyone can do it, have it or whatever. Of course, if I don't have the latest thing trending at the moment, it's the most coveted state imaginable, and I yearn for it.

That type of thinking is found in groups of all ages, sexes, socio-economic strata, and every other classification into which we divide human beings. It's sad the lengths to which people will go to attain that artificially created, can't-live-without-it lifestyle.

I read a while ago about the growing number of Asian women having plastic surgery on their eyelids to make them look more American or European. Of course, it's easy for me to pass judgment on such an act as ridiculous, sitting on my perch with my Caucasian eyelids. But, I'm the same person who dyed my hair blond for decades so I could bump up my fun level. If you don't believe me about that perk, just ask Miss Clairol.

Look at the success of Botox because it has been fed to us for decades that youth is in and wrinkles, those town criers of aging, are out. What other animal in the world deliberately ingests poison into its body?

The popularity of liposuction is fueled by the current ideal of concentration-camp thin bodies, making zaftig thighs, hips, whatevers so unattractive. By the way, save that fat they suck out of you, people. Kim Kardashian (never thought I'd print her name in my blog) is changing that fashion, and big hips are coming back into vogue. I'll bet your liposuction guy will give you a deal on reinjecting the fat he removed from your (fill in the blank) a few years ago and you saved in a bottle in your closet, way in the back hidden out of sight behind your luggage.

Of course, you could cut your lipo guy (or dermatologist, or plastic surgeon, or whomever) loose and start being okay with yourself and making your own decisions about how you'll live your life—what an idea! Think about it. Someone is creating our insecurities and making a fortune off of them. And, it only works because we cooperate so willingly.

Slowing Down **(April 29, 2016)**
For so many of us, it's hard to slow down. We've been used to a certain pace in our lives for years—decades. It's a rhythm we follow and have honed to a comfort level. We may be overcommitted: classes, jobs or volunteer positions, dates with friends, meetings, etc., all requiring us to show up according to a certain schedule. Yes, we enjoy it. Yes, it makes us feel important. When our bodies, stamina, health, and other circumstances force us to move at a slower pace, it can be frustrating, upsetting, and discouraging. After all, there are so many responsibilities, so much to do, so much to accomplish.

However, we must take it easier. We are often forced to do

so as our energy wanes. Then, it's time to reverse direction—replace our current activities with others not as demanding or continue with our regular pursuits but to a lesser degree. There will be forces working against that. After all, if others depend on us, it is not to their advantage for us to do less.

You must take care of yourself. You must survive and thrive with a new lifestyle, a slower lifestyle. The best way to do so is to look ahead. Think about all that you can do rather than all that you can no longer do. Cut out unimportant things. It's okay to step down from all the responsibility. Nothing will collapse. There are over seven billion people in the world, and there will be someone else to step in and carry on.

Tell friends and others that you can't commit for sure and may have to cancel with little notice. Explain why so they won't be upset or hurt such as: you don't always sleep well, you don't always feel well, things sometimes become overwhelming, etc. Delegate. Hire someone to do the heavy lifting: cleaning, shopping, bill paying, and other taxing chores. Buy prepared foods instead of doing all the cooking yourself. Get rid of your car and the stress of driving. Take a bus, metro, or subway. If they're not convenient, take a taxi or a ride sharing service; the cost will probably end up being about the same as driving your own car when you consider the amount you spend on gas, insurance, and repairs.

You can do it the easy way or the hard way. You can lament what used to be and no longer is, or you can embrace what is and what you still have. Choose the latter. It's easier, healthier, and more fulfilling.

First World Problems (April 14, 2016)

I was complaining to my son about my washing machine conking out and needing to buy a new one. I bemoaned having to search for a replacement online, having to call different appliance stores to check their stock, having to stay home to get the delivery, and figuring out how to use it. He listened patiently and then put it all in perspective.

"Mom, this is a first world problem."

That shut me up immediately. How petty and ungrateful we can become with the minor inconveniences in our otherwise privileged lives. We're not being bombed like some people in the world. We're not starving like some people in the world. We're not being exposed to horrendous diseases, being mauled by animals, being beheaded or having a relative who is. You get the idea.

It's easy to get caught up in the minutiae of our lives, stressing about having to buy a new washing machine and the like. I'm certainly guilty of it. But, it illustrates how any situation can be looked at in a different light. How lucky I am that I have the money, availability, and ease to buy a new washing machine. Not everyone does.

Yes, our problems are significant to us, but we must keep some perspective. Practice looking at problems from a different angle and see if their importance doesn't diminish. Too many people complain too often about too many things. Stop complaining folks and make it work for you. If you go shopping for something and they are out of it, get something else and move on. If you've made plans with someone and they are late, stop grumbling and read a book or magazine until they arrive. When you can't get what you want, choose something else at that moment. When things aren't going like you had in mind, "go with the flow" as they say.

Complaining is easy. Dissatisfaction is rampant. Why can't we take the opportunity to improve our swimming when the water gets choppy? There are so many positive, interesting things going on all around us constantly. Choose to get into that mind frame. It makes life gratifying and so much easier.

Beer and Diapers (March 30, 2016)

An article in the newspaper a few months ago mentioned that companies like Walmart track purchasing patterns. One thing they found was that beer and diapers are often purchased together. Yes, it brings a laugh. However, in analyzing it a bit further, it's not so funny.

Having a baby is a significant stressor. Resorting to alcohol, drugs, over-eating, and worse on a regular and maybe excessive basis to handle that tension can be counterproductive and dangerous. Substance abuse to cope with stress doesn't just happen to new parents, it occurs across the spectrum of age, sex, race, and every other classification. We are bombarded with it all the time. Sometimes it's externally driven and sometimes internally. However, it creates anxiety, nervousness, and a search for a solution, too often in the form of ever-encroaching, addictive behaviors.

We can't eliminate all pressure from our lives. But, we can try to lower it. Look carefully at what causes you stress. Are you babysitting too often and too long for grandchildren who wear you out? Do you have too many activities and obligations scheduled and just yearn for some relaxation time? Do you (fill in the blank)? Learn to assess your personality and abilities. Admit if you can no longer keep up the pace you did when you were younger. Maybe things that didn't used to bother you do now.

Practice prioritizing. Learn to tell others "no." Learn to tell yourself the same. When life becomes overwhelming and you find yourself sinking into substance abuse or other self-destructive behaviors just to function, find another, less harmful "drug of choice"—an alternative, more beneficial means of managing it.

Exercise is one example. Join a gym, attend it, and work out on a regular basis. Take long, brisk walks. Climb stairs whenever possible. Writing is another way to deal with stress. We used to write in our diaries; today it's called journaling. It's therapeutic and calming. Use the old-fashioned, paper and pen method or compose it on your computer. Think of other non-self-destructive means of attacking the aggrevators that life throws at you. Be your own advocate. Handle life rather than the other way around.

The Art of Senescence (March 16, 2016)

While reading an article in a scientific journal, I came upon this word which I knew but had forgotten: senescence. It simply means aging. Senescence happens to all living things; it is a normal trajectory of nature.

Many things that are alive practice senescence artfully. For example: as trees age, they become more beautiful, majestic, and regal. Applying this to humans, some people are able to recast the act of aging into an art form. Unfortunately, so many aren't. They bemoan the inevitable rather than accepting and growing into it.

I recently saw a movie, "The Lady in the Van," starring the wonderful actress, Maggie Smith, as an elderly woman who, although successful when younger, had fallen upon hard times and was living in her van. The actress portrayed her character with authenticity, joy and dignity just as she did with the polar opposite character she portrayed, an English dowager noblewoman, in the television series, "Downton Abbey." The most important take away from this observation is Maggie Smith, the person. She has aged naturally, embracing her wrinkles, sagging neck, and faltering voice. They are her trademark, and she wields them with skill. She has discovered the art of senescence.

Another example of such a person is Iris Apfel, the 97-year-old fashion icon (born in 1921). A documentary about her, "Iris," was released in 2015. As is evident from the movie, Iris Apfel does not hide herself from public exposure because her youthful looks and stature have eroded. She is proud of her accomplishments as a designer and as a businesswoman. She has created an image of an elderly person who is positive, sharp, and respected.

Rather than fighting growing older with one elective surgical or dermatological procedure after another, both of these women have used their own aging process to their advantage. They are the human equivalent of a senescent, awe-inspiring Morton Bay Fig tree I encountered. That tree and these women challenge the rest of us to follow in their footstep and not fear and fight aging but to investigate it, embrace it, and make it work for us.

Let Your Children Teach You (March 2, 2016)

I often get advice from my son who is an adult with children of his own. He's bright, and I learn from him. He enjoys counseling me, and I enjoy our interaction.

No matter how old your children get to be, it's hard for a parent to switch from the teaching mode into the learning mode. I've heard parents say to their adult children something along the lines of "Don't tell me; I'm your father (or mother)." What does that have to do with hearing sound advice?

I suspect that what's really going on is a power struggle. The parent doesn't want to admit that their child may surpass them in any way. It's also a sign of aging which so many distain—passing the baton when a child is old enough to be the adviser to a parent. But, the flip side is that it allows the aging parent to have an adult-to-adult relationship with their child. This scenario can be extrapolated to any relationship between an aging person and a much younger person whether it be an aunt/uncle relationship with a niece/nephew, a boss-employee relationship regardless of which person is in which role, and so many others.

What a wonderful gift to receive at this stage of life. Embrace it! Be grateful for it! Don't push it away just because your ego becomes a little bruised or you don't want to give up being the pack leader.

It's also a wonderful gift to your child. It lets him/her know that you admire them and have confidence in them when you listen to and/or accept their counsel. What an empowering experience for a child to know how much they've succeeded in their parent's eyes. What a boost to their self-confidence. That's probably one of the things they crave the most.

Remember to thank them. Remember to verbalize how proud of them you are. Too many parents forget to do so. Be aware of the gift you are giving each other. Not all parents get such a reward in the later stage of their lives.

Impatience (February 18, 2016)

Do you "fly off the handle" on a regular basis? Do you know others who do? As I get older, I find myself becoming more and more impatient. I get antsy when I have to wait for service; I feel irritated with inane chatter; I'm uptight when anything takes too long. It's hard to remain patient when others are inefficient, screw up, or are lackadaisical.

I've never been particularly patient, but I'm getting worse. Does that happen to others, or am I the only one? My gut as well as stories I've heard and personal observations suggest that it's common in the boomer and senior demographics.

What does impatience do for the practitioner? Does it really make the inciting situation any better? What is the downside of such behavior? When I do it, it just causes me to be more upset for a longer period of time. When I am the recipient of it, I become angry and feel like defending myself or engaging in payback. Impatience is a destructive emotion to the sender and to the receiver.

Certainly, one cause of impatience has to do with aging. Another contributing factor, though, may be living in a technological world. We have become used to immediate gratification in so many areas that did not exist in previous times. We can grab our smart phones and find out within seconds the answer to almost anything that used to require consulting an expert or making a physical trip to the library. We can communicate instantly by email what used to require a letter or a phone call with its concomitant telephone tag games and actual conversation starting with time-wasting niceties.

Living in a town or city of thousands or millions, however, still requires patience. None of us can get immediate gratification on everything. We still have to wait our turn in the queue. So, what do we do when we become impatient?

As many do, we can whip out our technology to entertain us, burying our heads in virtual reality. But, here's another, old fashion idea: we can actually look around and enjoy our environment. We might watch a child play as we wait in line at the bank; feel the rain, the sun, the wind as it touches our skin while walking from the parking lot to our doctor's appointment; observe the passersby and notice what they look like, what they are wearing, how they behave; listen to conversation while we wait for service at a retail establishment; and on and on.

There's a free floor show out there, folks. From time to time, don't forget to check out the non-virtual world, also known as the real world. You may find it far more fascinating, enlightening, and instructive than staring at little rectangular devices. And the upside is that it helps you to be more patient which is so much better than the opposite.

The Power of Touch (February 4, 2016)
Touch is one of our five major senses. We usually don't think about it because the senses of sight and hearing seem so much more important. They are, of course, but don't underestimate

the power of touch. It allows us to experience temperatures, textures, pressure, and other tactile sensations.

Touch also helps make human connection. When communicating with another, we often include touching: patting someone on the hand, poking them in the chest, clapping them on the back. We use such expressions as: touch a nerve, touch base, and touchy to describe feelings and behaviors.

It feels good to be touched and to touch another. We do it in intimate contact as well as social communication. We shake hands to connect more closely upon greeting each other. We link arms when walking which both helps us steady ourselves and feel closer to our companion. We may tap a listener on the hand or arm to emphasize a point which not only commands attention but also conveys a closer feeling between the two parties.

We derive comfort from touch. Parents touch their children as much as possible, or should, conveying to them a feeling of protection and love. Animals touch each other in herds, packs, pods, and all the other collectives, conveying a sense of belonging to a group. I saw a lovely video a while ago showing the first steps of different baby animals including the human kind. I remember the long black tongue of the giraffe mother licking her newborn to encourage it to try standing up. Other mothers of various breeds did the same or similar, sometimes nuzzling their young. None stood back while their offspring struggled alone. Touching them was urgent to aid in their progress.

We as self-contained, I'm-just-for-myself human beings can connect to one another using touch when other means are not within our comfort zone. For example, clapping someone on the shoulder encourages them. Holding hands enables bonding.

Another form of feel-good touching is hugging. There's a camaraderie to that gesture. Hugging friends or even acquaintances in a non-threatening but heartfelt way conveys a warmth, an acceptance. Hugging upon the initial encounter as well as the termination sends a message: "I'm happy to see you," or "It's been so nice being with you."

Check out the wonderful, online video of a man in a well-trafficked, London square holding up a sign saying, FREE HUGS. People regarded him strangely at first, but soon someone took him up on his offer. Within a short time, a crowd gathered, and he had a lot of takers. Everyone seemed to be positive, upbeat, and enjoying the experience.

Some people have grown up in situations where touch was very limited, or touch feels offensive to them. If that describes you, practice slowly to bring touch into your life. Start with just one quick tap with your fingertip on another person's hand or knee during a conversation. Take baby steps to increase your touch contact with others.

Don't forget the importance of touch. Incorporate it into your life. It's a win-win for both the touchor and the touchee. Start touching people in a non-threatening yet warm, caring manner. It's a benefit for each party to the transaction.

Take Time for Those Less Fortunate (January 24, 2016)

Most of us are normal physically and mentally. Most of us are so much more adept than the disabled, disfigured, handicapped, or less competent in our society. Can we stop our busy lives for a moment or two to connect with another, less fortunate human being? Can we take an instant to be kind to those in that group? Can we be grateful that we can share of ourselves?

Yes, we can. Yes, we must. Probably, most of us have been touched by someone in our lives who was born disabled or became so through illness, disease, or an accident. I have, and it has made me humble, made me so much better than the self-absorbed teenager I once was.

Do you ever wonder how you escaped that fate and it befell another? We have an obligation to be kind and gentle to such people. A variation of a famous expression attributed to sixteenth century preacher, John Bradford, is: "There but for the grace of God go I."

If you encounter a disabled person when you're out and about, approach them and make a point of saying "hello." Compliment them on something, anything: "That's a nice shirt you're wearing," "That color looks so attractive on you," "I like your smile," "It's nice to meet you." Touch them: shake their hand; pat them on the arm or shoulder. That could make their day. It could also make yours.

Maybe when your turn comes to be less able than you are now, and it will come, someone will take a moment to engage you. How wonderful that will feel. After all, inside, you're still that nice, creative, competent person you once were, or at least you feel that way.

I have a dear friend who has severe Parkinson's disease. I remember how feisty she used to be. I remember our days of riding our bicycles along the bike path at Santa Monica Beach. Now, I visit her from time to time at her assisted living home.

I call her as often as possible to chat for a moment. The conversation is short, simple, and not world shaking. However, it brightens both our days.

Stop your very important business to connect with someone who will appreciate it so much. Make time to give of yourself. It will reap benefits to you.

Rekindling Toxic Relationships (January 13, 2016)

Have you ever had a friendship or relationship end because it was too toxic, often anxiety provoking, or the cons greatly outweighed the pros—you know the drill? It has probably happened to all of us. It might involve a relative, a friend, a spouse, a significant other, a parent, a child, etc. When you look back, you realize that you're better off out of that relationship. Some time may pass, years even, and without him or her in your life, you become aware that you've grown–you're healthier.

But, when life gets boring or you feel lonely, you may think about reaching out to that person. After all, there was something about the relationship that was magnetic, that brought experiences or qualities into your life that you craved. Conversely, one day the other party might reach out to you, trying to rekindle the relationship? They, too, probably miss what they gained from their involvement with you.

Perhaps you'll get a phone message, a Facebook friend request, a letter, or some other means of communication. Maybe you'll have mixed feelings, remembering the good times as well as the painful ones. If it happens when you're in a vulnerable place in your life, however, you might start focusing on how nice it would feel to bask in the warmth of those sunny days again. The temptation is great to click that "accept" button on the friend request. After all, what harm can a little social media communication do?

Before you jump back in, take a breath or two or ten or a thousand. Assess why the relationship fell apart in the first place. Remember how the bad times began to dominate. Do you really think the other individual has changed enough to no longer behave as they once did? Have you changed enough to no longer let it bother you? What benefit is it to you to resurrect the relationship? Might it soon devolve into the toxicity that characterized it the last time? There are all kinds of expressions describing this scenario including, "let sleeping dogs lie."

The most important thing is for you to remain healthy. The pain following the termination of a close relationship lasts quite a while and regurgitates regularly as experiences spark memories. If you have finally reached a point of well-being, why would you want to put yourself back in that stressful position?

"Well, people can change," you might say. Yes, that's true. However, there is a limit to how much anyone can change. Consider if that particular person could have changed enough to become a positive rather than a negative influence in your life? Think about how many people you know or know about who keep reconciling only to split up again and again. Be careful before you grab at hopes and wishes which are not now and never were reality.

BLOG POSTS FROM 2015

Be Careful What You Wish for (December 30, 2015)

Yes, 'tis the season for wishes. We wished for presents on Christmas, Hanukkah, and at other sacred and secular ways of celebrating this holiday time. Perhaps you blew out candles at your birthday and made a wish as I did. New Year is approaching, and we're now making New Year's resolutions which are also wishes: I want to lose ten pounds, start writing that novel, get a new car, hairdo, nose... Often, attaining that wish or desire only makes us want something else. When are we ever satisfied? When are we okay with what we already have–with what we already are?

There is nothing wrong with setting goals and working toward them. The problem comes when you are never fulfilled, always striving for the next thing–the not yet attained. The basis of those seemingly unattainable aspirations is not being okay with yourself.

A while ago, I was complaining to a friend about who knows what, and she responded, "Be careful what you wish for." I've thought about that many times. Yes, you might get that coveted thing you yearn for or envy in others: an object, attention, recognition, fame, money, power, etc. However, follow its logical progression. What also comes with that gain? There might be responsibilities, expectations, requirements, additional baggage, and other unwanted consequences.

People with lots of toys must maintain them, warehouse

them, upgrade them—all time and cost consuming. People with a plethora of attention often burn out and yearn for privacy and a spare moment to themselves. People with a high status are objects of constant expectations by others: attend our affair, donate to our cause, do this, do that. People with great wealth must expend tremendous effort handling and manipulating it; maintaining vigilance so others don't siphon it off; and keeping current with new changes and advances to be sure their money does not dribble away unknowingly, lost in a technology void somewhere.

If you're dissatisfied with your current life, envy another, or pine for something else, think about what goes along with it. Or, perhaps you have thoughts such as, *When can I get off this speeding highway and just rest?* If so, consider how important it really is to keep up with the proverbial Joneses or the currently trendy Kardashians? Are you really inferior or deprived if you don't? Who decides this? How about if it's you?

Renovations (December 15, 2015)

Our lives are filled with good times and bad times, ups and downs, positives and negatives. Way too often, we focus on the negatives and forget that we ever had any positives.

Some years ago, my high school graduating class had its fiftieth anniversary reunion. I wasn't going to miss that! Five decades after graduating high school, I was a completely different person. No longer the withdrawn, scared, worried-about-what-everyone-is-thinking-of-me teenager I had been, I was confident and comfortable with myself. I wanted to attend the event to expose myself to peers who had intimidated me so long ago—to test myself. I wanted to see how others had turned out and whether they had been as frightened and bewildered as I had at that vulnerable age.

What happened unexpectedly was that I connected with fellow students I had not been friends with back then and re-connected with some I had. In this late stage of our lives, we have formed adult friendships—senior friendships, as though fifty years had not even passed.

We get together periodically, share old times, and laugh about current times. We met one time at Clifton's cafeteria, an old standard in downtown Los Angeles where so many of us had eaten as children and teenagers. It had been closed for renovations for some years and recently reopened. Of course, a few of my high school classmates and I had to check it out. We each shared our remembrances of the old Clifton's and marveled at how the renovations have been true to the origi-nal while adding modern, updated features.

Can we renovate ourselves? Can we add new, modern, updated features to our own mix while remaining true to the original? I'm not advocating a quick fix such as a vacation, elective surgery, a new house, a new car, a new whatever. I'm suggesting behavior changes, confidence building changes, connecting and reconnecting changes.

Think about the good times in your life. Think about the positive things that have happened to you. See if you can re-connect with them and bask in them. Save them and build on them to enhance yourself. Be the same but even better. Too hard, you say? I say, all you have to do is want it, and then let yourself do it.

Trees Afire (December 7, 2015)

Oranges and reds, pale greens, golds, pinks, and yellows. These are the shades of nature in November in the beautiful retirement community where I have been staying. They are the trees changing their colors in the fall season. Not natives, not wild, but breathtaking, cultivated imports that calm the mind, distract the thoughts, share their peace.

Those magnificent, arboreal giants dressed in their autumn costumes stand in line like belles at a ball waiting to be claimed by the next partner on their dance cards. Their falling leaves float down like rainbow flakes, surrounding me gently as I walk, treading on the ones that have already made it to the ground.

It is my first experience living with this particular free gift of nature. I'm a Southern California girl, not used to such a display. Some of you have probably grown up with this magnificence. Even so, I can't believe it ever gets old. As I drive down the streets, I'm constantly pulling over to snap another photograph. One is not enough; certainly ten is not enough. Snap, snap, snap as my cell phone battery runs lower and lower.

I've tried to visit such places in years past. However, I've never hit it dead on, always arriving when just a few branches show a bit of color or the trees are already bare. I like it; I love it! I must have more of this in my life.

What I saw when I looked out of the window of my rented condo was a tree afire—a metaphor of what we must do for ourselves. There are many profound aphorisms and proverbs to that point. These days, they are bundled into a less dramatic term: self-motivation.

How do we do that; how do we motivate ourselves to press on, to keep going when we're down, discouraged, or times are hard? Yes, it's so difficult, but think of the alternative. That's even harder. Pulling inward, ducking down–burying your head in the sand, your hands, the pillow, a bottle. No, don't do that; be kind to yourself. Give yourself permission to move ahead, to try for what you've always wanted.

We're so afraid to take that step. We're frightened of the possibility of failure and even more frightened of the possibility of success. What would you say to your son, your daughter, your grandchildren, the kid next door? Why is it always for others but never for you? You deserve a shot just like everyone else.

The Power of Clothing (November 19, 2015)

"Clothes make the man." It's true; dressing in a specific manner affects how we feel. We wear different clothes for different occasions.

When we put on a pair of jeans, we're of a casual, getting-ready-for-physical-work mindset. When we dress in formal wear, we get into the spirit of a party or special occasion. A bathing suit prepares us mentally to go swimming or to the beach. All of those articles, of course, can be worn for other things, but we've associated a particular behavior with each, and our thoughts go to that place. Some people have their favorite jacket, gloves, hat, or some such item to relax them, stimulate them, get them ready for some specific undertaking.

Buddhist monks wear soft-colored, lightweight, non-binding garb–so much easier for prayer and deep contemplation. Business people arrive at work in suits and ties to present a certain persona. Many jobs require employees to wear uniforms often with accompanying badges or insignias to establish expectations on the part of both the wearer and the observer. When I come home from a taxing day with no plans to go out again, I usually change into my old, comfy robe and slippers. Instant calm and tranquility!

Children know all about this. I love to watch my young granddaughters playing dress-up as they dive into a basket of well-worn, "fancy" clothes which they use to concoct outfits for themselves. Princess and fairy are the favorites this week. They are transformed into the role, staying in character while wearing their costumes.

Clothing tells a story. It conveys profession, attitude, pursuit, leaning, wealth, poverty, and on and on. People are judged by their clothing. It is often the first thing noticed by others.

Manufacturers and the advertising industry are very aware of the power of clothing, and it has made them rich. For example, as each new sport catches on, clothing companies create a line of wear which they tout as essential for that activity. Remember when you could just climb on a bicycle and ride off? My preferred dress to cruise down the bike path at Santa Monica Beach as a teenager was a tee-shirt and jeans with a cord tied around each ankle to keep the bottoms from getting caught in the bicycle chain. Now, the sporting goods stores sell form-fitting Spandex pants, matching shirts, bicycle helmets, special gloves, and more. First, you have to buy the bicycle for hundreds of dollars. Next, you have to fork out hundreds more just to get on the thing.

It's unsure whether special clothing for the task at hand justifies the cost or whether it's just an image we've succumbed to perpetrated by Madison Avenue types. The point, however, is that clothing does put us in a particular mental mode and affects how we feel about ourselves as we perform the designated behavior. That's not necessarily good or bad. It's just something to be aware of.

Help yourself reach a desired state of mind. Wear clothing that assists you in getting there.

People Whisperer (November 3, 2015)

Buck Brannaman was the model for the 1998 movie *The Horse Whisperer* starring Robert Redford. He was a man with a sensitive way who could "talk" to horses, calm them down, gentle them.

Can a horse be a People Whisperer? I think so because I met one. We were a group from the Horse Enthusiast's Club who took a behind-the-scenes tour at a local race track.

We saw the trainers trotting the young horses around the track, accompanying them astride an older, more experienced horse. We watched the horses being bathed, swaddled in blankets, and hooked to a huge, circular device called a hot walker reminiscent of old-fashioned, revolving clotheslines. This allowed them to walk slowly around in a circle to relax and cool down their muscles after a demanding workout on the track.

We then went into the stable area where some horses were in their individual stalls with their heads and necks poking out over the half doors. That's where we met the "people whisperer," a three-year-old, thoroughbred filly aptly named: She's a Charmer, and she was. That sweet equine refused the horse treats offered to her, instead placing her head against the chest of any of us who approached her. When it was my turn,

I was relaxed, calm, and in the moment as I cuddled with She's a Charmer.

We were so enamored with our new, hoofed friend that we hatched a rescue scheme. We would each contribute a like amount of money and buy her, freeing her from her life as a racehorse and bringing her into our fold. Although soon abandoning our plan as completely unrealistic for an almost thousand pound, high maintenance animal, we have continued to think about her, talk about her, and check up on her. These endeavors alone perpetuate the contentment and good feelings she brought to each of us.

Horses are used as therapy animals for the disabled, children with emotional or behavioral problems, and veterans with post-traumatic stress disorder. There have been wonderful stories of bonding between autistic people and horses. Yes, their size might seem intimidating. However, just being in their presence is a privilege and can be soul-cleansing.

Try hanging around with horses. See if their magic works on you.

Moving Along (October 21, 2015)

It's scary to try new things, especially when they are big things. Any major life change, even a positive one, creates anxiety. The more the change diverges from your usual routine, the more intimidating it is.

I'm on a new adventure right now. I'm trying out an active retirement community hundreds of miles from where I've lived since childhood. I've been here a few weeks, and I have another few months to go before I return to my comfort level back in my own home and neighborhood.

Everything about this experience is a challenge. Nothing comes automatically; nothing is routine. I have to concentrate on each thing I do, each place I go. I'm constantly confronted with big learning curves: how to find my way around this community, where to buy food, how to work the convection oven (thank you Google for a convection converter), and so much more—sigh.

Why am I doing this? I've thought to myself more than once.

The answer: because I want to live near my son and his wife and children (my adorable grandchildren); because if I'm ever going to do it, I must do it while I'm still healthy. I want to make this work if I possibly can. So, I stumble on, and each day it gets just a bit easier.

On the upside, I'm having experiences I've never had before. I've encountered wild turkeys wandering around the neighborhood. What a delight! Of course, I had to follow them as I whipped out my cell phone to take photo after photo. Where I live in the heart of a large, metropolitan city, I've never even seen a wild turkey. I've also seen deer here. As far as I'm concerned, one can never see enough deer.

What was so strange just a few weeks ago has become less so. I have attended a few club meetings, classes, and events which tap into things that interest me (acting, writing, horses, and more). I made a few acquaintances who have the potential of becoming friends. I bought a senior subway card. I have navigated my way around using the amazing GPS technology. There were and continue to be lots of getting lost moments, lots of screw ups–typical trial and error when everything is unfamiliar or unknown.

I can feel my progress; I'm moving forward. I'm beginning to enjoy where I am and seeing it as my possible future. I'm proud of myself for undertaking this journey. Just the doing of it gives me strength and the confidence that I can succeed.

Start thinking whether it's time for you to make new plans for the rest of your life. Make decisions rather than avoiding them. Take action and move forward. It's hard, but with persistence, it does become easier.

Getting Noticed (October 6, 2015)
We all want attention of some kind for all sorts of things in our lives: personal, social, business, and more. The competition to get noticed is vicious.

What are you willing to do to get noticed? Rachel Dolezal, an American author, passed herself off as being black even though she was born of white parents. A few years ago, a white, male poet, Michael Derrick Hudson, submitted a poem under an Asian, female pen name and got his work published after it had been rejected numerous times under his real name. There has been a lot of online chatter in writer's groups as to whether what he did is ethical. In my opinion, these moves are probably not any less ethical than what George Eliot (over 150 years ago) or J.K. Rowling (of modern day "Harry Potter" fame) did to disguise their sex and maybe give the impression that they were male, thereby offering them a better chance to be noticed, so their thinking probably went.

People use a plethora of methods to get attention onto themselves: unusual dress, affecting an odd laugh, dying their hair, talking loudly or excessively, becoming a great dancer, intellectual and academic achievement, and on and on. There's not necessarily anything right or wrong with any of these methods or hundreds of others you may think of. However, some might not be within your comfort zone or might bring about the opposite result by driving attention away instead of attracting it. The secret is to find the thing that is your particular style and accomplishes your purpose. How do you do that?

First you have to identify methods that work for you in your quest for that elusive attention you're seeking. Gather ideas from reading magazines, newspapers, and books. Do research by going to the library, navigating the Internet or networking (asking friends, relatives, acquaintances, and even strangers for advice). Finally, observe what others do. Try out in small ways and in safe places those things that appeal to you. See how they feel. Discard the ones that don't work. For those that do, ramp them up and try them out in more places—cut a broader swath.

If what you're doing is not illegal and isn't hurting anyone else or yourself, keep at it. If you find that you're getting the payback you're seeking, go for it!

Jargon (September 23, 2015)

"Manny-petty" was the word (or was it a phrase?) that the woman yelled out to me from the back of the crowded room after I walked into the nail salon. I thought she was speaking another language and for some reason assumed I was fluent in it, too.

"What," I shouted back, not understanding what she was talking about?

"Manny-petty?" she repeated in her singsong manner.

I finally got it; she was saying: mani-pedi, salon-speak for manicure-pedicure. She had boiled our pending transaction down to its essence.

"No, just mani," I responded, getting into the trendy shorthand; I'm a fast learner.

Each job, profession, avocation, pastime, pursuit or hobby has its own jargon. One must learn it to survive and thrive there.

I had been booked for a hand modeling job for jewelry. (Yes, even aging hands are sometimes needed for such gigs.) I had only had a professional manicure a few times in my life, the last being at least two decades ago. I didn't even know where to go and had to call friends for referrals.

I've always manicured my own nails, never liking other people fussing with my body for cosmetic purposes. (I'm not crazy about doctors or dentists either, but that's a whole other blog.) I don't do well with massages, and even encounters with shoe salesmen are iffy.

Somehow, I feel that by being the one serviced, I'm being placed in a position of privilege being attended by underlings and putting the one delivering the service in a subservient position. I even cut and style my own hair–natural curls are very forgiving to answer your question.

A glance around the salon revealed a lot of clients with one hand on a small table being worked on by a manicurist while in too many cases the other hand held a cell phone jammed against its appropriate ear. Several of these princesses also had their feet on small stools with cotton crammed between their toes to hold them apart while another worker took care of the pedi part.

Help! Let me out of here. This is not my world.

My inquirer and all of her fellow manicurists were Asian, and I remembered reading that the industry has become dominated by immigrant Vietnamese women, at least in Los Angeles, California. With limited English skills and a need to support themselves and their families, they have found a niche. With niches comes jargon. In this case, their opening line is: mani-pedi, thereby avoiding a long, taxing discussion in English which might be a challenge.

I soon overcame my aversion to the experience as I watched the manicurists working efficiently while laughing and chatting with each other in their native tongue. I don't know if they felt demeaned being in a position of cosmetically servicing the digits of others. However, while I was there, they seemed calm, pleasant, dedicated to their task, and proud of their work.

Can we learn to be like that, even when we are tasked with work duties we don't like or that others consider undesirable or demeaning? Yes, we can. Use jargon to help you do it. A stewardess has become a flight attendant, no longer an airborne, female server of food, drinks, and pillows, but now a position for both genders and a part of an integrated flight team. Garbage collectors have become sanitary engineers–same job, different mindset. Try a change of jargon to elevate and enhance yourself.

Meandering (September 8, 2015)

What a wonderful word: meandering. It evokes thoughts such as: lazy times, no pressure, free flowing.

I was on vacation last month at a dude ranch in Wyoming. I spent a lot of time atop my black steed, Prince, a gentle giant who had been matched to my riding ability. As our little group headed by our guide was meandering through an Aspen grove, the Grand Tetons mountain range was our backdrop. That package really pulled my attention away from the usual stuff crowding my brain.

We all need to meander occasionally, some more, some less. We use other terms to describe it: downtime, chilling out, having your own space, etc. You don't have to travel to another country, to another state, or even to another city to meander. You don't even have to do it on horseback. You can meander anywhere, even at home and in many different ways. Meandering can happen while reading a good book, making a new recipe, strolling through a store, anything that diverts the mind from the usual stuff.

Sometimes, when I am overwhelmed by the demands of life, I take what I like to call a "mental vacation." I cancel my appointments, put on hold any serious decision making, and clear my life of everything that causes pressure. Just a day or two usually does it for me. Even a few hours of mental meandering can be significant.

Conversely, too much unstructured behavior can be destructive. We can find ourselves drifting, without purpose, unstimulated. We must seek that balance so we don't work ourselves to misery, but we also don't lead purposeless lives.

It takes discipline to put aside everything jockeying for your attention and get into meandering mode, but it's worth it. Find stimulating, meaningful, fulfilling work and activities with just enough meandering time to regenerate.

It's the Right Thing to Do (August 25, 2015)
Why am I making an effort to conserve water when it's being wasted, squandered or stolen by others? Why am I still seeing so many very green lawns around my neighborhood in Los Angeles, California?

Within a one week period while driving, I came upon two broken water pipes, one in Beverly Hills and one in Sherman Oaks. The precious water was rushing down the street into gutters.

There was a news item a few months ago about someone filling up a water tank truck from a municipal water faucet and driving it to a property outside of that municipality for use in watering an orchard. I was so incensed that I wrote a letter to the editor of the Los Angeles Times newspaper which they printed in the Opinion Section.

The answer to my question at the beginning of this post: Because, for me, it's the right thing to do. Don't let your actions be dictated by the behavior of others. When you feel something is wrong, don't opt for that choice just because someone else does.

Live your life on the moral path that's right for you. Don't live it always trying to get away with something, trying to screw the next guy before he screws you, always worrying about being caught. You will feel better about yourself and glide more smoothly as you go. Play nice on the playground even when others don't.

Fortune Cookie Says (August 7, 2015)
My friends and I had just finished dinner at a local Asian restaurant. We moved to the obligatory next step and opened our fortune cookies.

"Here, Lee Gale, write a blog about this," suggested Sheila as she handed me her fortune.

The thin slip of paper said: "Develop an appreciation for the present moment." I put it in my wallet and forgot about it. A few weeks later, I noticed it hiding between a one-dollar and five-dollar bill.

What shall I write, what shall I write? I pondered.

Some days later, I had parked my car in the underground parking lot of my neighborhood corner shopping center and was running for the elevator. I squeezed in just as the doors were starting to close thinking, *Whew, I made it. These stupid elevators take so long to come.*

I turned around to face front as all good elevator riders are taught as children when I noticed an obese, crippled woman walking toward us. Without even thinking about it, my arm shot up between the doors and broke their pending contact, almost breaking my arm in the process. I forced the doors open and said, "Don't rush. We'll wait for you." Of course, I hadn't polled the other passengers, but I noticed one looking at me, smiling, and nodding. The lesson was that the present moment had presented me with an opportunity to do something nice for someone else and to feel good about myself—

no, proud of myself.

The woman stepped into the elevator and thanked me. Maybe she's used to people helping her out. She's also probably used to people ignoring her or even berating her for delaying them as they go about their busy and important agendas.

We exchanged a few idle, ice-breaker words as the elevator took off. When it arrived at her floor, she thanked me again as she exited. It should have been me who thanked her. I am sure I walked a few inches taller until bedtime.

Get some of those good feelings for yourself. It's easy; just be kind to others. Your acts might even splash onto bystanders, too, and remind them to slow down and appreciate the present moment.

Dare to Be Colorful (July 26, 2015)

Some know how to swath themselves in color; some don't. Have you ever noticed people who dress only in neutral or drab colors: blacks, whites, grays, beiges, browns, pale blues? Or, maybe you dress that way.

I've always wondered if those people feel they don't deserve to shine. Maybe they don't want to attract attention to themselves. Their color palettes often match their personalities.

In physics, color is a function of a specific wavelength of visible light. Black and white are not considered colors since they do not have specific wavelengths. White is made up of all wavelengths of visible light, and black is the absence of visible light.

We use the word color to denote a certain lightheartedness such as colorful jokes which are risqué, daring, and fun.

We describe something as being off-color if it is somewhat offensive. I've heard it said that color makes a statement, whereas lack of color only makes a suggestion.

There is a medical condition occurring mostly in the winter called seasonal affective disorder (SAD) where low light causes depression in those who suffer from it. One of the treatments is exposure to light boxes, which are small walls of light.

Color and light are uplifting, perky, jazzy, exciting. Color can be visual, auditory, emotional, and more. Some people dream in color.

A neurological phenomenon called synesthesia is where stimulation of one sensory or cognitive pathway creates automatic, involuntary experiences in a second such pathway. So, synesthetes (people with this ability) may feel, hear, or taste color, and it may aid their creative process. Artists such as Franz Liszt, Vincent Van Gogh, and Leonard Bernstein were synesthetes.

If your comfort zone won't allow you to dress colorfully, at least bring color into your life in other ways: flowers (not just white ones), colorful paintings, tropical fish, etc. Dare to lighten up; dare to brighten up; dare to make a statement. Maybe color will aid your creative process or at least bring some cheer into your life, and one additional perk: it's free!

NOTE: My response to comments from some of my blog followers:

1. What a shame that China used to encourage (or maybe still does) dark, drab colors for women over forty. That is so in many cultures of the world. Even more

shameful is when those women acquiesce, assuming that someone else knows better what is good or appropriate for them (like our fashion and cosmetics industries here). We need to start a movement: "Senior Women Are People, Too."

2. Another follower felt that senior women should not wear flashy colors but instead should dress conservatively exemplified by a black dress with pearls. Of course, I am not advocating neon chartreuse when I talk about celebrating color. Here was my response: I did not suggest that seniors should only dress in "flashy" colors. I certainly agree that a lovely black dress with white pearls can be striking. I have a few black and white outfits. What I'm talking about is the person who always dresses in a drab manner. I believe color can be uplifting to a person, and the constant choice of drab hues in clothing can be depressing. If, for example, you choose a black or brown suit, you could wear a nice blouse or scarf or jewelry with tasteful colors instead of a gray or beige blouse which makes you look all one color. Just because you're a senior doesn't mean that the rejuvenating benefit of color is not for you. The constant avoidance of color by some people deprives them of a small, uplifting bump in their lives. I suspect that most of these people are not even aware they're avoiding color.

Participate in Stimulating Experiences (July 11, 2015)

There are many ways to bring joy, excitement, and purpose

into your life. One thing I try to do is grab opportunities to be involved in stimulating experiences.

For ten years starting in 2005, I volunteered with a fireworks crew to set up the show on the golf course of the Big Canyon Country Club in Newport Beach, California. We built scaffolding to hold tubes for the fireworks charges. Then, we wired the tubes electrically and loaded the charges inside. An electric cord at the end of the center strip on top of the scaffolding was then plugged into a battery operated motherboard which was used to control the firing of the charges. That was a long explanation for something that might seem mundane or unimportant to some. To me and maybe a few of you, however, it was fascinating.

A few years ago, I worked the motherboard during the fireworks show. That was a real high! Think of the Wizard of Oz sitting at his control board in total charge of a display that captivated the enraptured attention of others.

The day of the fireworks shows, I leave my house at 8:00am and get home after 1:00am the following morning. It's hard work all day for no pay. *What is your reward?* you might ask. Answer: a good physical workout, stimulation in areas that excite me, a fun day at a gorgeous location, camaraderie with the other crew members, chow on hand the entire day, a fantastic seat for the fireworks show, and a satisfying sense of accomplishment.

Repayment doesn't always have to be monetary. Sometimes, it's worth doing a thing just for the pleasure of doing it. Find those kinds of opportunities for yourself. Live your life for the sheer joy of it.

Battling the Inevitability of Aging (June 26, 2015)

"Nothing is certain but death and taxes." We've all heard that quotation or a variation of it. Usually, the path to that certainty of death is aging. So, how do we deal with it?

Like most things in life, we have choices. We can rail against aging, try to defeat it, or accept it. No matter which method we chose, however, we can't avoid it.

Today, with so many tricks of medicine and technology at our disposal, people try to pretend that they are not aging. There is makeup to allow us to hide blemishes, enhance dull features, or just sparkle; hair dye to avoid revealing that telltale gray; hair implants to reverse balding; plastic surgery to do away with sagging skin; contact lenses to make the correction of poor sight invisible; hearing aids of various kinds including implants—the most invisible; clothing to make us look like teenyboppers; and shoes with too-high heels pathetically worn by women with foot problems and fragile bones teetering to keep their balance. The list goes on and on. For years, I missed much of what was being said because I refused to consider even exploring hearing aids; the idea made me feel old.

Many turn themselves into caricatures: the fake looking face which is now so common it's almost a norm; the old guy with the too-young girlfriend, another almost norm; the baby boomer with the too tight pants and tee shirt. So, do we keep chasing after that elusive youth, do we just throw up our hands and let whatever happens happen, or do we choose some middle path? Each person must make that decision for him/herself, of course.

Let's consider one additional factor: happiness. Are we happy with ever escalating procedures, devices, and fashions? Some will insist they are. However, under that facade still lurks failing hips and knees, pain from arthritis, waning strength and vigor, and all the rest.

Is there a way to age gracefully and be okay with who you are? Some thoughts are: we can strive to be as healthy and fit as possible; we can dress nicely but age-appropriately; we can accept that we need glasses or hearing aids to enhance the quality of life—or a cane, or a walker, or whatever.

Let's at least try to avoid health endangering procedures such as invasive elective surgery done only to chase that hyped youth. There was a case a few years ago of the mother of a famous entertainer being rejected for cosmetic surgery by various doctors due to an existing health condition until she finally found a willing one. He did the surgery she so hungered for, and she died.

Must we put our lives or health at risk only to pretend we're something that we're not? Let's battle to be okay with who we are rather than battling against nature.

Unstressing at the Airport, One Dog at a Time (May 28, 2015)

I love dogs of all stripes, colors and persuasions. Tell me off, and if you're a human, I'll be right back at ya. Tell me off, and if you're a dog, I'll beg for more.

Whenever I see a dog anywhere, I'm drawn involuntarily as if beckoned while in a trance, powerless to resist. Just to be able to look at them, pet them, hang out with them is a privilege and calms me immediately. So, imagine my surprise a few weeks ago when I was part of the craziness that is Los Angeles International Airport.

I was waiting to board an airplane for a flight to visit my family. I had already navigated parking, walking to the terminal, checking in, and making my way to the gate. I found a place to sit in a crowded area and, with great difficulty, was trying to relax and read. I glanced up for a moment and saw a big, curly dog walking toward me followed by a few humans. Naturally, I sprung out of my seat to investigate.

I was greeted by Sofie, a Golden Doodle (Golden Retriever and Poodle mix) resplendent in a red cape, who was next to her owner. I was all over Sofie—calm, patient Sofie. Other passengers sidled up to make her acquaintance. Sofie nonchalantly tolerated her admirers—just another day's work.

Heidi Huebner, who was part of Sofie's entourage, explained that the PUP (Pets Unstressing Passengers) Program at LAX has been operating since April, 2013. For years, dogs have been used elsewhere in such duty providing stress relief and comfort to people at hospitals, homes for seniors, schools, and other similar facilities. (I used to be a pet therapy team with my dog at a local hospital.) Now, dogs are doing it at airports, those high stress generators.

The dog/owner volunteer teams are trained and then registered with Therapy Dogs, Inc. Heidi added that similar programs are now operating at 26 airports throughout the nation. To volunteer at the PUP Program and other VIP (Volunteer Information Professionals) Programs at Los Angeles International Airport, visit their website at: www.lawa.org/vip.

Now, I'm just wondering where the human Sofies are trained and registered? I need a few of those in my life.

Irritants Can Be Advantages (May 16, 2015)

Last week I was sitting at my computer, busy, busy, busy. I went to grab for my pencil, missed, and knocked it off the computer desk.

Oh, I don't need this now! I muttered to myself.

I bent over and groped for it on the floor. No luck. After a few choice expletives, I activated the flashlight on my cell phone (a nice feature BTW) and bent over even further, shining the light around.

I finally spotted the blasted pencil. Of course, it had rolled completely under my desk to the far end, tightly jammed up against the wall molding behind the computer cord, like a kitten hiding under the bed. I had to bend over to the point where my head was at the same level as my feet and reach to my arm's length to grab it. As I was doing so, I realized how good it felt to stretch my spine. My errant pencil had offered me a little free exercise.

Why can't we extrapolate those kinds of experiences to larger ones in our lives? How many times are we inconvenienced by unforeseen circumstances which annoy, irritate, or anger us? We're less able to tolerate them when we're on a deadline, tired, running late to an appointment, and on and on. That's when each of our own versions of "expletives deleted" kicks in.

Some opt for the "F" word, the "S" word, the "D" word, or the "H" word, and that's just in English. Others downplay it such as what a childhood friend's father used to say: "Oh, feathers and moose meat!" I always liked that. I wish I had found out the origin, but I was just a kid and not so fascinated by words and phrases as I am now. Anyway, that was just as powerful for him as the current popularity of the "alphabet" words.

There's that old expression, "When life hands you a lemon, make lemonade." Well, that's not just for the big, oppressive stuff of life. It can also be for the little things, too.

When something interferes with your plans for a minute, an hour, or a day, see if you can turn it into an advantage or opportunity. Don't let the small irritants you encounter take a few more seconds off your life span. Those seconds are valuable and finite. Save them for the rewarding things. If you must, throw that pencil on the floor deliberately to open new possibilities.

If You Don't Age Gracefully, Think of the Alternative–Yikes! (April 30, 2015)

Aging gracefully is hard work. We have to motivate ourselves to eat healthy, exercise, be positive, seek interesting activities, and so much more. When I begin to falter, I think of the alternative: if I eat too much junk food, I feel bad physically; if I skip exercising, my body hurts; if I get into negativity, I feel sluggish and non-productive. So, although it seems easier to just vegetate and withdraw, it's much harder in the long run.

There are many paths to aging gracefully. Some people think it's in their physical appearance alone and spend huge chunks of time and money running to hairdressers, makeup artists, plastic surgeons, clothes shopping, etc. Yes, our physical appearance is important to a degree. However, our attitude, behavior and pursuits are just as important if not more so.

A young looking, well dressed, well-coiffed outer shell is barren when matched with an angry, negative, judgmental mind-set. Such an outlook spills out and colors everything else in our lives.

Have you ever had the experience of meeting a physically attractive man or woman only to discover they had a very off-putting way of acting? You suddenly begin to notice their physical attributes that are not so attractive which you hadn't seen at first. Conversely, have you ever met someone whom you found physically unattractive, but who had a warm or charismatic personality? You soon forget about their physical appearance and are drawn to them. Remember the phenomenal success and influence of Eleanor Roosevelt, a woman who truly reinvented herself as she aged.

So, remember how fortunate you are to be alive and have the opportunity to age gracefully. Do it by working from the inside out.

Oh, I Can't Do That (April 16, 2015)

Many people encounter something new or different and say, "Oh, I can't do that." Then, there are others who say, "Oh, I can do that."

Sheila, a member of my gym, is seventy-nine years old and in the latter category. She is able to do a yoga exercise called "the plow." Sheila has never taken a yoga class. She simply saw someone a few months earlier doing that maneuver and decided to try it. Yes, Sheila has been exercising for a long time, and yes, she's naturally limber. However, she had never done the plow, but she was willing to give it a try.

Not everyone will be able to do the plow. However, maybe we can at least take a lesson from Sheila and try things that seem difficult rather than backing off immediately with an "Oh, I can't do that" attitude.

This pertains to all types of behavior, not just a yoga exercise. Do you shy away from such actions as taking a class, volunteering, or going somewhere to make new friends? That's typical behavior. It's uncomfortable to venture into the unknown. However, we miss so many opportunities and life enhancing possibilities by retreating into our comfortable cocoons.

It's so easy to automatically say, "That's too hard for me," or "I've never been good at that kind of thing," or whatever your excuse is. What about doing what Sheila did? What about seeing or hearing about something interesting and saying "I think I'll try that?" Let's work toward overcoming that little voice inside our heads that always tells us we can't do things. Remember the mantra which I've discussed before: if you think it's too hard, do it anyway!

You won't be proficient the first time you try something new. But, you can certainly work up to it. The secret is: small, manageable portions. The program is:

1. Think of something that intrigued you, but that you resisted trying with all your reasons and good excuses.
2. Approach that something with baby steps and keep at it slowly and consistently.
3. Give it a try for a given period of time, say two weeks.
4. Check your progress at the beginning and at the end.

Have you gotten a little better? Is it a bit easier?

5. Keep going and give yourself another couple of weeks to reassess.

Remember, it's not a contest, and you don't have to become an expert. The goal is to find more joy, excitement, and purpose in your life. You might not be successful in all your new endeavors, but at least you tried, which puts you a lot closer to success than not making an attempt in the first place. I promise that if you don't like it, you can always go back into your cocoon.

Hanging Out via Technology (April 3, 2015)

In my last post, I wrote about taking a break from your technology. This time I'm going to focus on a wonderful, underused way to use your technology.

Hanging-out time with a cherished person in your life is precious. Hanging out is just being together doing nothing in particular. Just the closeness, even if the conversation is minimal, unimportant, or non-existent, is nourishing.

Several years ago, I visited my aunt who lived in Las Vegas at the same time her two sons, my cousins, were visiting. Her third child, a daughter, was living in Thailand.

When we sat down to dinner, one cousin opened his laptop computer. With the click of a few buttons and the magic of Skype, he connected with his sister in Thailand. He placed his laptop on the table in front of an empty chair, and my aunt, my three cousins, and I all had dinner together. We talked, laughed, and just engaged in typical dinner patter like most families sharing a meal together. It was an amazing experience! I watched my cousin in Thailand on the computer screen as she participated in the conversation just like the rest of us.

I talk often on the phone to my son, Richard, who lives hundreds of miles away. He calls me when he has free time which can be while walking to the subway, driving to the store, or whatever.

A few days ago, I went technologically with Richard to Home Depot. He needed some wood and hardware for a cabinet he was building. I was on the Bluetooth stuck into his ear, and I could hear him talking to the salesman as well as the sound of the wood being cut on the skill saw in the background.

When Richard walked to another department, we spoke briefly about the type of cabinet handles he was looking for—nothing of great importance. I'd hear him laughing with an employee about some consideration or another dealing with the proposed cabinet. Just listening to his laughter buoyed me up.

I remember hanging out with Richard years ago when he was distributing flyers door-to-door for some neighborhood campaign he supported. I was in Los Angeles on my cell phone as he was knocking on doors and talking to neighbors hours away from me. I still remember listening to the flapping of his sandals as he walked the streets while we chatted. I was right there with him.

Hanging out with my son is a privilege, doing nothing special but just being together. Hang out with your special people whenever you get the chance. Don't terminate the telephone conversation because it doesn't seem important enough; it's valuable! Spend more time with those who cheer you up. Use the power of today's technology to help you do it.

Disconnect from Your Technology (March 18, 2015)

Do you need more quiet time in your life and can't figure out how to get it? We live in an age of too many distractions, and we are constantly multi-tasking and anxious. Everyone and everything seems to be vying for our attention. We don't even have time to think, contemplate, or wind down.

To preserve our health, both physical and mental, we must disengage periodically, preferably a few times per day. I've blogged here on similar subjects before. (See my blogs of September 9, 2014: "Scheduling Downtime," and February 28, 2014: "Decompressing in a Compression Age.") This time, I'm going to focus on our technology devices.

Many people have their cell phones hanging around their necks in phone slings so they are close to them at all times. Some of those necklace-like pouches are decorative and also serve as a fashion statement. And, how about the even trendier Bluetooth earpiece, seemingly a permanent feature protruding from an ear of some perpetually-connected types? They can't even wait the few seconds to retrieve their cell phone and push the talk button.

One long-time, close friend puts her cell phone on the table when we meet for lunch at a restaurant. The moment the phone rings, she looks at the monitor to see if it's a call she must answer. The reality is that she answers almost all calls "just in case it's something important." My reaction to that is: *What am I, chopped liver?* Obviously, that "just in case" phone call is more important than our quality time together for the hour or so we've allotted in our busy schedules.

This happened to me once on a first (and last) date. We met at a restaurant whereupon Mr. Wonderful plunked his phone next to his plate for easy access. He didn't like it one bit when I suggested that we turn off our cell phones during dinner.

I have a former friend whose motherly role to her husband and grown children included serving as the family information hub. All day, every day, her husband and children would check in with her several times on the phone, and she would convey the family news and plans from one to another. As you might guess, when I was with her, I spent a lot of time just sitting there like a lox while she waxed on via phone technology. When I once suggested that she not answer the phone during our short time together, she became distraught and defensive. As you might guess, that's why she's a former friend.

Another addiction is listening to the car radio or a CD while driving. Have you ever considered turning off those gadgets from time to time? Just ride in silence and bask in the quiet; it's rejuvenating. To help you with that task, I've found this amazing method to disconnect, which is quick, easy, and free. What more could you ask for? I've used this method for a while now and found that it works, so there's no need to check Urban Legends to see if it's a myth. With some extrapolation, it can be applied to most electronic devices. Just follow the simple instructions. With a little practice and patience, I'm sure you'll be able to grasp it. If I could, you can.

Fool proof instructions for turning off car radio:
1. Hold index finger out in pointing position.
2. Aim finger toward on/off radio knob.
3. Slowly propel arm forward until tip of finger makes contact with aforementioned knob.
4. Apply additional arm muscle pressure to compel finger to push knob.

5. Listen to determine if sound still emanating from radio. If so, start again from Step 1.

Once you've mastered your car radio, try that method on your other technology paraphernalia. They may work a bit differently, but with a little tweaking, you'll get the hang of it. Some will have to withdraw from their devices like an addict. I know it's hard, but it's also calming, liberating, and gratifying. Take charge of yourself, people! No one else will.

On Death (March 5, 2015)

Our own death is a subject that is the proverbial elephant in the room. Most people are in denial and don't want to talk about it. But, most of us in the baby boomer and senior age ranges think about it a lot. Maybe we have our own health issues, or maybe our peers and loved ones have died or are dying. We can't help thinking that we're next.

I recently talked with a friend, Dr. Janet Maker, about this subject. Janet battled breast cancer a few years ago, which had a permanent impact on her. Now in remission, she is writing a book: *The Thinking Woman's Guide to Breast Cancer: Take Charge of Your Own Recovery and Remission*, about her difficult experiences navigating the medical world. Janet feels strongly about preparing and thinking about her own death.

"I want to do it right. I don't just want to go out kicking, screaming and afraid."

Janet suspects that people avoid thinking and talking about their own death because they fear the unknown, feel sadness about losing everything they love, and have regrets about things they did or did not do.

"If you knew you were going to die tomorrow, what would you regret not having done?" she asked me.

I had never thought about it. Identifying those things might motivate people to do them. Do you feel like you have done what you came to do?

I realized that one of my needs is to help others—to give back to the community. I use my blog and my public talks as a vehicle to do so. I hadn't really identified it that way before.

Janet's pending book is toward that same end. She wants to pass along the information she learned the hard way to make it easier for women who find themselves on a similar journey with breast cancer. She also wants to bring as much joy as possible into her life. That includes being kinder to herself and others. With that goal, she plans to create an online newsletter, "Janet's Good News," where each month she will feature a person and charity that is doing something to make the world better.

What do you need to do? How might you go about doing it? When?

The Health Obsession Spiral (February 19, 2015)

Are you obsessed about your health or that of someone else such as your child, spouse, or parent? Do you always manage to work it into the conversation? People spend so much time focusing on health issues: thinking about them, reading about them, discussing them, going to doctors, taking medicine, getting treatments, and on and on.

I'm not saying people don't have legitimate conditions and concerns. Sometimes health issues totally interrupt our lives. I'm talking about becoming obsessive about it—making it into your whole life.

I don't want to use the "H" word (that's hypochondriac to you), but some people are or come pretty close. Maybe they learned that behavior as children from some influential adult in their lives who behaved that way. Or, maybe they found that they got a lot of sympathy and attention when they had ailments, and now it has just become a lifestyle without their realizing it. Those who obsess about the health of another may get attention onto themselves that way, too (shades of Munchausen by Proxy).

People who engage in this obsessive behavior seem to think that subject is also fascinating to others. One day, as she waxed on about her husband's latest health issue, a friend started discussing his bowel movements.

"Okay, stop right there," I screamed.

That snapped her back to the moment. She hadn't even realized how inappropriate her discussion had become, and that most people are simply not interested in hearing about other people's elimination patterns.

It always amazes me how often sickly people rally when there's something fun or interesting to do. They manage to get themselves dressed and to an event, and they don't seem to think about their health issues until the event is over.

The constant discussion of health issues weighs on me, whether my own or the health of others. Does it on you? Or, are you the one who discusses it ad nauseam, totally ignoring those raised eyebrows or glazed looks in the eyes of anyone within the sound of your voice?

When I was a young mother, much of my conversation centered around my children including their health issues. I'd discuss with other mothers things like pediatricians, shots, and typical childhood illnesses. It often got to be a subtle pissing contest of "my pediatrician is better than your pediatrician." I learned then that those types of discussions become tiresome, to me anyway. As people get older, many focus more on their own health and play a version of "my health problems are worse than your health problems." Another popular game is "my therapist said" as I get often from a relative who uses it as her weapon of choice to beat any opponent into submission. Therapy can be very beneficial. However, used in that manner, it is counterproductive.

Then, there's the crowd that focuses on the health of their pets. I was at a luncheon recently, and some of the women there lapsed into discussing the size and consistency of their dogs' poop. Although I love dogs and all animals for that matter, there are some issues about them I'm not interested in discussing.

In her final years, my mother's only focus became her declining health. It was all she wanted to talk about, and she'd get angry if we didn't want to discuss it constantly. On the other hand, there was my friend, Priscilla. She refused to give in to her cancer; she rarely discussed it. Four months before she died, I went on a trip to Alaska with her and another friend. Yes, Priscilla had to rest more than we did. Yes, she was sometimes quiet. However, she participated in activities to the best of her ability and got real joy from the beauty around her.

I have another friend with serious Parkinson's disease.

She calls me to give me book recommendations. When I ask her how she is, her answer is usually, "fine."

When my dog and I were a pet therapy team visiting patients at a local hospital, the patients usually perked up when we came in and forgot about their health issues for the five or ten minutes we were there. The diversion took their minds off their conditions.

If you have health issues, you don't have to moan and dump on others as a regular practice. You can create your own diversionary activities and make yourself into someone people want to visit and be with rather than avoid.

I'm not implying that health issues aren't important nor advocating ignoring them. What I'm saying is that there must be something else of value in life than just that. Certainly talk about your health briefly from time to time, but be sensitive to whether others want to hear long, detailed discussions about it. Consider the reverse: are you really interested in a constant diet of hearing that type of information from them?

Being a Good Listener (February 5, 2015)
Are we all buzzing around on send-mode but rarely on receive-mode? My forty-four-year-old son taught me this distinction. One time, when he was upset about something and was telling me about it, I immediately segued into my problem solving role. He became irritated and defensive.

"Mom, I don't want you to fix it. I just want you to listen."

I'm definitely a problem solver—the "fix-it" type. Are you that type? Do you find that when you're just trying to help someone with your sage advice, worldly wisdom, or unsolicited opinion, they become defensive and suddenly dump all their anger on you? Maybe they don't want your advice, wisdom, or opinion. Maybe they just need to rant.

Learning to be a good listener is an art. That's why counselors, therapists, life-coaches, etc. get paid the big bucks. They have mastered the art of just listening with an occasional "oh," or "uh-huh," or "I see."

Occasionally, we all need a sounding board. There isn't necessarily a solution to what we're upset about. We just want to verbalize it. Somehow, doing so to the wall or a chair just doesn't cut it. Why an inert human being hearing our angry commentary seems so comforting is a mystery. Maybe it just makes us feel valid that another sentient being, preferably a human one, cares enough to spend time with us and just listen.

Now, when my son discusses something that is bothering him and I slip into fix-it mode, I try hard to remember to ask, "Do you want my input, or do you just want me to be a good listener?" I don't always catch myself and am still a work-in-progress, but when I do, it has avoided so many arguments, misunderstandings, and hurt feelings. I show that I'm being supportive, that I respect him for being able to handle it himself, and that I'm not being intrusive.

Try it, even if you have to put a piece of tape over your mouth while you're doing so. It may save a lot of friction in your relationships.

Having a Bad Day (January 19, 2015)

Have you ever had a bad day? I can almost guarantee the answer is, "yes." I don't think anyone can get through this life without having one. Well, last week I had a doozy. I set my alarm for 7:30am to allow plenty of time to get dressed, have breakfast, and drive carefully over a one-lane, winding, canyon road to pick up my friend for a writers' club meeting.

She answered the door dressed in an old sweat suit.

"It's tomorrow, Lee Gale."

"What?" I responded without comprehension.

After she repeated it a few more times knocking me out of my denial, I fished out my calendar book. Yup, she was right. I had arrived at her house a full twenty-four hours before our date.

I couldn't believe it; I was really bummed out. I didn't have anything to do until 11:30am. I could have slept another few hours; I could have avoided a twelve-mile drive via a treacherous route; I could have done a million other things with my life.

I did some shopping to kill the time and made my way back over that horrible canyon road, fighting a traffic snag which made me late. When I got to the restaurant for my real first appointment that day, all the parking spaces in the lot were taken. I found one on the next block and had to pick my way with my sore toe through an unevenly paved alley. When I walked in to join the senior center "dining out" class as an invited guest of some friends, there were about thirty people seated at a very long table made from several placed railroad car fashion. My friends had been unable to save me a seat next to them.

I had been to the same restaurant once before, and I wasn't too crazy about the food. Because this was a large group, the restaurant had set a fixed price menu costing almost twice what I paid previously. That would mean I'd have to sit at the far end from my friends and eat a mediocre, expensive meal with strangers.

Right at that moment, I went on overload. I had to have a time-out from my so far bad day. I whispered in one friend's ear that I was going to leave, and I did. I drove home and had lunch, some quiet time, and a rest.

That's one of the few times in my life I've been able to do something like that. Of course, the circumstances allowed for it: I was alone with my own car, I was close to my house, and I didn't know anyone at the event except for a few people. Nevertheless, the lesson was that I assessed my needs and acted to meet them.

It made up for the fact that the week earlier I had done just the opposite at a social gathering and brooded over it for the next few days because I hadn't been able to take care of myself. It's so difficult to learn how to take care of ourselves yet so worth it.

Every Time I Drop a Spouse, I Blossom (January 6, 2015)

Someone emailed me recently suggesting I write a blog about suddenly finding yourself single in your senior years. She is in her late sixties and getting a divorce.

Loss of a partner be it a spouse, live-in relationship, or significant other, whether by death, divorce, or mutual agreement, is a blow at any age but maybe even more so in your later years when your resiliency has decreased. Such a shift is a major passage of life; we face the unknown future alone, scared, naked and shaking. I've experienced it, and what I've found is that no matter how hard it seemed at the time, my life eventually became better than before.

I'm certainly not advocating termination of a relationship if each party is enhanced by it. However, in my case, I blossomed after my two divorces. I found myself freed from a constraining existence which only served to restrict and diminish me. After the initial shock, fear, and devastation, I gathered my resources, struck out on my own, and flourished. The first time, I became much more independent, made new friends, and learned to ski. The second time, many years later and as a senior, I became an actress, author, motivational speaker and blogger—whew!

Although I make it sound easy, it was anything but. Each blossoming happened slowly over some years, and there were a lot of periods of self-doubt, misgivings, and lack of motivation. However, I finally did it, and I can honestly say that those new, wonderful things in my life would not have occurred within those marriages.

Divorce or a breakup of any type of relationship usually happens when it changes from one of nourishment and support to one of toxicity and isolation. If the deterioration comes gradually, we at least have time to get used to it. If the termination was sudden such as in the case of an unexpected death, the devastation can seem much worse. Nevertheless, in both instances, even if the relationship was positive, there might be an element of relief if it made you feel oppressed and stifled or forced you into the role of submissive underling (laborer to his/her CEO), full-time caretaker, etc.

Regardless of the reason you find yourself single, the healing process is the same. After grieving the loss, you must look inside yourself at your strengths (yes, you have them) and move forward with the goal of becoming healthy. You may have to alter your lifestyle: lower your standard of living, move to other quarters, or find a job. However, in the process, you might find those strengths you never knew you had.

Go check out that local senior center you've heard about. Sign up for a class others have mentioned or sounded intriguing. Take a trip with a friend or group. Follow up on a hobby, pastime, or something you always thought you might try some day but never had the time.

As I've emphasized so many times in my blogs, you have choices. You can become mired in your grief and turn it into a life-style, constantly discussing it with everyone you encounter until they start avoiding you. Or, you can proceed to carve out that new identity for yourself and blossom. This is your chance!

BLOG POSTS FROM 2014

What Do You Do When the Happy Holidays Aren't So Happy? (December 22, 2014)
So, what do you do when the "happy holidays" aren't so happy? Well, you bake cookies, of course (further discussion below).

Yes, it often looks like what the other guy has is so wonderful compared to what you have. This is the season where that's especially true with seemingly everyone discussing all the wonderful things they're going to do over the holidays. Maybe your plans or lack of them look pretty paltry next to theirs. How can we be happy with what we have and embrace it?

I had an experience a few years ago where I was feeling envious of a friend. It doesn't matter what it was about–just fill in the blank. The point is: what she had seemed better, more desirable, and more appealing than what I had, and I was jealous.

I was telling my sad story to another friend who commented, "Be careful what you wish for." Ah yes, it's so true and so easy to forget. When I took a good look at my coveted friend's whole life, I realized I was cherry-picking. Yes, I was envious of "Thing A" that she had, but I certainly didn't want "Thing B" in her life.

So, folks, when envy strikes, and it will, think about whether you'd really be willing to switch places with another person if you had to take the whole package and not just cherry-pick.

To cheer you up a bit if you're feeling down at holiday time, and lots of people are, here's a guilt-free cookie recipe that's super healthy and yummy. You can also freeze them and, with a 20-second zap in the microwave, they're ready to serve last-minute guests or pack in sack lunches.

"NO SUGAR, SALT, BUTTER, EGGS, FLOUR, BAKING SODA" COOKIES

3 average, over-ripe bananas

2 cups regular rolled oats

1 cup golden raisins

1/3 cup oil

1 teaspoon vanilla

1 teaspoon cinnamon

Preheat oven to 350 degrees

Mash bananas in large bowl; add rest of ingredients; mix well; let sit for 15 minutes; place large, teaspoonfuls onto cookie sheet (mold into desired shape as they don't change during baking); bake 20 minutes (NOTE: Cookies can be frozen and defrosted in microwave.)

Happy Holidays, your style!

Do You Have Something to Say? (December 8, 2014)

A few months ago, a woman bought my memoir. I ran into her recently, and she told me she had really enjoyed it.

"I knew you had something to say when I first met you," she commented.

There's a trendy term for that: "finding your voice." It means getting in touch with and revealing your innermost feelings—expressing your real self. It's a hard thing to do. After all, we keep so many things private fearing that if others learned about them they'd misuse the information, and we'd be harmed in some manner: rejected, ostracized, manipulated, criticized, lose control…

Have you found your voice? When is it finally your turn to do so? In my case, I was too inhibited by social constraints: this isn't acceptable; I might hurt someone's feelings; someone might get angry at me; I might be judged; someone might find fault with me. So, I went for years without saying what I had to say. I was so good at keeping my true feelings hidden that I even did it from myself.

I finally decided to write a memoir. It was just supposed to be a lightweight, father/daughter bonding book about when my father and I attended a senior acting class together when I was sixty and he was eighty-five. However, as I wrote, things appeared on the page almost involuntarily. Sometimes, I would sit back and ponder what I had just written: *I didn't realize I felt that way. I haven't thought about that incident in decades.* I was finding my voice through the process of writing about a small piece of my life. My sweet, little memoir became much more than that; it became a catharsis. The hidden feelings I was writing about are universal feelings, I'm sure, filtered through my own unique experiences.

How do you feel about things, about life, about your own life in particular? When is it time for you to start saying it? You don't have to write a book like I did. There are many ways to say what you have to say. If you like writing, then keep a journal or diary, write a letter to a friend (remember letters?), write a letter to the editor, write an article for a publication. If your preference is verbal, then tell it to a friend, acquaintance, group, therapist, the world.

We all have something to say. It's gratifying to finally say what you feel inside without having to mask it for society's approval. Try it. It may take baby steps, but with some practice, it will become easier.

It's Not All about You (November 25, 2014)

Everyone craves attention, even the quiet ones among us. In each encounter between people, there's only a finite amount of it, and everyone deserves some. Human interaction is a competition with attention being the prize.

Have you ever been on a first-time encounter (date, business meeting, etc.) with someone who spends the whole time yapping about him/herself? That can get old very fast. A friend told me about a man she met recently who spent the whole date talking about himself and never asked anything about her. I'm sure when he called for another date and she turned him down, he didn't have a clue as to why.

Everyone is vying for the floor, and the stronger ones usually prevail. When one person grabs that coveted platform too often, others can become resentful.

Although not a hard and fast rule, we tend to choose our friends, partners, spouses, or significant others based on our needs. Introverts often seek extroverts to be the entertainment committee or shield them from the world. Extroverts, conversely, find calm and relaxation with introverts. Needy types seek caretaker types, and vice versa. I'm sure you can think of many more examples. It's subtle, but it exists. In this arrangement, there's an unspoken agreement that one person gets more of the attention than the other. After a while, though, the pauper of the duo can get tired of the protocol and want to break that old treaty.

If you're usually the main attraction, try to let the other guy have some attention. Ask, "How's it going?" or "What have you been up to?" Then, watch his face light up as he starts talking about himself. And, remember not to jump in and dominate the conversation again which usually goes something like this: "Oh yeah, when that happened to me I…" Just be a good listener for once.

If you're the guy who usually ends up with a dearth of attention, be proactive and get some of it; it's valuable stuff—makes you feel important. You might have to be bold and even rude by saying something as blatant as, "I'd like a turn to speak" or "I wasn't finished yet."

Remember children, play fair on that playground of life. Everybody deserves a turn on the swing.

Taking Advantage (November 12, 2014)

I've become more and more aware of how valuable and precious my time is. I have to pick and choose what's important to me. That brings me to today's topic. There's usually nothing wrong with taking advantage of an opportunity within reason. We all try to do that. However, that's not the kind of "taking advantage" I'm talking about.

Some people take advantage of the precious time of others. These are a few synonyms for that behavior: impose upon, exploit, use for one's own sake, milk. Of course, friendships and relationships require some giving of time and energy to each other. However, the problem is when it's taken to an extreme.

Do others take too much advantage of your precious time,

or do you take too much advantage of the precious time of others? Taking advantage excessively can come in so many forms: unrealistic expectations of you, asking you to do too much and too often, dumping their problems on you, and so on. It doesn't matter that they might do so very sweetly, maybe with apologies. They are still draining your valuable time and energy.

There reaches a point where we have to be assertive no matter how difficult it is. I know someone who has a literary skill which earns her money. A friend of hers often asks for help with various writing projects but doesn't pay what the work is worth under the guise of "we're friends." That might fly once or even twice, but when is it time to put a stop to being taken advantage of, even by a close associate? It's our own responsibility to set boundaries. We must be the one to "call a halt." If you don't do it, you send the message that the status quo is okay with you.

How can we be assertive without damaging or ending the friendship or relationship? First, be honest with yourself. Are you tired of being taken advantage of and are starting to harbor resentment? Then, be honest with the other person. To use the aforementioned example: tell her that your time is valuable and limited, that you choose to use it on other things such as your own jobs that pay you a fair wage, and that you can't accept her projects anymore.

Adapt that template to your own situation. Write out your speech so you'll remember what you want to say. Practice it so you'll hit your key points. It's difficult telling others what they don't want to hear. It's even more difficult living with the consequences of not doing so.

Have a Potlatch (October 26, 2014)

A potlatch, practiced by some Native Americans, is a tribal ceremony highlighted by the giving away of material and non-material (ex: titles) things. Status is achieved not by who has the most "stuff" but by who gives away the most. Yes, the Native Americans sometimes took it to extremes with the giving-away part turning into a competition or by expecting a similar payback. However, let's not throw out the concept of potlatch with the bath water. Maybe we can take the good parts.

We need to give away some of our stuff. We accumulate and hoard too much. Must we have more and more possessions, toys, money? When is it time to divest rather than invest? As the saying goes, "You can't take it with you." Of course, as a teenager who thought she knew everything, I'd point that out to my father, and he would respond, "Then I'm not going." Dad did, however, become more generous as he aged.

If you don't have "stuff" you can give away, then give away intangibles such as compliments, attention, help, advice (sparingly on that one). Giving away feels good to the giver as well as the receiver.

Are you familiar with the idea of helping others when you can't repay the benefactor of kind acts done in your behalf? The potlatch I'm suggesting is a version of that. Sometime in your life, someone probably gave to you. The way to reciprocate is to give to someone else. The winner in that competition will be you.

The Secret Benefits of Exercise (October 13, 2014)

We all know or have heard or suspect that exercise is good for us. It keeps you toned, fit, firm. I started exercising years ago at a gym because I had lower back pain. Boy, has it helped with that! But, I found a hidden benefit: it helps with my stress level and when I'm feeling down.

I'm a Type A personality and always on the go—doing lots of things—trying new stuff. However, even if you're a Type B, we all have stress. It's life's little gift to us for the privilege of being alive.

So, think about enrolling in a gym. Start out slowly doing what you can. It's not a contest. There are no winners and losers. You don't have to beat that person next to you doing their Jack LaLanne impersonation. Exercise for me seems to work best in a group situation. I guess I like to be among fellow sufferers. That's why I go to a gym. Also, the music in the background helps to motivate me.

You might get a kick out of a commercial I made a few years ago advertising gym equipment. Google my name to find all of my online acting work.

If it's too expensive to join a gym or you don't like the regimen, then get outdoors and start walking. That doesn't cost anything. Or, do your power walk at your local mall. It's safe, interesting and free with air conditioning thrown in at no extra charge. Replicate the musical accompaniment of a gym by listening through earbuds on your favorite technology device.

It's too boring, you say? Find some friends to walk with; you can socialize as you go. I have a group of friends who walk twice a week at the beach. No friends, you say? Check out Meetup.com, and find a group of walkers in your area. Many of them walk at the local malls.

What about your dog? It needs walking and loves it most when it's you on the other end of the leash. When did "dog walker" become a profession? Why aren't you walking Blondie or Milo or BooBoo yourself? Think of it as dog/owner bonding with exercise thrown in as a bonus.

When I had a dog and walked her in my neighborhood, I met neighbors I had never met before walking their pooches. As an aside, dogs sniffing each other is also a perfect icebreaker for their owners to get to know one another. If you don't have a dog, one sniffing your crotch is an opportunity to start a conversation with its human. You just might make a new friend. Then, you could walk together and get some conditioning and socializing.

You can't miss your daily daytime dose of (insert your favorite soap opera), you say? Record it and watch it in the evening. Use the daylight hours to be out there exchanging your stress and depression for some rays and a physical tuneup.

Surviving Irritating Behavior (September 28, 2014)

More and more as I get older, so many little things seem to irritate me, draining too much of my time and energy. However, harboring upset feelings hurts ourselves much more than the ones who caused them.

Recently, it was the voice quality and conversation of a woman at an exercise class I attend that annoyed me. I've heard her speaking before, and she has a certain pitch which seems to shatter my ear drums. Her usual non-stop, rapid-fire conversation about some innocuous thing in her life, projected loud enough to wake the sleeping in the back row of a large theater, results in her delivery landing on the ears of many who aren't interested, including me. She is a drama queen and seems to crave attention, so she has honed her skill well.

Perhaps you've been the receiver of such behavior or maybe even the sender? How do we survive irritating people whom we encounter so often in our crowded society? The first thing, in my opinion, is to accept that we can't change them. I certainly couldn't have approached the woman in my class and asked her to change the quality of her voice and, in fact, her entire personality.

What I can do is change myself. I have learned to carry earplugs with me. I quietly donned my orange neon plugs and went about my exercise routine calmly and contentedly. If my tormentor noticed them poking out of my ears, maybe she got the idea that they were my firewall against her, but I doubt it.

The point of all this is that you have choices as I've emphasized many times in prior blogs. Don't just let life happen to you. Take charge.

If you're around irritating people: family, friends, acquaintances, or strangers in your personal life, your work life, your leisure life, or wherever, decide what you want for yourself. Do you want to suffer silently and be the loser, do you want to confront the situation head-on, or do you want it to change with as little effort and stress as possible? If it's the last on that list, then alter yourself in some manner so the irritating behavior no longer affects you. It just might add a few more minutes to your life or at least make that life less agitated.

Scheduling Downtime (September 9, 2014)

Give yourself a day, a half day, or a few hours of decompression. You've been swimming out there in life's ocean, fighting the sharks and treading water. You need to relax. Don't come up too fast or you might get the bends.

Yes, it's important to rest from the daily, frenetic rush. I tend to schedule too much packed into my day. By evening, I'm wiped out and on overload. The things I do in the early part of the day get much better attention than those at the end. When I have too many days like that in a row, I become overwhelmed and a little ditzy.

If you're like me, it's urgent to program relaxation into your schedule. Sometimes, I just crave a day alone at home with nothing planned, padding around in my sweats. Even then, I tend to be in high gear: on my computer, making a new recipe, cleaning, doing my nails, talking on the phone—always on. It's so hard for me to stop. I have to make a conscious effort to do so.

If that also describes you, you probably wear yourself out just as I do. We have to force ourselves to calm down, chill out.

A friend recently told me that he's been taking classes in breathing because he has a medical problem with his oxygen intake. The new breathing technique works well for him. Now, his biggest problem is remembering to breathe in the new manner.

Like my friend, when I consciously think about it, I do take a rest. My problem is the remembering part.

We Are All Herd Animals (August 24, 2014)

Humans are social animals. We have a natural instinct to stay together; we need each other. Make it work to your advantage. Figure out how to interact with your fellow beings so that you don't become upset, agitated, or stressed out. You can't change the behavior of others. You can only change your own behavior. So, go ahead and change your behavior.

Analyze what you're doing that causes you to be the loser, the victim, the ostracized one—whatever typically happens to you during many interpersonal encounters. Try some behavior modification techniques on yourself.

If you have a hard time interacting with people, getting along with others, or making new friends, observe those who do it so easily. What do they do? Once you figure that out, start imitating them. Yes, it will feel artificial at first. But, it's like breaking in a pair of new shoes. Slowly, it will fit. You'll start to be comfortable with your new behavior, and it will become incorporated into how you act.

You must persevere to make your life better. If you're passive and just let life happen to you, you take what you get. To aim your life in the direction you want it to go, be proactive. Go ahead, give it a try. If it doesn't work, you can always go back to being passive.

Seek Environments That Calm and Uplift You (August 9, 2014)

I went to a wonderful exhibit recently at the Los Angeles County Museum of Art. I toured the display of Alexander Calder's airy, spellbinding mobiles and was transported to a fairyland. For those few moments, I forgot about the crushing heat here in Los Angeles, California; my personal issues and anxieties; and the world and its demands. I hung out with Calder's gifts to us all. The mobiles float, they waver, they tremble like the fragile human beings we all are.

Each was a jewel in its own right and was accompanied by a description, some poetic, which set the stage for the awe and amazement the work inspired. One I remember in particular had a vivid narrative written by Jean-Paul Sartre in 1963 after a visit to Calder's studio. He described the magical mobiles he saw as lyrical, technical, and mathematical symbols of nature, unable to ascertain if they were a result of cause and effect or the evolution of an idea.

Calder, who studied mathematical engineering as a young man, died in 1976. I was in my thirties then.

The lesson I took away: enjoy the natural and man-made beauty around you. It transports you for an instant and enables you to take shelter from that hurricane that is your life and focus on something other than your own, self-involved self.

Why Are People So Tough? (July 24, 2014)

Tough! Strong! Aggressive! Angry! As a child in junior high school, it was a big deal who was the best at put-downs—verbal violence, kill or be killed. Where do kids learn that—at home, in the community? One thought: sports are games of aggression, even seemingly innocuous ones like board games or chess matches, not only for the players but also for the spectators. As we watch, we are whipped (a very aggressive verb) into a frenzy of excitement. We want to see pain; blood is even better. Athletes are our avatars. They do what we can't do for ourselves: vanquish, destroy, win.

A few weeks ago, I heard a radio report about the running of the bulls in Spain. It's a prelude to the bullfights, one of the cruelest of modern-day sports. I attended a bullfight in Mexico about 40 years ago, not having any idea what I was actually going to see. Observing the audience was as eye-opening as the bullfight event itself. Whole families were in the stands from grandparents to toddlers to witness the spectacle. They had picnic baskets to dine while being entertained by the ceremonious goring of the bull with spears to weaken it for the eventual kill by the matador.

This is just a variation of the ancient, public gladiator performances where someone's death was the prize, I thought.

I recently read about the proliferation of elephant poaching to harvest their tusks for the lucrative world market in ivory. There was a description in the article of a baby elephant that was taken to a village and tied to a post as a toy for the local children to torture. What is this twisted behavior all about—teaching children how fun it is to torture a helpless animal and perhaps by extension another human being? The old "nature vs. nurture" puzzle still puzzles: Is cruelty inherent in human nature, or do we teach it? If the latter is predominant, why?

People don't have to thrust the bullfighter's sword to be cruel. They can do it very subtly. They can snub others; they can post mean social media comments; they can one-up each other, and on and on. We think we're so civilized, sophisticated. How does aggression and cruelty jibe with that? Do we get better perks in life being contentious and brutal? Are we happier?

Why I Write (July 10, 2014)

A friend commented recently that in my writing, I seem to understand and express so much about human nature, and she wondered how I was able to do that. I told her that I had learned a lot about the human condition from my probationers when I was a probation officer for 37 years. They often revealed their feelings to me, probably because I wasn't a part of their personal lives, and they felt safe in doing so. That helped me understand my own fears, joys, frailties, goals, desires, and other feelings.

I've always been introspective, and that's probably why I was drawn to a job working intimately with people. It's only been a handful of years since I discovered that when I write, thoughts, feelings, and emotions spring forth that I didn't even realize I had.

Writing is an incredible process for revealing yourself to yourself. Even those who write fiction insert so much that is personal. As I've mentioned in a prior blog, that's why therapists recommend their clients keep a journal. We each think we're unique, and we probably are in small ways. However, I believe that life's processes are universal; most of us have had the same experiences in one form or another. I like sharing my own personal discoveries because if I'm able to help a fellow traveler on this planet, I feel satisfied, and that I'm giving back to the community.

Someone else asked me why I reveal so much about myself in my writing. I had to think about that for a while, but here's my answer. At this stage of my life, I'm trying to confront and overcome the things that have controlled me for so many years, and I have used my blog as well as my published memoir, *Adventures with Dad: A Father and Daughter's Journey Through a Senior Acting Class*, to do that.

So, my motives aren't totally altruistic—are anyone's? I get a payback by passing along my thoughts to others. You might, too.

Giving with No Strings Attached (June 25, 2014)

Do you give with strings attached? Have you ever been the recipient of such giving? Giving (or gifting) with strings attached is demeaning both to the giver and to the receiver. It is a power play—the giver wants to control the receiver's behavior.

The commodity involved with giving is usually thought of as money or tangible goods. However, it can also be love, attention, effort, etc. For example, many people use love as a manipulative tool: I love you when you're good (i.e. when you do what I want or act the way I want you to act), but I will withdraw my love when you are bad (i.e. when you don't do what I want or act in a way I don't like). This often occurs between spouses, significant others, parents and children, and other close relationships.

The giving-with-strings-attached scenario usually goes something like this: Okay, I'll give you X, but in return I expect Y from you. That's fine for a formal, contractual agreement or a gift for a specific purpose previously agreed upon by both sides such as college tuition for your child. However, in more casual giving, it is the control freak's agenda and is resented by the receiver.

Of course, the potential giver has the choice of not giving in the first place. If you are asked to give and choose not to do so, just say "no" and go about your business. You don't have to turn your "no" into a lesson, admonition, or verbal manifesto. However, if you do commit to give (once, an extended period, a lifetime), don't use your promised gift as a power tool, cancelling it if you get mad or don't get your way. Keep your word, or it will result in the recipient never trusting you again.

If your gift is unconditional, it will benefit both parties so much more than if it is retractable upon your whim. If you give unconditionally to loved ones, the benefit you receive is knowing that you gave out of love or sincerity and not the quest for power. The benefit the recipients get is the same. They know you trust them to make decisions for themselves. Their decisions may not be what you would have chosen, but you've shown respect for them which, in the long run, is the much more valuable message.

If you give to strangers (an organized charity, a homeless person on the street, etc.), behave the same. Don't admonish the street beggars that they must use your handout for food and not alcohol or drugs. Treat them with respect so they can make their own decisions about how to live their lives. Maybe one day someone will give to you in your time of need. Wouldn't you prefer it be on terms of love and/or respect rather than power and control?

Why Do People Criticize Others (May 16, 2014)

A few years ago, I went on a wonderful, often very rustic trip to Papua New Guinea. After returning, I got together with the man I had been going out with for a while. I was very excited to show him my photos. As he was looking through them, he stopped at one, held it up to me, and commented, "Well, you certainly don't look your best."

Technically, he was right, I guess. I had no makeup on and my hair was in total disarray as I was caught on film climbing out of a dugout canoe on a brackish river. My point here is not the correctness of his statement which, by the way, was the truth as "he" saw it, but the fact that he chose that statement to make among so many others he could have said.

Here are a few possible proclamations he might have opted for: "Gee, what a neat dugout." "Boy, that looks like it was fun." "You look tired." Instead, he chose to trash my looks, albeit subtly—a vulnerable position for anyone.

I knew I looked a mess; he didn't have to tell me. It's really hard to look great floating down a river in PNG in a dugout canoe in the hot, humid jungle after having slept in a bare-bones structure with no air conditioning, no electricity, no indoor plumbing (think a hole-in-the-ground outhouse), and in a sleeping bag on the floor under mosquito netting.

I wonder why he chose to make the comment he did. What satisfaction did it bring him? Was he sending me a message that he only liked me when I looked well-groomed and attractive? Was he feeling insecure that he was dating a woman who could look scuzzy sometimes?

Those types of statements—subtle put-downs—only serve to put pressure on the receiver: *I'm unattractive, unlovable, un(fill in the blank) unless I'm always perfect; I always have to be on.*

What I'm advocating is that you examine your own motives when you criticize someone. If the purpose is to help correct their behavior, appearance, etc. for their benefit, then your commentary might be justified. However, if the purpose is to assuage your own discomfort, maybe that's your problem and not a shortcoming of your chosen reprobate.

Before you throw out potentially hurtful comments, think if a positive response might be more effective than a negative one. Demeaning another person doesn't only demean them, it demeans you as well.

Learning from Animals (April 29, 2014)

I've written about animals before. (See my blog of January 17, 2014: "The Therapy of Pets.") Animals are the ultimate stress reducers.

Last weekend, I went on a day trip to visit an unusual, animal rescue compound near Solvang, California. They had a variety of animals including miniature donkeys; I never knew such a creature existed. The full-grown mini-donkeys came up to my waist. Then, I bonded with Princess, a Vietnamese Potbellied Pig.

While I was scratching Princess' belly, currycombing a donkey, or petting a tortoise, I forgot about all my commitments, obligations, must-dos, and everything else in my life that stresses me out.

Many animals are so calm, placid, easy-going, and relaxed. (Those terms may all mean the same, but I couldn't stop with the descriptors.) When hanging around them, those qualities spill over onto you. That's why hospitals and other institutions often bring in animals to interact with the occupants; it's therapeutic. It is so much better, cheaper and has fewer negative consequences than many of the methods people use to reduce stress such as alcohol, prescription medications, illegal drugs, smoking, and excessive caffeinated drinks.

Because of the danger to our lives, health and happiness, we must reduce the stress that life hands each of us. One thing I use is exercise. When I'm working on the exercise machines at my gym, I'm concentrating on the workout and not on my stressors. Animals have that same effect on me. Since I don't have an at-home pet in my life right now, I'm always going up to people walking their dogs to get my "animal hit" for the day. I ask the owner first if I can pet their dog. Afterward, I always thank the dog and the owner for sharing.

Try an "animal hit" whether it be your neighbor's dog, cat or bird, or a more exotic variety such as Princess. Let their calmness wash over you and accompany you throughout the day. Somehow, it puts in perspective all of the little concerns we think are so important and that we allow to drain so much of our energy.

Getting Cut from the Lineup (April 13, 2014)
Have you ever been cut out of something you were sure was a shoe-in for you like a job promotion, a relationship, or even an appearance on a TV program as happened to me last week?

I am one of sixty women profiled in Marlo Thomas' new book, *It Ain't Over…Till It's Over*, about reinventing ourselves. I was contacted a few weeks ago and told I was one of the subjects chosen to be on the Today Show in a video clip in conjunction with Marlo Thomas' appearance to discuss her book.

I jumped though all the hoops they asked for with a very

short deadline. I taught myself how to make a brief, selfie video on my iPhone. I taught myself how to upload it to a file sharing website as it was too big to email. I searched for some requested photos buried in my desk drawers of myself at my office when I was a probation officer, which I then scanned and emailed. My stress level was way up there as you might imagine.

On the day of the show, I watched only to discover that I had been cut out. I was very upset as well as embarrassed because I had told everyone I knew that I was going to be on the Today Show; posted it on some online, group discussion sites; and blogged about it right here.

After indulging in "poor me" for a while, I was able to put it in perspective and turn it around. What had I gained? Well, there was my photo and a lovely story about me tracing my journey from probation officer to actress in Marlo Thomas' book; I learned how to take a selfie video for when I might need to do it another time; I learned about file sharing websites; and I got a blog subject out of it.

When something like this happens, we all wallow in self-pity for a while; that's human nature. But, wallowing for too long is unproductive and destructive. We do have choices; we can choose to move on and get over ourselves. How long it takes is up to us.

The Fear of Being Alone (April 2, 2014)

I always used to be so afraid of being alone. I don't mean alone for a few hours; I mean alone in life. That fear seeped into my everyday activities and still influences me. How many more decades is that going to continue? I don't have that many of those left. I must do something now.

I'm sure some of my poor decisions in a few prior relationships stemmed from that fear—better someone than no one. How many people remain in bad, destructive marriages, relationships, or friendships because the alternative, being alone and unloved, seems worse? I did.

I remember in junior high school that if you were seen by classmates outside of school engaged in activities like clothes shopping or going to the movies by yourself, or worse—with your mother, you'd be considered as someone who didn't have a pal to go with—a loser. A friend recently confirmed that she'd had the same fear and still does.

Now, as a senior, I've learned to do many things by myself without a second thought. However, there are still some activities that I avoid if I don't have a companion. I don't travel alone; I don't go to a movie alone; I don't go to a restaurant alone. I reject those pursuits automatically without consciously thinking about them.

Recently, I wanted to see a movie that all my friends had already seen. I simply told myself that I'd catch it on Netflix, and I moved on to thinking about something else.

I know a lady who travels all over the world by herself. I admire her—envy her. I'd like to be able to do that—just call a travel agent and be done with it. Even though I'm a personable woman and attract people easily, deep down inside I'm afraid that if I travel alone, no one will talk to me; they'll look at me with pity or scorn because I don't have someone to be with. On a conscious level, I know that's ridiculous. On a subconscious level, that old lesson from junior high school still controls me.

I've vanquished so many old restraints and blossomed as a result. I want to break some others. How about you?

Ending a Friendship (March 19, 2014)
Have you abruptly terminated a long-time friendship or relationship in sudden anger at something your friend did? Have you had that done to you as was done to me a while ago?

I wonder, was the offending behavior really the felony you imagined, or just a misdemeanor? Maybe your friend unknowingly pushed a button that you're hardly aware of yourself. Perhaps the action reminded you of something hurtful that someone else did to you in the past. However, just because the behavior was similar, were the motives the same? For example, did your friend stand you up like that other person did because he/she got a better deal, or was it for another reason? Did he do it with malice, or was it without realization that it would hurt you? Did you tell him that his behavior was painful to you and give him a second chance? Or, did you just expect him to read your mind and know?

These are all things we must think about before terminating a long and valuable relationship. Everyone makes mistakes sometimes (both the droppor and the droppee). We have to be more forgiving of each other's mistakes. On the other hand, if you terminated the friendship because the offense was just one more of a long, established pattern of behavior (or some other motive such as jealousy), then that was a relationship you had been wanting to end but didn't fully realize it or didn't know how.

I have described two very different scenarios that resulted in the end of a relationship. Be careful in ending a worthwhile friendship in anger because you might be hurting yourself as much as the one you dropped.

Decompressing in a Compression Age **(February 28, 2014)**
In my last blog, I wrote about the benefits of solitude. This post piggybacks on those thoughts.

Life is so tumultuous and becomes more so with each so-called advancement. What looks like something that will benefit mankind often turns out to just put more stress on we humble humans that populate it. For example, the automobile has proliferated to the point of almost constant gridlock. Our commute by car now seems as long as by the horse carriage it replaced.

Today's modern technology makes us more connected, able to work 24/7, able to access more and more data, and on and on. What happens to our slower evolving bodies in the meantime? I like the notion of viewing your body as a house you inhabit, and your well-being depends on how you care for your abode.

So, what do we do with everything bombarding us for our valuable and finite time and attention? We decompress! We must put up a mental gate—a barrier to protect ourselves from the ravages of that avalanche. It's hard to do; it takes willpower.

How do we turn off that cell phone, computer, or TV which have become addictive and so much a part of our lives? Here are a few ideas: You can make a schedule and allot some quiet time during the day. You can take a vacation to a place off the grid. There aren't many anymore, but seek them out and re-member to leave your technology toys behind. I have a friend who refuses to get a cell phone or computer as she wants to enjoy life without the barrage of technology—smart woman.

Do we really need hundreds of virtual friends on Facebook? Can we give ourselves permission to opt for a slower, gentler journey? Maybe.

The Benefits of Solitude (February 20, 2014)

In great quantities, solitude can be isolating and destructive. However, in small quantities, solitude can be comforting and cleansing.

I always used to fear solitude. It left me alone with my thoughts. It meant that I didn't have anything to do. It meant that no one wanted to be with me. Now, I find that it replenishes me. It gives me space from the demands of the world—downtime.

Solitude enables my creativity. When I'm alone, my mind is free to wander. That's when I come up with some of my best thoughts. Sometimes, solitude helps when life becomes too overwhelming. During that time, I give myself permission to take a mental vacation. I try hard not to make any big decisions, not to have any conflicts, engage only in non-demanding activities, and just let my mind drift.

Solitude in limited amounts can be refreshing, like sleep. It can help you pace yourself, stop your hectic running, get off the race track for a while. Don't fear solitude. In controlled amounts, it can be your friend.

We Don't Have Time for Negativity! (February 7, 2014)

Do you know anyone or are you someone who is often negative or complains a lot? Now that we're baby boomers or seniors, we don't have that much time left. Do we really want to spend it mired in contentiousness or bellyaching?

If that's been a lifestyle, it's hard to change. But, being conscious that you're like that and morphing into a more positive person can pay dividends. I have a relative who has raised complaining to an art form. It comes so naturally to her, I'm sure she doesn't even realize how much she does it and has no idea why people avoid her. It's sad. She'd love to have more friends, but she's such a turn-off.

Conversely, I had a group of friends, one of whom had cancer. She would join our various activities whenever possible, working it in between chemotherapy treatments. It seemed to give her a reason to keep going, and she contributed to our good time as much as she could.

I have another friend who has a debilitating disease. She calls me to tell me about a good movie she just watched on her iPad. I love talking to her.

These two women are my role models. Why does negativity come so easily to some? I suspect that people who fall into this category learned at a very early age that doing their "poor me" routine yielded a big payoff—attention. We all crave attention. We engage in all sorts to behaviors, tricks, and pursuits to get it. Being negative or complaining excessively does work for a while until the receiver has had enough and realizes they're ineffective in helping you overcome your problems, and that all their relationship with you does is bring them down.

If you've had a history of a lot of short-term friendships which seem to fizzle out, maybe you're driving your friends away with negativity or complaining. We all complain or are negative sometimes. I'm talking about those who are compulsive about it.

You have a choice in the matter. Upsetting or bad things don't just happen to you. They happen to all of us. On the other hand, we all have positive experiences, too. Maybe they're not earth-shaking, but we can let even small, upbeat episodes drive our lives if we choose. Did someone smile at you? Did someone give you a compliment? Talk to your friends about those incidents or maybe about a good movie you just watched on your iPad.

The Therapy of Pets (January 18, 2014)

I love animals; a lot of people do. We've all heard how therapeutic animals can be for us. Why is that? Here are some words/phrases to describe animals as a general rule: content, calm, hang-loose, loving, go-with-the-flow, devoted, live in the moment. They embody so many of the things that so many of us humans lack or have in short supply.

When we need a friend, our pet or someone else's pet or some horses at a stable or some wild birds are there for us. I was in a park the other day and chose to sit on the lawn near some migrating geese. I felt calm just watching them as they watched me.

Years ago, I hung out with some gentle cows in a field in England. Their curiosity overcame them, and they walked slowly toward me—boxcars on legs. It was special; I still remember it vividly.

I used to be half of a pet therapy team with my dog at a local hospital. We'd visit patients who had requested a dog visit. I'd put Fergie on their bed so they could pet her. The patients loved it, often launching into a discussion about their pet at home that they missed. None ever found the need to mention why they were in the hospital. We were also barraged by staff and visitors.

Once, there was a big, burly patient who looked terrified when he saw Fergie. When I questioned him thinking I had the wrong room, he explained that he'd always been frightened of dogs ever since he was a child and witnessed his best friend being mauled by one. He was amazed when Fergie started licking his hand.

"Oh my God, a dog is licking my hand," was all he could say over and over.

Fergie and I visited him a few more times over the next several weeks. Just before he was to be released, he told me he was planning on getting his own dog.

Even if you're not a pet person, maybe a bird or a tank of fish could bring you some joy. Try it out.

BLOG POSTS FROM 2013

Embrace Your Age, Don't Fight It! (December 26, 2013)
I haven't blogged for a while because I had bunion/arthritis surgery on my left big toe and have been recuperating. That really made me feel old. As a younger person, the words "arthritis" and "bunions" were associated only with old people. These days, an old woman has been stalking me. She follows

me wherever I go. She also has the audacity to jump into every mirror I look at and mimic my antics. Although she seems vaguely familiar, I don't know her, and I wish she'd go away.

Yes, "getting old sucks" is the prevailing attitude. It is to be avoided at all costs including pushing ourselves toward age-inappropriate behavior, dress, and the exploding popularity of surgery toward that ever-elusive youth ideal we've been sold.

Although I try to fight it, I'm certainly a victim of it. My hearing began to deteriorate a few years ago. However, I resisted even exploring hearing aids; it smacked of being old. I went around missing part of what was being said in conversations, lectures, movies and TV, and, of course, asking people to repeat. When I finally got hearing aids, a whole new world opened up to me.

What a jerk I was, playing the "youth" game. We don't resist getting glasses as we age because lots of young people wear glasses. However, we'll shun a cane as we teeter off-balance, chancing a fall and a broken bone. It's only after the bone is broken, we're in pain, and we spend months in a nursing home getting daily physical therapy that we admit to "I should have…."

Where did this all come from, this pathological race toward eternal youth? Is it Madison Avenue, Hollywood, what?

It hasn't always been that way. So many prior and current cultures of the world embrace aging. The elders are the wise of the tribe and are to be respected and emulated. Why can't we go back to that? The answer is: we can, each in our small way.

We can admit that we tire more easily and choose not to over-schedule just to keep up with our fictitious, youthful self.

We can use hearing aids, canes, low-heeled shoes for women, whatever, and have a better quality of the life left us. No one will hate us for it. No one will shun us for it.

Some years ago, I let my dyed-blond hair color grow out. It wasn't an easy decision, and I was nervous about it–about looking old. I had been dying my hair since my twenties, and I didn't even know what color it was naturally. It grew in a snow white.

Skeptical friends started admiring it. Friends and strangers would comment on it in a positive manner. A well-known actress in her sixties with whom I worked in a production for the baby boomer and senior market remarked that I was the only one there without dyed hair, including her.

I was becoming a pace setter to other friends. Some started letting their dyed hair grow out. We have all survived the experience, and no one has ostracized us. We still have a good quality of life and lots of fun.

Once, a friend gave me a left-handed compliment: "Lee Gale, you look so good. Imagine what a knockout you'd be if you had your face lifted." I felt only sadness for her. My purpose in life is not to be a knockout by the "youth" definition. My purpose is to be as healthy as I can, to embrace life as it is now, and to enjoy it. I don't have to wear the facade of youth to do so.

The Importance of Friendships (November 26, 2013)

Friendships are important to everyone. However, they're especially important to baby boomers and seniors. It's all too easy to feel depressed and isolated when we get to that stage of our lives. Friendships will help ease those feelings. Friends will care about you. Friends will share your good times. Friends will help you when you need help. Friends will talk you through hard times and will be there to listen. Sometimes, having a good listener is all we need. And, always remember to be a friend back.

If you're lucky enough to have long-term friends, don't ignore them. Remember to cultivate them, even if it's just an occasional phone call to ask how they're doing or even an email reminding them that you're thinking about them. You might not have friends or many friends or enough friends for a variety of reasons such as: you've moved to a new location; your old friends have moved away or died; your former friends have found new interests that don't include you; you were never very good at making friends; and so on.

One way to cultivate new friendships is to attend groups or join organizations. Don't be afraid to approach someone you meet there; just start talking to them about the group interest or about admiring what they're wearing or just about anything. People are usually flattered by your interest. Of course, some might not be or might even be rude or ignore you. You won't know why. Maybe life's not easy for them, either, or they don't feel well or don't hear well.

It's easy to let an unpleasant encounter deflate you. Try hard not to give up. Move on to another person. Sometimes, when you go to a new group, people already have their cliques. It's hard to break into an established circle. Keep at it. There are usually some group members who don't stick to that clan mindset, and you might engage one of them.

I have a friend who relocated to a large retirement community. She found it very cliquish. It took her a few months to start making friends. She was quite discouraged at first, but she kept at it and now has several new buddies.

Seek out special interest activities that attract a lot of people. You might see them posted at such places as senior centers, schools for seniors, libraries, and in senior magazines and online newsletters. Always keep networking by asking neighbors, acquaintances and others about activities they might recommend or have heard of.

If you like outdoors activities, look for local walking or hiking groups. I'm a long-time member of the Sierra Club, and I've made many wonderful friends through their activities.

Volunteering (which I blogged about in my last post) is another good way to find friends. If you attend a religious organization, look for their affiliated senior groups. I've mentioned meet-up groups in previous blogs. Go online to: meetup.com. Look for a group near you which focuses on something that interests you. You'll meet like-minded people there and possibly make a friend.

One caveat: friendships are fragile, so don't just make it all about you; you must give as well as take. The opportunities are there. The hard part is motivating yourself to start with the first step. You have to do that, however, to yield results. As I've said before: if it's hard, DO IT ANYWAY!

Volunteering (November 6, 2013)

Volunteering is a wonderful way to get involved in an interesting activity and to give back to the community at the same time. Another benefit is that you can make new friends who enjoy the same activity that you do.

There are so many volunteering opportunities available in every community—enough to fit every personality type and comfort level. The secret is to volunteer at something that is interesting and exciting to you. That way, it can become a passion and motivate you to embrace life (a theme I stress repeatedly in my speeches and blogs).

Are you a people-person? If so, then you might choose a pursuit that brings you in contact with humans such as at the help desk at a hospital, museum, police or sheriff department, etc.

I'm a people-person, and I love to perform. I also love science and animals, and I live close to the world famous La Brea Tar Pits. So, I guide tour groups around the La Brea Tar Pits and inside its concomitant Page Museum. My group talk is like performing a monologue in front of an audience. My group members are all so appreciative, and I love the experience. It's definitely a win-win for everyone involved. I had to study hard to learn my subject, but I'm passionate about it, and it's been very rewarding.

Maybe you're a one-on-one person. My dog and I used to be a pet therapy team visiting patients at a local hospital.

Maybe you're the reserved, private type. There are lots of behind-the-scenes, volunteer activities. I have a friend who used to volunteer in the "bone room" of the local Natural History Museum sorting ancient animal bones.

Maybe you like children. I have another friend who volunteered in a classroom at a nearby grammar school.

Do you like animals? There are lots of volunteer opportunities at local animal shelters or animal rescue organizations. I have another friend who used to be a tour guide at the zoo.

If you like art, check out the local art museum. Here are a few more ideas where you might volunteer: public gardens, local festivals, theaters, aquariums, senior centers, etc. Just drive around your town and see what piques your interest. Then, get on the phone, call them, and ask if they are seeking volunteers. Better yet, go in person.

Ask friends, acquaintances, neighbors or the librarian for ideas of where to volunteer. I know it may be difficult, embarrassing or uncomfortable, but as I've said before: If it's hard, do it anyway!

Is It Too Late for Baby Boomers and Seniors? (October 5, 2013)

I was at a meeting recently where we were all seniors. We were going around the room each telling a little about ourselves. It was my turn, and I told my story of retiring from my career as a probation officer and becoming an actress, author, and speaker.

The next person was a woman who mentioned she was working at her brother's law office, but she didn't sound very excited about it. She said her dream as a young woman had always been to get a college degree. I spoke up: "Why don't you do it now?"

"Now?" she responded in a shocked and defensive tone.

I dropped that discussion quickly; she obviously didn't want to hear it.

The woman seemed aloof toward me after my remark. I

thought that maybe she was jealous. My suggestion that she revisit her youthful dream was apparently the last straw for her. She made it a point not to talk to me during the rest of the event. I think I touched a nerve.

During my speaking engagements, I deliberately touch nerves. I encourage baby boomers and seniors to find something to be passionate about as a motivation to embrace life. Why should we do this at our age? Do it for the challenge of it–the sheer joy of it.

Why should we seniors go quietly into the night? There is still plenty of life to be lived. Now is the time to do it! Don't just take the easy way out–the same boring way out.

You don't have to follow my path. If you've always wanted to try something, do it! You might have to modify it, but see if you can figure out a way to connect with that thing that excites you. Maybe you can't become the doctor you'd always wanted to be, but maybe you can volunteer at a medical facility helping patients in some manner. Maybe you can't go trekking into the jungles after animals, but maybe you can volunteer at an animal shelter. Don't just settle. Find a passion!

Try Something New (September 21, 2013)

Life can get stale, just like bread. Try something new. If you don't like it, don't run back to the old, boring stuff you've always done; try another new thing. Eventually something might grab you.

That's how I got into acting. I retired from my 37-year career as a probation officer and immediately signed up with the department to work as a retiree on an as-needed basis doing the same thing I'd been doing for years because I didn't know what else to do in my retirement.

Luckily for me, a friend told me about a local senior community program. I saw an acting class listed in the catalog and thought I'd try it, as it was something I had never done in my life—something new.

I know it's comfortable to stick to the tried and true, both in activities and friends. However, trying something new might open doors for you that you never knew existed.

That acting class changed my life. As a result of just deciding to take a chance on doing something different, I am now an actress, author (I wrote a book about attending that class with my 85-year-old father) and speaker (about the book and about inspiring baby boomers and seniors to find a passion as a motivation to embrace life).

Gratitude (September 8, 2013)

I read a self-help book a while ago because a friend raved about it. Those kinds of books are usually not my thing, but I checked it out. It had a lot of interesting things to say, but others didn't resonate.

Rather than ignoring everything because it didn't all work for me, I chose the things I liked and discarded the rest. The part I liked best talked about being grateful. I've incorporated a few minutes of "gratitude reflection" into my morning back-exercise regimen. I sit back on my heels, take a deep breath, and say out loud: What am I grateful for today? I think of five things and say them out loud. Verbalizing that way helps me focus on them. When my attention strays, I notice that and gently bring it back.

I try to find different gratitudes for each day. They might sound the same as previous ones (example: my son called me last night), but it's new for today even though it was the same gratitude I verbalized last week after he called. Doing my daily gratitudes helps me stay positive in my life. I have so many good things and don't want to spend my senior years focusing on the not-so-good things.

We all have a choice. If you get off on complaining and rehashing each negative, upsetting thing that happens, then go for it. However, if you want to embrace life, stop whining and focus on what makes you grateful.

Meetup Groups (July 21, 2013)
Today, I want to discuss meetup groups. Have you heard of meetup.com? It's a wonderful website. You can find groups near you of people who all share a common interest. I have a friend who has connected with a meetup group just for going to the movies.

I went to a meetup group near my home of people who were interested in speaking Spanish. We met at a restaurant, and we all conversed in Spanish the entire time. People had varying degrees of fluency, but everyone was tolerant and helpful toward everyone else. The ages of the participants also varied greatly. That didn't matter as we all shared a common interest.

Just google "meetup groups" or put meetup.com into your computer address bar. It's not hard to do. If you're not computer literate, ask for help from a friend or relative who is.

If you don't have a computer, the library has computers. You can sign up to use them for free, and the librarian can be helpful in showing you how to get to that website. It's a great way to connect with others.

I know it's hard to reach out. Remember my motto: DO IT ANYWAY!

Genealogy (June 23, 2013)

Today, in my ongoing discussion of things baby boomers and seniors can do to develop a passion as a motivation to embrace life, I'm going to talk about pursuing genealogy.

I have a retired friend who has been charting his genealogy and that of his deceased wife. He was able to go back several generations on his own by visiting various websites. Then, he hired a professional to go back even further. My friend has contacted distant relatives he finds, and he travels around the world to meet them and visit old cemeteries where ancestors are buried.

The Mormons are passionate about keeping genealogical records on everyone they can as it corresponds with their religious beliefs. They are very welcoming at all their churches to allow anyone to check their genealogical archives, and there are volunteers there to assist. You don't have to be a Mormon to take advantage of their help. Best of all, it is totally free.

I visited the Mormon Temple in Los Angeles, California many years ago and found my mother's name along with all her parents and siblings in a 1920s census record. She was only five years old. It was very exciting. Distant family members have found me because someone spent a lot of time pursuing the family genealogy.

Is genealogy something you could become passionate about as a motivation to embrace life?

Singing (June 10, 2013)

I have a horrible voice and wish I could sing. I think there was a mistake on the drawing board, and someone else ended up with my voice. Maybe it was you.

Have you always loved to sing? Now is your big chance. There are all sorts of singing opportunities for baby boomers and seniors. Senior citizen centers have singing classes and groups. Religious institutions of most faiths have choirs. I know a senior who has gotten great satisfaction singing in a barbershop quartet group for years.

Community theaters produce musicals. You don't have to be the main attraction (unless that appeals to you). You could be in the chorus.

Get on the computer and google something like "singing opportunities in (fill in the name of the town or city where you live)." Or, ask a friend, neighbor or relative.

I know it's intimidating. Remember my motto: Do it anyway!

Gardening (June 4, 2013)

It's so easy to tell someone else to get a life–find something to do. It's so hard as the recipient of that advice to know where to start. One might secretly ask themselves: What would I even do? Where do I go to do it? Will I look foolish? Will I be rejected?

In my last post on this subject, I suggested looking for classes and senior programs in your community. Today I want to talk about gardening as a pursuit.

A friend, who is a senior, retired a few years ago and turned to her prior hobby of gardening. She is now a member of two rose societies, one of which tends the rose garden on the grounds of the Rose Parade headquarters in Pasadena, California. She is always going to some gardening meeting or another, often with plant cuttings in her car trunk. I have contributed cuttings from my own yard to her cause. She has become passionate about this pursuit. It gives her life joy, meaning, and excitement and provides a social outlet, interacting with other devotees.

There is a Cactus and Bromeliad Society in my area. They have club meetings, competitions, and other events. I once got involved for a while in an organization for carnivorous plants after I was gifted a tropical pitcher plant.

Have you always enjoyed gardening? See if there are any public gardens (flowers, edibles, etc.) where you live and if they're looking for volunteers. And, remember my motto: even if you're scared, do it anyway!

Get Passionate About Something as a Motivation to Embrace Life! (June 2, 2013)

It's so important to reinvent yourself so you discover and learn new things. It's a way to get excited about life and want to get out there. I've met so many baby boomers and seniors who are bored and depressed. Now that they've retired and the kids are grown, they don't know what to do with themselves.

In my life, I've gone from being a mother, wife and career woman (I was a probation officer for 37 years) to becoming an actress and author as a senior. So, I'm going to start blogging about activities you can do to find something to be passionate about—something to make you want to get out of bed, get dressed, get out of the house and embrace life!

Today, I'll talk about classes and senior programs. There are senior citizen centers and learning-in-retirement programs in just about every neighborhood. They offer wonderful classes, activities, and events.

Just ask friends about them or google "senior citizens center in (your city)." Then, find their website or better yet, go in person to see what it looks like. However you do it, get their Schedule of Classes or their program or whatever they call it. Find a class, event, bus trip, etc. that sounds interesting, sign up, and go to it.

It's hard walking into a roomful of people where you're alone and everyone else seems to know each other. Do it anyway! Remember, just about everyone there was where you are at the beginning. It gets easier the more you do it.

HINT: Try something you've never done in your life. That's how to grow, expand, and find a new passion in life. That's what I did, shaking in my shoes at the beginning. I write all about my journey in my new memoir, *Adventures with Dad: A Father and Daughter's Journey Through a Senior Acting Class*, including the scared, shaking in my shoes part.

About the Author

Lee Gale Gruen ("Lee Gale" is her first name) lives in the East San Francisco Bay area. She has two children and three grandchildren. She grew up in Los Angeles, California, graduated college from UCLA, and had a 37-year career as a probation officer. After retiring, she became a professional actress appearing in television; commercials; short films; theater; music videos; voiceovers; print jobs; and live, interactive roles. She has been performing for 15 years at medical schools portraying patients for student training. She was one of six supporting exercise/dancers in the 2011 "Jane Fonda Prime Time Firm & Burn" workout DVD. Her transition to becoming an actress in her senior years has been written about in *Time* magazine, the *Los Angeles Times* newspaper, AARP, and Marlo Thomas' 2014 book highlighting women who have reinvented themselves.

Lee Gale's memoir, *Adventures with Dad: A Father and Daughter's Journey Through a Senior Acting Class* (available on Amazon.com), was published in 2013. She writes a free blog, "Reinventing Yourself in Your Retirement Years" at: LeeGaleGruen.wordpress.com where she shares her thoughts, observations, and experiences which she believes are universal to the retiree and senior demographic. She also lectures publicly on senior reinvention. Her goal with her blogs, lectures, and this book is to help retirees, those soon to retire, baby boomers and seniors find joy, excitement, and purpose in life after they retire. This book resulted from audience members at her lectures requesting a book about it.

Books/Speaker Website: LeeGaleGruen.com
Acting Website: LeeGaleGruenActress.com
Blog: LeeGaleGruen.wordpress.com
Email: gowergulch@yahoo.com